Wontner's Guide to
Land Registry Practice

Eighteenth edition

Patrick J Timothy LLB
Solicitor

Longman Group UK Ltd 1991

ISBN O 85121 7931

First Published 1928
Eighteenth edition 1991

Published by
Longman Law, Tax and Finance
Longman Group UK Ltd
21/27 Lamb's Conduit Street
London WCIN 3NJ

Associated offices:
Australia, Hong Kong. Malaysia, Singapore, USA

All rights reserved. No part of this publication may be reproduced, stored in a retrieval system, or transmitted in any form or by any means, electronic, mechanical, photocopying. recording or otherwise. without the prior written permission of the publishers, or a licence permitting restricted copying issued by the Copyright Licensing Agency Ltd, 90 Tottenham Court Road, London W1P 9HE

No responsibility for loss occasioned to any person acting or refraining from action as a result of the material in this publication can be accepted by the author or publishers.

A CIP catalogue record for this book is available from the British Library

Printed in Great Britain by Biddles Ltd, Guildford and King's Lynn

Contents

Preface ix
Editor's Note xi

Chapter 1: General Features
1 Introduction 1
2 What interests can be registered? 3
3 Who can apply for registration? 5
4 Delivery and priority of applications 5
5 Classes of titles 7
6 The register of title 9
7 Land and charge certificates 10
8 Index of proprietor's names 11
9 Computerisation 11
10 Rectification and indemnity 12
11 Judicial powers of the Chief Land Registrar 12
12 Stamp duty and production of documents (L(A)451) 13
13 Requisitions raised by the Registry 14
14 Forms 15
15 Fees 15
16 Information 15

Chapter II: Plans and Maps
1 Official plans generally 17
2 The filed plan 17
3 The Land Registry general map 18
4 Field numbers and areas 19
5 Deed plans 19
6 Ownership of fences and walls: 'T' marks 20
7 Boundaries 21
8 Metrication 23

CONTENTS

9	Official searches of the public index map	23

Chapter III: First Registration
1	Compulsory first registration on sale	27
2	Voluntary first registration	29
3	Before completion	29
4	The application for first registration	31
5	Incorporeal and other hereditaments	36
6	Official examination of title	36
7	Completion of registration	37
8	Acquisition of title by possession	37
9	Title shown procedure	38
10	Public authorities: certificates of title	39
11	Public sector housing	39
12	Housing Defects (Housing Act 1985, Part XVI)	41

Chapter IV: Covenants and Other Interests
1	Covenants	42
2	Overriding interests	46
3	Easements	51
4	Minor interests	54

Chapter V: Inspection, Office Copies and Searches
1	Inspection of the register	55
2	Inspection of the index of proprietor's names	55
3	Inspection in the case of certain crime, receiverships and insolvency	56
4	Personal inspection	56
5	Office copies	57
6	Certificate of official inspection of the filed plan	58
7	Official searches of the register	59
8	Searches in the Land Charges Department	68
9	Local land charge searches	69

Chapter VI: Dealings Generally
1	Dealings expressly authorised by the Act	70
2	Production of certificates	71
3	Documents placed on deposit	72
4	The application forms	72
5	Acknowledgment of dealings applications	75
6	Associated dealings	75
7	Forms of dispositions: approval of draft instruments	75

8	Deeds and their execution	76
9	Execution by attorney	78
10	Alteration of instruments	80
11	Change of name, address or description	80
12	Plans 'for the purpose of identification only'	81
13	Requisitions from the Registry	81

Chapter VII: Transfers

1	Sale of registered land	82
2	Forms of transfers: implied covenants	87
3	Transfer of part: plan	87
4	Easements: covenants	88
5	Transfers to two or more transferees	88
6	Transfers to give effect to dealings with undivided shares: fees	89
7	Particular parties to transfers	89

Chapter VIII: Leases

1	Leases of registered land	92
2	Easements and restrictive covenants in registered leases	95
3	Options in leases of registered land	95
4	Registered leases: endorsement of registration with lessor	96
5	Office copies of registered leases	96
6	Variation of leases	96
7	Mergers and surrenders of leases	98
8	Leases determined by effluxion of time: Landlord and Tenant Act 1954	101
9	Agreement for lease	102
10	Leasehold Reform Act 1967	102

Chapter IX: Charges and Liens

1	Registered charges	110
2	Charges subsisting at the time of first registration	120
3	Public sector housing: discount charge	121
4	Equitable charges	123
5	Notices of [intended] deposit	126

Chapter X: Rentcharges

1	The Rentcharges Act 1977	129
2	First registration of rentcharges	130
3	The rentcharge certificate	133

4	Rentcharges incapable of substantive registration	133
5	Notice of rentcharge	134
6	Dealings with registered rentcharges	134
7	Apportionment and redemption of rentcharges	135
8	Extinguishment of rentcharges	136

Chapter XI: Conversion of Title

1	Conversion of good leasehold to absolute leasehold	138
2	Conversion of possessory titles	139
3	Conversion of qualified titles	139
4	Inquiries before conversion	140
5	Application form and fees	140

Chapter XII: Trust and some Special Cases

1	Settled land	141
2	Trusts for sale	144
3	Sole trustees	147
4	Charities	148
5	Minors	154
6	Mental disorder	155

Chapter XIII: Death

1	Death of sole or sole surviving proprietor	157
2	Death of a joint proprietor not being the survivor of joint proprietors	160
3	Inheritance tax: capital transfer tax: death duties	161

Chapter XIV: Protection of Third Party Rights

1	Notices	164
2	Cautions	166
3	Restrictions	170
4	Inhibitions	172
5	Priority notices for first registration	172
6	Protection of non-local land charges, pending land actions, writs and orders, deeds of arrangement	173
7	Local land charges	174

Chapter XV: Matrimonial Homes

1	Matrimonial Homes Act 1983	176
2	Is the matrimonial home registered?	176
3	Application for notice	177
4	Rights continued by order of court	177

CONTENTS vii

5	Renewal of registration of a notice or caution	178
6	Change of matrimonial home	178
7	Charges to secure further advances	178
8	Cancellation of notice	179
9	Cancellation of caution	179
10	Rights of occupation of a bankrupt's spouse	180
11	Rights of occupation of a bankrupt	180
12	Search by mortgagees	181

Chapter XVI: Insolvency
1	Bankruptcy	182
2	Liquidation	186
3	Administration orders	187
4	Company receivership	188
5	Administrative receivers	193
6	Inspection of the register on insolvency	193

Chapter XVII: Building Estates — 194

Chapter XVIII: Lost or Destroyed Deeds and Certificates
| 1 | Lost or destroyed title deeds | 200 |
| 2 | Lost or destroyed land or charge certificates | 202 |

Chapter XIX: Rectification and Indemnity
1	Correction of minor errors	205
2	Rectification	205
3	Applications and fees for rectification	206
4	Indemnity	207
5	Costs and expenses	208
6	Applications for indemnity	208

Appendices
I	District Land Registries	209
II	Areas served by District Land Registries	214
III	Register (Non-computerised form)	217
IV	Register (Computerised form)	219
V	List of Forms	222
VI	Practice Leaflets Issued by HM Land Registry	226
VII	The Land Registration Fees Order 1991	227

Index 243

Preface

Two radical and a number of other important changes are reflected in this edition of the Guide.

The radical changes are the opening of the Register to public inspection by the Land Registration Act 1988 (Commencement) Order 1990 and the extension of compulsory registration to the whole of England and Wales by the Registration of Title Order 1989. The 'Open Register' led to other changes in the rules including the Land Registration (Open Register) Rules 1990, the Land Registration (Official Searches) Rules 1990 and the Land Registration (Matrimonial Homes) Rules 1990. The completion of extension of compulsory registration was followed by the Land Registration (District Registries) Order 1989.

Other changes include the Land Registration Rules 1990 which cover, among other changes, Searches of the Index Map and delivery of applications by facsimile transmission; the Land Registration (Execution of Deeds) Rules 1990 which deal with the form and execution of deeds following the Law of Property (Miscellaenous Provisions) Act 1989 and the Companies Act 1989 and the Land Registration (Charges) Rules 1990 relating to documents incorporated in charges by reference, obligations to make further advances and evidence of discharge. The Land Registration (Solicitor to H M Land Registry) Regulations 1990, following the removal of the requirement that the Chief Land Registrar be legally qualified, specify certain acts of the Chief Land Registrar which may be done by a legally qualified Solicitor to H M Land Registry.

Inevitably there have also been a number of Fees Orders the latest of which, the Land Registration Fees Order 1991, which comes into force on 1 November 1991, is the one referred to in this edition.

I have taken this opportunity to reorganise the contents in what I consider to be a more logical order.

PREFACE

As always, my thanks are due to colleagues in the Registry for their assistance and to my wife, Anne, for her continuing support.

30 JULY 1991   Patrick J Timothy

Editor's Note

Throughout this work (unless otherwise indicated) references to 'the Act' and to section numbers relate to the Land Registration Act 1925; references to 'the Rules' and to the numbers relate to the Land Registration Rules 1925; and references to 'the Fees Order' relate to the Land Registration Fees Order 1991 a copy of which is set out in Appendix VII.

Any reference to a 'solicitor' should be read as though it included reference to a licensed conveyancer and a recognised body within the meaning of s11 (2) of the Administration of Justice Act 1985 (see r2 of the Land Registration Rules 1989).

The expression 'the appropriate district land registry' is used throughout in place of the statutory words 'the proper office' as to which see p 6.

Chapter I

General Features

1 Introduction

Her Majesty's Land Registry is a government Executive Agency the principal aims of which are stated to be:
— to maintain and develop a unified and reliable system of land registration throughout England and Wales which offers users a speedy, inexpensive and secure service and
— to achieve progressively improving performance targets set by the Lord Chancellor, so that high quality services are delivered promptly and at a lower cost to users (see the Registry's 'Framework Document' published by HMSO on 2 July 1990).

Land registration is carried out under the authority of the Land Registration Acts 1925 to 1988 and various rules and orders of which the Land Registration Rules 1925 are the most important.

The central feature of the system is the preparation and maintenance of a register and a plan for each title and the issue of a land certificate to the proprietor of the land. The register is open to public inspection.

The title to unregistered land in certain areas must be registered on the occasion of a sale, the meaning of which in this context is defined on pp 28-29, and may be registered at any time.

When the title to land is registered, it is given a title number, and the land in the title should then be dealt with by reference to that number.

Registered titles may be absolute, qualified or possessory or, in the case of leasehold land, good leasehold (see pp 7-9). The class of title governs the extent to which the Registry provides a guarantee of title.

The register of each title is divided into three sections, namely, the property register, the proprietorship register and the charges register. As their names indicate, these describe respectively the land in the title, its owner and burdens upon it.

In general, the register does not show matters which would not be disclosed by an abstract of title. In addition to the charges and other incumbrances set out in the charges register of the title, registered land may therefore (like unregistered land) be subject to:

(1) such rights as may be ascertained by:
   (a) inspection of the land, eg, rights of way, rights of drainage and other easements;
   (b) inquiry of the owner, eg, leases not exceeding twenty-one years in length;
(2) rights arising under Acts of Parliament:
   (a) affecting land generally, eg, rates and taxes of a general nature; and
   (b) affecting land in a particular district, eg, rights under the Public Health Acts, as to which inquiry should be made of the appropriate local authority;
(3) local land charges.

Simple forms for effecting dealings with registered land are set out in the schedule to the Rules. They may be modified to suit particular transactions, but it is desirable that they should be followed without unnecessary embellishment. Many of the scheduled forms, and others designed by the Chief Land Registrar, are printed and sold by HM Stationery Office and the principal law stationers. A list appears in Appendix V.

The conveyance or assignment of unregistered conveyancing is replaced as regards registered land by an instrument of transfer which, in form, is in most cases as simple as a transfer of shares. Where part of the land in a title is transferred, it is usually identified by a plan bound up in the transfer.

When a transfer of all the land in a title is registered, the Registry amends the register of the title by cancelling the entry of the name and address of the transferor in the proprietorship register and entering the name and address of the transferee. In the case of a transfer of part of the land in a title, a new title (with a new title number) is opened in respect of the land transferred, and the register of the parent title is amended to show that the land transferred has been removed from it.

Registered land can be charged by way of legal mortgage. A form of charge appears in the schedule to the Rules, but, in general, any form may be used provided that it clearly identifies the land charged. It should of course refer to the title number. When the charge is registered, the chargee's name and address are entered in the register to record that he is the proprietor of the charge, the land certificate is retained, and a charge certificate is issued. Leases of registered land must refer to the title number and, if only part of the land in the title is demised, contain an adequate plan, but otherwise may be in any form. Changes of proprietorship on death can be effected by the registration of simple forms of assent.

2 What interests can be registered?

Substantive registration is confined to legal (as distinguished from equitable) estates and interests.

The estates and interests that are capable of being registered are:

(1) a legal estate in fee simple absolute in possession;
(2) a legal leasehold term (ie, a legal term of years absolute)
   (1) of which more than twenty-one years remain unexpired at the date of the application (see p 4 for the position where only twenty-one years or less remain of a registrable term granted out of a registered reversion) (s 8(1)); or
   (2) which is caught by the compulsory provisions of s 123 even if having less than twenty-one years to run at the time the application is made (see below) (s 8(1A) as added by the Land Registration Act 1986); or (iii) under the right to buy provisions of the Housing Act 1985 and related legislation even if granted for a term of twenty-one years or less (see p 39), except:
      (a) a mortgage term where a right of redemption is subsisting; and;
      (b) an agreement for a lease;
(3) a legal rentcharge;
(4) a legal easement, right or privilege in or over land (eg, a right of way or a right of drainage) being held for the equivalent of an estate in fee simple absolute in possession or a term of years absolute. Such an interest, however, can only be registered as appurtenant to registered land.

The definition of 'land' in the Act includes manors and mines and minerals severed from the surface. These can accordingly be the subject of applications for first registration.

The following interests are incapable of substantive registration:

(1) A mortgage term where there is a subsisting right of redemption.
(2) An agreement for a lease or a contract to buy freehold or leasehold land.
(3) Land held under a lease for a term of years absolute of more than twenty-one years of which only twenty-one years or less remain—except:
   (a) a lease granted pursuant to the right to buy provisions of the Housing Act 1985 and related legislation (see p 39);
   (b) where a lease is caught by the compulsory provisions of s 123(1) when granted or assigned (see p 27) an application may be made for its registration within the two month period allowed by s 123(1), or any authorised extension of that period, notwithstanding that the term has less than twenty-one years to run when the application is made (s 8(1A) as added by the Land Registration Act 1986); and
   (c) a lease granted for a term of years absolute exceeding twenty-one years out of a registered reversion must be completed by registration (ss 19(2) and 22(2)) and it will normally be accepted for registration even though twenty-one years or less remain at the date of the application.
   It should be borne in mind that:
   (d) where a lease in possession and a reversionary lease to take effect in possession upon, or at any time within one month after, the expiration of the first lease, are so held that the interest under both instruments belongs to the same person in the same right, such leases, so far as they relate to the same land, may be treated as creating one continuous term for the purposes of an application for first registration (r 47); and
   (e) a leasehold term cannot come into effect before the date upon which the lease is executed; so that in calculating the length of the term any period prior to the date of the lease should be discounted.
(4) A lease originally granted for twenty-one years or less, except a lease granted pursuant to the right to buy provisions of the Housing Act 1985 and related legislation (see p 39). The first two points in sub-paragraph (3) above should be borne in mind in connection with such a lease.

(5) Any interest in land declared to be 'souvenir land' by the Chief Land Registrar under the Land Registration (Souvenir Land) Rules 1972. The effect of such a declaration is that compulsory first registration does not apply to the land and that, whether the land is registered or unregistered, the Chief Land Registrar may refuse applications under the Acts relating to it. Souvenir land is land all or most of which has been or is proposed to be disposed of in souvenir plots.

3 Who can apply for registration?

The person to apply for registration either personally or through his solicitor is the estate owner, ie, the person who owns the legal estate or interest the title to which is to be registered. The capacities in which he can hold the estate or interest include those of:

(1) a person absolutely and beneficially entitled;
(2) tenant for life;
(3) statutory owner;
(4) trustee for sale;
(5) personal representative.

If the applicant is absolutely entitled, he may apply to have a nominee registered in his place. The written consent of the nominee, and confirmation that the applicant is not in a fiduciary position, are required in support of the application.

4 Delivery and priority of applications

The Land Registry's headquarters office at 32 Lincoln's Inn Fields, London WC2A 3PH, is an administrative headquarters, and the work of registration is organised on a regional basis and carried out at district land registries, a list of which is set out in Appendix I. All applications and correspondence should therefore be delivered to the appropriate district land registry, which can be identified from Appendix II which contains a list of areas of local government in England and Wales and the district land registries serving them.

It is provided that no application shall be duly delivered until it is delivered at the proper office, namely: (*a*) where an application relates to land wholly within a district, the district land registry for that district; (*b*) where an application relates to land in two or more districts, any one of the district land registries for those districts (the Land Registration (District Registries) Order 1989 and rr 24 and 83 as amended by the Land Registration (Delivery of

Applications) Rules 1986 and the Land Registration Rules 1990). In this book, the expression 'the appropriate district land registry' is used in place of the statutory words 'the proper office'.

It is unnecessary to attend personally at any district land registry to deliver applications for registration or to make searches. The post or document exchange can be used to deliver all applications. Their use is officially recommended; and, as explained in Chapters II and V, certificates of the results of official searches of the public index map and of the register can be obtained through the post or document exchange.

Applications for first registration (including priority notices under r 71 and cautions against first registration under s 53) and applications for making, rectifying or cancelling any entry in the register of a registered title delivered at an appropriate district land registry after 9.30 hours on one day and before or at 9.30 hours on the next day are deemed to have been delivered at the same time, namely, immediately after 9.30 hours on the second day (rr 24 and 85 as substituted by the Land Registration (Delivery of Applications) Rules 1986 and the Land Registration Rules 1990). They are dated as of the day on which they are deemed to have been delivered; and they are completed as of the day on which and (subject to the effect of any provision of the Act or of any rules made thereunder) of the priority in which they are deemed to have been delivered (r 24 as so substituted; r 42; r 83 as substituted by the Land Registration Rules 1978 and amended by the Land Registration Rules 1990). 'Day' here means a day on which the Land Registry is open to the public (r 1(5B) as added by the Land Registration Rules 1978). The Land Registry is not open to the public on Saturdays, Sundays or public holidays.

Where two or more applications relating to a particular registered title are deemed to have been delivered at the same time, the order in which they should rank in priority as between each other is commonly clear from their content. However, r 84 as substituted by the Land Registration Rules 1978 provides for the determination of priorities in such situations.

See Chapter V as to the deemed times of delivery of applications for official searches of the register and as to the priority conferred on applications for registration by official certificates of search.

5 Classes of titles

(a) Absolute titles

An absolute title is the best form of registered title. In the case of freehold land, the grant of such a title on first registration vests in the proprietor the fee simple in possession, together with all appurtenant rights (whether mentioned on the register or not), but subject to (s 5):
  (1) the entries on the register;
  (2) overriding interests (see p 46) unless the contrary is expressed on the register; and
  (3) minor interests (see p 54) of which the proprietor has notice, where the proprietor is not entitled for his own benefit.

The rights of a beneficiary against a trustee registered proprietor would be an example of such minor interests.

In the case of leasehold land, registration with absolute title is deemed to vest in the first proprietor the leasehold interest described on the register, with all implied or expressed rights, privileges and appurtenances, but subject to the matters mentioned in (1), (2) and (3) above and to all implied and express covenants, obligations and liabilities incident to the registered land (s 9). To remove any uncertainty as to easements granted and reserved by registered leases a note setting out the position appears at the head of all modern registers of leasehold titles (see p 95 for the wording of the note).

An absolute title to leasehold land is only granted when the lessor's title can be examined by the Registry and the Registry is satisfied as to his title and his power to grant the lease. Where the superior title or titles up to and including the freehold are unregistered, these titles must be deduced, and the power of the lessor and any superior lessor to grant the lease or leases must be proved. Where the superior title or titles are registered, the examination of them is effected internally in the Registry, and here also the power of the lessor and of any superior lessor to grant the lease or leases must be established. Where the lessor's title is registered but is less than absolute, it may be impossible for the Registry to establish that the lease to the applicant was validly granted without raising requisitions relating to the superior title. The Registry will not raise such requisitions. Instead the applicant will be told that his application involves requisitions relating to the superior title and that for this reason an absolute leasehold title cannot be granted unless an application is (successfully) made by the lessor for conversion of his title to absolute.

It is, of course, advisable to apply for an absolute leasehold title wherever the superior title can be proved. Not only does the proprietor of land registered with an absolute leasehold title enjoy the security arising from the Registry's acceptance of the lessor's title to grant the lease (cf good leasehold title); he also has the advantage that the register of his title, unlike the register of a good leasehold title, gives notice of any restrictive covenants, adverse easements, and rentcharges appearing on the title to the reversion; and the absolute title extends to any easements validly granted by the lease. Moreover, by the acquisition of an absolute leasehold title on first registration, subsequent requisitions (eg, by building societies) relating to the class of title will be avoided.

(b) Good leasehold titles

The best title that a lessor or assignee of Leasehold land can obtain when the superior title is not proved as explained above is a good leasehold title. This is granted when the Registry can guarantee the applicant's title to the lease, but not that the lessor had power to grant it. The registration of a person as first proprietor of leasehold land with a good leasehold title does not affect or prejudice the enforcement of any estate, right or interest affecting or in derogation of the title of the Lessor to grant the Lease, but otherwise it has the same effect as registration with an absolute title (s 10). The advantages of an absolute leasehold title are discussed above and conversion of good leasehold to absolute leasehold title is discussed in Chapter XI.

(c) Possessory titles

A possessory title carries no guarantee that the first registered proprietor is or was entitled to the registered estate (ss 6 and 11). Thus, a person investigating a possessory title must also investigate the title prior to first registration. However, a possessory title is dealt with and guaranteed as to all subsequent ownership after the first registration as if it were an absolute title. So, although a possessory title carries no guarantee of the first proprietor's title, it will guarantee that all subsequent proprietors validly acquired such title as he had.

The Act permits the conversion of possessory titles to absolute or good leasehold. Generally, an application for conversion can be made when the title has been registered for a prescribed number of years, or sooner on the production of sufficient evidence of the pre-registration title. Conversion of title is discussed in Chapter XI.

The number of possessory titles is comparatively very small, and almost all applicants for first registration obtain an absolute or good leasehold title.

(d) Qualified titles

If, on an application for absolute or good leasehold title, title can only be established for a limited period or subject to certain reservations, the title may, at the request of the applicant, be registered with an appropriate qualification in the register. A title so registered is known as a qualified title. Subject to the qualification shown on the register, the grant of a qualified title has the same effect as the grant of an absolute or good leasehold title (ss 7 and 12). Qualified titles are uncommon. Conversion of qualified titles is discussed in Chapter XI.

6 The register of title

The register of title consists of three parts:
(*a*) the property register;
(*b*) the proprietorship register; and
(*c*) the charges register.

The *property register* contains a description of the land in the title, with a reference to the official plan of the land. It also commonly contains entries relating to easements, including on 'leasehold' registers the note set out on p 95, the inclusion or exclusion of mines and minerals, and the addition of land to the title or the removal of land from it. Statements in conveyances and transfers relating to party structures, the ownership of boundary walls and fences, and rights of light and air and other easements, are often set out or referred to in the property register.

The property register also states whether the land is freehold or leasehold. When it is leasehold, short particulars of the lease are set out, a note is made of any provision against alienation in the lease, and the lessor's title number is stated if that title is registered.

The property register of the title to a rentcharge contains short particulars of the deed creating the rentcharge and particulars of any overriding rentcharges.

The *proprietorship register* sets out:
(1) the quality (absolute, good leasehold, qualified or possessory) of the registered title;
(2) the name, address for service and description of the registered proprietor of the land; and
(3) any cautions, inhibitions or restrictions affecting the registered proprietor's powers of disposition.

The *charges register* gives particulars of incumbrances subsisting at the date of first registration and subsequent charges and other incumbrances. It contains such notes as have to be entered relating to covenants, conditions and other rights adversely affecting the land, and records such dealings with registered charges and incumbrances as are capable of registration.

Registers of title in non-computerised and computerised forms are illustrated in Appendices III and IV.

Usually a separate title is opened for the land comprised in a single application for first registration or a single transfer of part out of an existing registered title. Where several plots of land are vested in the same proprietor, however, they may be registered under one title number or several as the Registry may consider most convenient for the purpose of saving expense and facilitating future transactions. If the proprietor has any particular wish in the matter he should inform the Registry of it but should be prepared to pay any additional expenses incurred in meeting his wish. The Registry will also, when practicable and desirable, clear the register by opening a new edition containing only subsisting entries. This is only done when all certificates relating to the title are in the Registry. The certificates are then cancelled and new ones are issued. A computerised register will only contain current entries.

7 Land and charge certificates

A land certificate contains a copy of the register of title and a copy of the title plan. It may also contain documents, or copies or abstracts of documents, referred to on the register.

A first charge certificate contains the charge and copies of the register and the title plan and any documents, or copies or abstracts of documents referred to on the register. Second charge certificates normally only contain the charge and a copy of the regiser.

Each certificate bears the Land Registry seal and is admissible as evidence of the matters contained in it. At any given time it does not necessarily correspond exactly with the register, although it can be made to do so. This important matter is discussed in Chapter V.

No one should alter, add to or otherwise tamper with any land, or charge certificate or any document annexed thereto. If a land or charge certificate is lost there is a straightforward procedure for its replacement (see Chapter XVIII).

8 Index of proprietors' names

The Registry keeps an index of proprietors' names in accordance with r 9 as substituted by r 2 of the Land Registration Rules 1976.

The index shows in respect of the register of each title the name of the proprietor of the land and of the proprietor of any registered charge together in each case with the title number: provided that it is not necessary for there to be entered in the index either:

(1) the name of any building society, local authority or Government Department as proprietor of a charge, or
(2) until such time as the Lord Chancellor shall direct (no direction has been made), the name of any corporate or joint proprietor of land or of a charge registered as proprietor prior to 1 May 1972.

9 Computerisation

It is the long term aim of the Registry to computerise all its registers but this will take some years. The Plymouth District Land Registry was the first to introduce the new computerised procedures in autumn 1986. Since then a number of other district registries have followed. Now all the new registers created at those offices are stored on computer and existing registers at those offices are gradually being converted to computerised form. Computerisation will be introduced to each district registry in turn. Current plans provide that all offices will be computerised by the end of 1993.

The Registry is also involved in a feasibility study to investigate the extent to which computerisation of its maps should be undertaken. As part of this study a pilot project commenced in May 1986 at the Peterborough District Land Registry which involved the processing of all maps and plans for the district of Corby in Northamptonshire on computer. The system is based on the large scale National Grid maps published in digitised form by the Ordnance Survey. This project is now being taken forward at Plymouth.

Computerisation will not affect the general principles of land registration but there will be changes in form. Those proprietors whose registers are computerised are being issued with a new style of land or charge certificate (see Appendix IV). Apart from the fact that obsolete entries are not shown, this contains the same information as the old certificate but in A4 size. Filed plans prepared by computer on the basis of the digitised maps are on a larger scale than the plans prepared manually, and where references are necessary they may depart from the conventional colours and usages. There is of course no question of departing from the traditional red edging to show the extent of land in the title!

10 Rectification and indemnity

Those provisions of the Act which deal with the effects of first registration with absolute title and of dispositions of registered titles may suggest that once registration with absolute title is effected no alteration to that registration is possible (ss 5, 9, 20 and 23). This is not the case. Although, with a few limited exceptions, the register cannot be rectified against the proprietor of an absolute title who is in occupation, the Act and Rules contain a number of provisions which allow rectification or correction of the register.

Where a person suffers loss, either because the register has been rectified or where rectification is refused or in the event of certain errors being made by the Registry, he is entitled to be indemnified against his loss.

More detailed discussion of this topic is contained in Chapter XIX.

11 Judicial powers of the Chief Land Registrar

The Act and Rules give the Chief Land Registrar wide judicial powers in relation to land registration. The main provisions are contained in r 220 (as to cautions) and r 298 (generally). The Chief Land Registrar has power to award costs (r 321). Now that the Chief Land Registrar is not required to be legally qualified, these powers will in practice be exercised by a legally qualified person called the Solicitor to H M Land Registry (The Land Registration (Solicitor to H M Land Registry) Regulations 1990). The Registry will provide full guidance as to the procedures to anyone contemplating or involved in such a hearing.

12 Stamp duty and production of documents (L(A)451)

(a) Stamp duty

Where there is doubt about the sufficiency of the stamping of a document presented for registration, the Registry will insist on adjudication.

When the sole purpose of an instrument delivered for registration is to carry out on the register a transaction already effected by an instrument not capable of registration, the stamp duty must be impressed on the latter instrument. The registered instrument bears no duty; but before completion of the registration the stamped instrument must be produced to the Registry as evidence of the payment of the duty (r 94). The registered instrument then needs no denoting stamp.

(b) Adjudication

When the stamp duty on a document requires adjudication, the question may arise as to how this requirement can be reconciled with the need to deliver the document for registration within the period of two months laid down by s 123 in relation to documents inducing compulsory first registration (see Chapter III) or within the priority period of an official search of the register (see Chapter V). The Registry cannot accept an application to register the document, nor can it allow priority for the document, unless the document itself is lodged with the application. However, r 95 provides for the situation. The document should be sent to the appropriate district land registry, with the application to which it relates, within the two months' period or the priority period, as the case might be. There should also be sent with the application a certified copy of the document and a written request by the applicant's solicitor for the immediate return of the original coupled with an undertaking to return it to the Registry as soon as it has been adjudicated. If this is done, the application will be accepted, the Registry will return the original document to the applicant's solicitors, and the application will be stood over until the adjudication has been completed. When the document is returned to the Registry, duly adjudicated, the application will be completed as of the date on which it was originally lodged.

(c) Production of documents (L(A)451)

Transfers of registered land and transfers, conveyances and assignments inducing compulsory first registration which require a particulars delivered stamp, and are properly certified below the level at which ad valorem duty is payable, must be lodged direct at the appropriate district land registry with form L(A)451. The form L(A)451 should be properly completed and any plan referred to must be attached. The form will be checked by the Registry and forwarded to the district valuer. It must, therefore, be capable of being read on its own and should not rely for completeness on references to other documents lodged for registration. A plan should be attached in all cases where the property description does not clearly define the property (ie where it does not include a postal number).

Leases, documents which need adjudication (even if no duty is payable) and documents without a certificate of value must be sent to the Stamp Office for the particulars delivered stamp.

Where a transfer is made after a conveyance or assignment which induces compulsory first registration but before that conveyance or assignment is lodged for registration, only the transfer is caught by these arrangements. The conveyance or assignment in such a case should, therefore, be presented to the Stamp Office for the particulars delivered stamp.

13 Requisitions raised by the Registry

Rule 317, as substituted by r 11 of the Land Registration Rules 1978, provides that if an application is not in order the Registrar may raise such requisitions as he may consider necessary and may specify a period (being not less than one month) within which the applicant shall comply therewith. If the applicant fails to comply with the requisitions within the period specified, the Registrar may cancel the application or may extend the period when this appears to him to be reasonable in the circumstances. If an application appears to the Registrar to be substantially defective, he may reject it on delivery or he may cancel it at any time thereafter.

In general, the Registry allows an initial period of two months for complying with its requisitions and an appropriate note appears on the printed forms of requisition. The initial period is readily extended if the applicant shows that it would be difficult for him to comply with the requisitions within that period.

In general, fees paid on cancelled applications are not refundable (Fees Order, art 9(3)) and accordingly, on any renewal of a cancelled application, a fresh fee will be required together with, in the case of a first registration, a new form of application.

Documents enclosed with requisitions received from the Registry must be returned with the reply, unless the requisitions state otherwise.

14 Forms

Forms are prescribed for most Land Registry transactions. A list of those most likely to be needed is set out in Appendix V.

15 Fees

The fees to be paid to the Land Registry are prescribed in the Land Registration Fees Order 1991, the text of which is not out in Appendix VII, which is referred to in this book as 'the Fees Order'.

The detailed application of the Fees Order is referred to in the relevant parts of this book.

Fees are normally required to be paid on delivery of the application to which they relate by means of a cheque or postal order crossed and made payable to HM Land Registry (Fees Order, art 14). If payment is made by a cheque which is not honoured the application may be cancelled (r 317(3) as added by the Land Registration Rules 1990).

Any person or firm, if authorised by the Registry, may use a credit account for payment of fees on applications and services of such kinds as the Registrar may direct (Fees Order, art 15). If the use of credit accounts is authorised in respect of a particular type of application or service the relevant part of this book will so state.

When two or more instruments relating to the same land are delivered for registration as parts of the same application, a separate fee is payable in respect of each; but when a sale and a sub-sale are effected by one instrument of transfer only one fee, assessed on the price paid by the sub-purchaser, is payable (Fees Order, art 2(3)).

16 Information

(a) Inquiries

Inquiries as to Registry practice may be made in writing, by telephone or by personal visit to a district land registry which in the case of an inquiry relating to a specific title should be the appropriate district land registry. Time may be saved by using the practice leaflets and practice notes referred to below. In the absence of a substantive application for registration (together with the appropriate fee) the Registry is not in a position to express any opinion about an unregistered title, whether as regards its length or the form or sufficiency of any document or otherwise. Nor will it commit itself in relation to any contemplated dealing with registered land, except so far as it may advise in general terms on a point of practice or approve a draft document (see pp 75 and 199).

(b) Practice leaflets and Registered Land Practice Notes

The Registry issues a numbered series of practice leaflets, each dealing with a particular topic. A list of these is set out in Appendix VI. Copies may be obtained in reasonable quantities free of charge from any district land registry.

As a result of meetings of the Joint Advisory Committee of The Law Society and HM Land Registry more than sixty current practice notes have been issued. These are published in the Law Society's Gazette from time to time and the entire set is also published in book form by Longman. The notes provide guide lines for practitioners in relation to everyday points on land registration.

Chapter II

Plans and Maps

1 Official plans generally

Registered land, whether freehold or leasehold, or a rentcharge or other incorporeal hereditament, is described in the register verbally and by reference to an official plan filed at the Registry. The official plan for each registered title is prepared from (*a*) the plans and verbal descriptions in the title deeds, (*b*) inspection and survey of the land where necessary, and (*c*) such inquiries as may be needed to establish the identity of the property. The Ordnance Survey map is used as the basis for all official plans prepared and issued by the Registry.

An applicant for first registration must give the Registry sufficient information by plan or verbal description to enable his land to be identified with precision on the Ordnance Survey map or the Land Registry general map (r 20(iii)). If the boundaries of the land are not shown on those maps or questions as to the extent of land to be included in the title arise, a survey may be needed. If the boundaries of the land can be identified from the information supplied the official plan will be prepared without a survey.

Land certificates and charge certificates in respect of first charges contain a copy of the official plan.

2 The filed plan

The system of having a separate title plan called the filed plan for each registered title is now in general use, replacing the general map system of composite title plans referred to on pp 18–19.

Each filed plan is based on an extract from the latest revision of the ordnance map. It shows the land in the title, usually by red edging, and it is marked with such colours, symbols and other markings as may be necessary to explain entries in the register relating, for example, to restrictive covenants, easements and leases. Dimensions are shown when necessary to tie the positions of unfenced boundaries or otherwise to clarify extents of land. Parts of the land that have been removed from the title are indicated by green edging and their new title numbers are shown in green.

The scale of 1/10560 or 1/10000 is sometimes used for the registration of mountain, moorland and marshland, and areas of a like nature that are most unlikely ever to be developed or actively cultivated. The scale of 1/2500 is used for land in predominantly rural areas such as farms and other medium-sized units that are unlikely to be developed in the near future. The scale of 1/1250 is used for land in urban areas, and for developing building estates, small houses, single building plots and so on. The scale of 1/1056, which was extensively used in the former County of London, is now being progressively superseded by the scale of 1/1250.

Enlargements are provided when necessary to show and clarify detail beyond the scope of the normal Ordnance Survey scales—to show, for example, small juts in boundary walls and overlaps at different floor levels. Supplementary plans can be annexed to filed plans to show parts of buildings, or to carry complicated reference markings that would cause confusion on the filed plan itself, and for other similar purposes.

A study into the feasibility of computerisation of its map records and plans is being undertaken by the Registry (see Chapter I under the heading 'Computerisation').

3 The Land Registry general map

The Land Registry general map consists of a series of maps based on the Ordnance Survey map. Each parcel of registered land in an area covered by the general map system has a parcel number, which is shown on the map, and each section of the map is bound in book form with a parcels index. By reference to the parcel numbers, the parcels index shows the title numbers, distinguishing between freeholds, leaseholds and rentcharges. It reveals any cautions and priority notices against first registration and bears the letters 'FP' where a filed plan has been used for a particular property instead of a reference to the general map.

The individual registers of titles based on the general map without a filed plan describe the land by reference to its general map parcel number, and a copy of the relevant section of the general map is sewn up in the title certificate. A single section of the general map may thus serve as a title plan for a large number of registrations; and, together with its parcels index, it serves also as a part of the public index map (see p 23).

Changing circumstances have favoured the use of filed plans (see above) for individual registrations, and the general map system is obsolescent.

4 Field numbers and areas

Only the 1/2500 scale Ordnance Survey map shows Ordnance Survey parcel numbers and areas. The great majority of filed plans are based on the 1/1250 scale Ordnance Survey map and consequently do not show these numbers and areas. However, where a filed plan is based on an extract from the 1/2500 scale map on which the numbers and areas are shown, they will not be deleted, except where only part of a parcel is included in the title.

It should be borne in mind that the numbers and areas shown on one edition of an Ordnance Survey map may differ from those shown on another.

5 Deed plans

(a) Use in land certificate

The question is sometimes raised whether the parties' own plans attached to a conveyance or transfer should be bound into the land certificate as a matter of course. The Registry is not willing to do this in all cases, since many plans received are prepared to unsuitable scales or are poorly drawn or otherwise inadequate.

However, in cases of overlapping floors or party walls, for example, where a surveyor or architect has prepared detailed plans on larger scales which approximate almost to architectural drawings, the Registry will consider using such plans, either as an adjunct to, or in substitution for, the filed plan.

(b) Plans 'for the purpose of identification only'

Where an instrument deals with part of the land in a registered title a plan described as being 'for the purpose of identification only' is unacceptable to the Registry.

(c) Reduced copy plans used in original deeds

Reduced copies of estate layout plans are sometimes used as plans to original deeds dealing with particular properties shown on the plan. Such copies are acceptable for registration if they are reduced copies of a layout plan drawn to a generally recognised scale, eg, 1/500, and if the copies themselves are to scale and are clear and unambiguous so that relevant details can be satisfactorily identified. Therefore, when a reduced copy plan is to be used in a deed that will be presented for registration, requisitions by the Registry may be avoided if:

(1) the original scale is deleted;
(2) the plan is endorsed with a suitable form of words to indicate that it is a reduced copy; and
(3) the actual scale of the reduced copy plan is calculated and shown on the face of the plan in place of the original scale.

With regard to (1) and (3) above, if the scale on the layout plan is drawn (by reference to metres or feet) the reduced image of the drawn scale that appears on the reduced copy plan will satisfactorily indicate the scale of the reduced plan; but an endorsement as at (2) above should always appear on the reduced copy plan.

(d) Information for surveyors

A Practice Leaflet (see Appendix VI) entitled 'Surveying housing development for registration purposes' is available as a guide for those involved in the surveying, setting out and preparation of layout plans for registered building estates.

6 Ownership of fences and walls: 'T' marks

The Registry will make an entry on the register in respect of a declaration as to ownership of fences and other boundary features contained in a transfer of registered land or in a conveyance of land about to be registered. Where 'T' marks are referred to in positive covenants that are set out on the register (because they are intermingled with restrictive covenants) explanatory notes are added as necessary, but it is usually unnecessary to reproduce the 'T' marks on the filed plan. 'T' marks may appear on the plan to a deed inducing first registration which contains no fencing covenant or other relevant provision. If in such a case the solicitor to the applicant for first registration specifically asks that the 'T' marks should be reproduced on the filed plan because he regards this as important in his client's interests, the Registry will usually comply with his request.

7 Boundaries

In this country nearly all holdings are enclosed by walls, fences, hedges or other physical boundaries. All physical boundaries have width. Legal property boundaries, however, have no width; they are imaginary lines which may coincide with one side or the other of a physical boundary or with the centre line, or may lie some distance within or beyond the physical boundary.

The boundaries normally shown on the filed plan or general map are general boundaries, and the exact property boundary is left undetermined, eg, whether it runs on one side of a ditch or through the centre, or (where the registered land abuts upon a road) how far the boundary extends into the road beyond the point shown on the plan of the title. This principle applies notwithstanding that a part or the whole of a ditch, wall, fence road, stream or other boundary is expressly included in or excluded from the title (r 278).

It is left for the owner to ascertain by inspection and inquiry on the site the exact position of the property boundaries in relation to the physical boundaries.

The position of boundaries is shown on title plans, as accurately as possible within the above limits, in the light of the information in the documents of title lodged and the results of a survey of the land where this is necessary. When appropriate, measurements from nearby features are shown. The definition of such general boundaries is as accurate as, and often more accurate than, the plans on the title deeds themselves. It must be borne in mind that (particularly on the small-scale plans) the width of a line on a plan may represent a space of one or two feet on the ground.

If an applicant requires that a title be registered with fixed and not general boundaries, a detailed official survey of the land is necessary, inquiries have to be made of adjoining owners, and their titles have to be strictly proved. The applicant has to bear the cost of this. It is an expensive process, and there is no guarantee that it will be possible, as a result of the investigations made, to fix the boundaries. In practice applications for fixed boundaries are almost unknown.

(a) The hedge and ditch presumption

The boundaries shown on the filed plan are general boundaries, as explained above, and like those shown on the Ordnance Survey map they follow the centre lines of hedges. In the case of agricultural land they may not be the property boundaries having regard to the hedge and ditch presumption. The explanation of the Registry's practice is to be found in the nature of a general boundaries registration, ie, that exact property boundaries are not defined on the title plans.

(b) Discrepancy between title plan and plan on transfer

Although registration with general boundaries does not guarantee the ownership of any boundary, it is the duty of the Registry to show as accurately as possible on title plans the position of physical features, including fences, hedges and walls, and where none exist to reproduce the boundaries shown on the plan to the conveyance or transfer with all available detail.

Accordingly, where a conveyance or transfer plan shows details which do not correspond with those actually existing on the ground, the Registry will consider the need to have either the deed plan, or the physical boundaries of the land, altered so that the two correspond and thus give effect to the bargain between the parties.

If the plan has to be altered (as will usually be the case) the Registry may ask that all the parties concerned sign a new plan, under a statement that it correctly represents their intentions, and an appropriate endorsement (referring to the new plan) on the defective deed plan. Or the parties may be invited to correct the defective deed plan and sign it, or to remove it, and substitute and sign a new plan. In these ways the task of preparing a formal deed of rectification is avoided.

However, if the deed plan is so badly drawn or so ambiguous that the Registry cannot decide whether or not it represents the fenced boundaries, either the application for registration will have to be cancelled, or the Registry will submit a draft filed plan for approval by all parties before the registration is completed. When a draft filed plan has been approved, the parties will be asked to sign appropriate endorsements on it and on the defective deed plan.

Where there are no physical features defining the boundaries of the land, the conveyance or transfer plan will be treated as the governing factor on which the registration is to be based, and the existence of survey pegs which do not conform with the boundaries shown on the deed plan will usually be ignored.

(c) Boundary disputes

Where a dispute concerns the boundary of a registered title the parties should contact the appropriate district land registry, at the first opportunity, to seek information and assistance in resolving the matter. The Registry will use its best endeavours to assist the parties to reach an amicable solution to the dispute. In such a situation the provisions as to rectification and indemnity (see Chapter XIX) may become relevant.

8 Metrication

In the Registry, as elsewhere, metrication is being introduced gradually. Either imperial or metric measurements on plans of deeds lodged for registration are accepted, but both forms should not be used in the same deed. When it is necessary to reproduce on official title plans figured dimensions shown on deed plans, reproduction is in the form used on the deed plan. Equivalent measurements in the other form are not shown, and no conversion factor is given. Metric linear measurements on official plans are expressed in metres and decimal parts of a metre. Where an estate developer changes to the metric system during development (and in some other cases) measurements in both forms may appear on a single official plan. In such cases, a warning is endorsed on the plan.

9 Official searches of the public index map
(a) The public index map

An index map is maintained by the Registry showing the position, extent and title number of every registered estate and the position and extent of all land affected by cautions and priority notices against first registration and souvenir land declarations (see p 5). This map is open to public inspection as described below.

The map differs in form and scale according to the area concerned. For some areas Ordnance Survey sheets are used; for the others the book form with parcels index as described on pp 18–19 above. A list of pending applications is also kept.

Objects of searching the public index map are:
(1) to discover whether any particular land is registered or affected by a caution or priority notice against first registration (a search is strongly recommended whenever an unregistered title is being considered);
(2) to find out the title number of a particular piece of land;

(3) to obtain a map reference in order to prepare a transfer (without plan) of part of the land comprised in a title registered by reference to the general map (see pp 18–19);

(4) to identify a particular property where there is some doubt which an examination of the Ordnance Survey map or the general map may help to resolve. Where questions of measurement or of scale are in doubt the plans official will always assist any applicant to identify the property with which he is concerned.

(b) Applications

Postal applications for an official search of the public index map must be made on form 96 addressed to the appropriate district land registry (Rule 3 of the Land Registration Rules 1990). Applications for personal searches must be made at the appropriate district land registry in writing on Form 96A copies of which can be obtained free of charge from the Registry. By concession, if the property is known to be registered but the title number is not known and office copies are required, the applicant may lodge Form 109 (see Chapter V) with the words 'Please supply the title number' written boldly at the top of the form. In this case Form 96 will not be insisted upon. Searches of the public index map cannot be made by telephone or telex.

A separate application form must be lodged for each parcel of land to be searched (Rule 3(2) of the 1990 Rules). Parcel of land is defined (Rule 2(1) of the 1990 Rules) as all or any part of:

(a) a 'dwelling' which means a building or part of a building occupied or intended to be occupied as a separate dwelling, together with any yard, garden, outhouse and garage belonging to it; or

(b) any other land which is separately occupied or if not separately occupied, in separate ownership; and for this purpose an owner is the person who (in his own right or as trustee for any other person) is entitled to receive the rack rent of land or, where the land is not let at a rack rent, would be entitled if it were so let.

(c) Description of the property to be searched

The application must fully and clearly describe the land to which it relates. The description should include the postal number or description, the road name, the locality, the town, the district or

London borough, the administrative county and the post code and/or Ordnance Survey map reference. When the land can be identified by a street number, a plan can usually be dispensed with. If there is any possible doubt as to the extent being searched and in all other cases, the application should be accompanied by a plan defining the land by colouring or edging. The scale and north point should be shown and the plan must contain sufficient details of roads and other features to enable the land to be identified on the Ordnance Survey map. If the search is in respect of a particular flat in a block of flats, this should be made clear in the description. If a search of a large area is required applicants are requested to contact the appropriate district land registry in advance so that special arrangements may be made to eliminate unnessary work.

(d) Fees

A fee of £7 for each registered title in respect of search is given or for each application where no part of the land to which the search relates is registered application (ie for each 'parcel of land') is payable under Part II of Schedule 3 of the Fees Order whether application is made on Form 96, Form 96A or by endorsement on Form 109. Alternatively a copy of an Index Map section can be supplied for a fee of £70. A credit account (see p 15) can be used for payment of fees on such searches. The Fees Order provides for additional fees in special cases but in such a case the applicant must be notified of the additional fee and given a chance to withdraw his application without fee if he so elects (Articles 7(4) and (5) of the Fees Order).

(e) Certificate of result

The certificate of the result of the official search will state whether the land is registered or not, and, if not, whether any caution against first registration or priority notice is registered. The certificate will also state whether any registrations are freehold or leasehold or of a rentcharge, and give their title numbers. The existence of any relevant souvenir land declaration (see p 5) will be disclosed. Details of any pending application for first registration will be given. Details of any registered leases will only be given if specifically requested. Normally this will be unnecessary as the search result will be followed by an application for office copies. If the details are required, 'Please reveal details of any registered lease' should be written boldly across the top of Form 96.

If the applicant specifically requests a plan covering the area searched with the result, it may be issued provided that (i) the Registry holds a copy of the current edition of a suitable ordnance survey map on which the property is defined and (ii) the property can be illustrated on a single standard A4 size print and the extent of the area searched can be readily determined from the public index map. No fee is charged. Applicants are requested to keep such requests to a minimum as preparation of such plans is time-consuming and causes significant delays in the issue of the search certificates.

Chapter III

First Registration

1 Compulsory first registration on sale

The following transactions with unregistered land make registration of the grantee's title compulsory (s 123, as amended by s 2 of the Land Registration Act 1986):
(1) a conveyance on sale of freehold land;
(2) an assignment on sale of leasehold land held for a term of years absolute having more than twenty-one years to run from the date of delivery of the assignment; and
(3) a grant of a term of years absolute (i) of more than twenty-one years from the date of delivery of the grant or (ii) pursuant to the right to buy provisions of the Housing Act 1985 and related legislation (see p 39);

provided, as regards (1), that the conveyance is of the legal estate, and, as regards (2) and (3), that the term is capable of substantive registration: see pp 3–5. Compulsion does not extend to incorporeal hereditaments or to mines and minerals apart from the surface, or to corporeal hereditaments parcel of a manor and included in the sale of a manor as such (s 120(1)) or to souvenir land (see p 5).

When a transaction of one of these three kinds has taken place, an application for first registration must be made by the grantee or his successor in title within two months of the date of the conveyance, assignment or lease. If this is not done, the conveyance, assignment or lease will become void as to the grant of a legal estate.

When the application for registration is made after the two months have elapsed, it should include a written explanation of the failure to register in time, and a request for an order of the Chief Land Registrar extending the time for registration. If a reasonable explanation for the delay is given, an extension will be granted. The explanation may be quite ordinary. No fee is payable.

It is the view of the Land Registry that an order is not essential where:

(1) the late application is for registration of the title to land demised by a lease granted out of a registered reversion or

(2) no disposition (eg, a charge or lease) by the applicant is disclosed.

It is never necessary to apply for an order in respect of any dealing with land already on the register.

Sometimes practitioners are in doubt as to whether a particular transaction is or is not made 'on sale' in the sense in which these words are used in relation to compulsory first registration. It is generally considered that the following are transactions as to which compulsory registration is:

Necessary	*Not Necessary*
Sale in the popular and commercial sense	Assent or appropriation
	Gift
Conveyance in consideration of shares or other securities	Mortgage
	Partition
Conveyance in consideration of a rentcharge or annuity	Voluntary settlement or settlement in consideration of marriage
Exchange where equality money is paid (s 123(3))	Exchange where no equality money is paid
Assignment of a lease by way of surrender for which the lessor pays money and which will not result in the immediate extinguishment of the lease	Conveyance of the legal estate to give effect to dealings with undivided shares whether for value or otherwise
	Assignment or surrender of a lease to the reversioner containing a declaration of merger (s 123(3))
Compulsory acquisition by deed poll	Conveyance or assignment of an interest which will immediately be merged (r 207)
	Conveyance or assignment of an equity of redemption made in consideration solely

of a covenant to pay the outstanding debt

The creation of a power of sale or trust for sale, as distinct from an actual sale

Compulsory acquisition by means of a general vesting declaration

The compulsory first registration provisions do not apply when the joint terms of a lease and a reversionary lease may be treated as creating one continuous term for the purpose of an application for first registration under r 47 (see p 4) if neither lease on its own is compulsorily registrable.

The provisions of the Act defining a conveyance on sale for the purposes of compulsory registration are contained in s 123(3). If, in cases of this kind, practitioners feel any real doubt, they may think it wise to register the title so as to avoid possible future difficulties.

2 Voluntary first registration

An application for the registration of the title to unregistered freehold land, or unregistered leasehold land capable of substantive registration (see pp 3–5), may be made voluntarily at any time.

3 Before completion

When an application for first registration is to be made either compulsorily or voluntarily, by a purchaser of freehold or leasehold land or by an original lessee, there is no special procedure to be adopted before the completion of the transaction in question. It proceeds on the lines customary in the case of unregistered interests, with the delivery and perusal of the abstract of title, requisitions on title, and the preparation and completion of the purchase deed, lease or grant. Besides the usual searches, an application should also be made to the appropriate district land registry for an official search of the public index map, as explained in Chapter XI, to discover whether any interests in the land are already registered.

Care should be taken to see that the extent of the land to be registered is accurately defined on the ground by boundary walls or fences or by reference to other physical features; and the conveyance or other assurance to the intending applicant must accurately identify the land to be registered in relation to the ordnance map. It is inadvisable to describe the land by reference to a plan to an earlier document of title unless the plan is known to correspond with the modern physical boundaries.

Particular care is required in the case of certain types of property. Examples are where a garden is separated from the house to which it belongs by a passage or road, where rooms or parts of rooms extend into an adjoining property or over a passageway or where the boundaries are not fully defined by features on the ground. A solicitor should ensure that he identifies such cases by discussing the layout of the property with his client and should bring the facts to the attention of the Registry, preferably by means of a plan, when lodging the application for first registration.

As one of the preliminaries to completion of the transaction the land should be inspected to ascertain its boundaries, and to discover, so far as this can be done by careful inspection, any rights of way, light or drainage, or other overriding interests (as to these see p 46 et seq) to which it is subject. Any persons in occupation of the land should be asked to disclose the nature of their rights and to whom rent (if any) is paid (see pp 48–50).

Rule 72 provides that a person who has the right to apply for registration as the first proprietor may deal with the land as though he were in fact registered as proprietor; and if he transfers the land the transferee is to be deemed to be the applicant for first registration. For example, if a purchaser of freehold land immediately re-sells the land, he may transfer it to a second purchaser. An ordinary form of Land Registry transfer should be used; it should refer to the document vesting the land in the transferor; and the transferee will be the person to apply for first registration. Rule 72 also covers charges by purchasers of unregistered land in the usual situation where there is a conveyance on sale followed immediately by a charge in favour of the building society or bank from whom part of the purchase money has been borrowed, the charge being followed in its turn by an application for first registration. Certain difficulties inherent in transfers under r 72 (definition of the land; rights and incumbrances; and indemnity covenants) are discussed in the Registry's Practice Leaflet No 5—see p 16.

4 The application for first registration

An application by solicitors for the first registration of freehold or leasehold land is made by sending, usually by post, to the appropriate district land registry a completed application form together with the necessary supporting deeds and documents. Application forms have been designed to meet the needs of the various kinds of applications. Appendix V contains a list of these forms, and some remarks about filling them in are on pp 31-33. The supporting deeds and documents are discussed on pp 33-35.

Care should be taken to choose the right application form and to complete it carefully. Three forms of application for first registration of land are published for use by solicitors. These are 1B for freehold land, 2B for leasehold land on behalf of other than an original lessee and 3B for leasehold land on behalf of an original lessee.

Forms of application are also available for use by the owner in person. These are IA (freehold land), 2A (leasehold land other than on the grant of a new lease) and 3A (original lessee).

Forms (apart from rentcharge forms—see Chapter X) cannot be obtained direct from the Registry but are available from HM Stationery Office and law stationers.

(a) Completing the application form

The following points should be borne in mind when completing the application form for first registration:

Class of title sought The form should be amended if a possessory or qualified title is being applied for. The leasehold forms provide for the alternative GOOD/ABSOLUTE to be deleted as appropriate.

Land Registry fees On first registration of land (other than by an original lessee) a fee under Scale A is payable (Fees Order, article 2(1)). On first registration of the title of an original lessee a fee under Scale B is payable on the amount of the annual rent and under Scale A on the amount of any premium (article 2(2)). Abatement 1 should not be overlooked. Attention is also particularly invited to:

   (1) the assessment of the fee payable on the registration of an original lessee in respect of a variable rent reserved by a lease or where there is no premium paid or annual rent (other than a nominal rent) reserved (article 2(2)(a) and (b));

(2) the assessment of the fee on the present value of land and buildings when the application is not based on a recent purchase (article 3); and
(3) the special provisions made for large scale applications (ie those involving 20 or more separate areas of land) (article 6).

When the application is made on behalf of a transferee who acquired the land by a transfer pursuant to r 72 (see p 30) the registration fee should be assessed by reference to this transfer, not by reference to the assurance in favour of the transferor.

If it is desired that an application should be specially expedited, a written request should be made and the minimum expedition fee of £35 (article 12) should be paid and entered in the fees panel of the application form. If the request for expedition is made by way of an endorsement on the application form, it should be made prominently; and if the request is made by letter it is advisable also to endorse the application form boldly, 'Please expedite'.

Name, address and occupation of applicant   The full name, full postal address and (not companies and corporations) description of the applicant for entry on the register are required. In the case of companies the registration number should be supplied. Postal codes should be given. The address must be an address in the United Kingdom (s 79) which in this context means England, Scotland, Wales and Northern Ireland, but does not include the Channel Islands or the Isle of Man. It is important that addresses on the register should be up to date, and accordingly, in the case of an ordinary householder who on completion of the purchase moves to the property being registered, the address to be entered on the register will usually be the full postal address of that property. Any person may have up to three addresses on the register, including the address of his solicitors (r 315). Registered proprietors who are not resident in the United Kingdom sometimes find it convenient to be registered c/o their solicitors. As the new application forms envisage this information being copied direct to the register particular care should be taken when completing this section.

Instructions regarding documents   It is essential that the relevant panels be completed correctly to ensure that the Registry's acknowledgement of the receipt of the application is sent to the right solicitors and that documents are issued to the persons entitled to have them.

Certificate and other statements as to the title The certificate relating to the capacity of the applicant(s) is printed in alternative forms. It is important to insert X in the relevant box or otherwise.

The certificates relating to company applicants should be completed or struck out as may be appropriate.

Attention should be given to the statement as to incumbrances created by the applicant (or applicants) and to the statement as to floating charges (company and other corporate applicants), the schedule of incumbrances being appropriately completed.

Failure to complete the certificate relating to entries in the Land Charges Department will probably give rise to requisitions by the Registry.

Merged leases The application that no note be made on the register of a lease that has been determined by merger should be completed or struck out as may be appropriate. When a lease has been determined by merger, this application should be completed even though there is a statement as to merger in a document of title.

Schedule of incumbrances It is important to complete the schedule of incumbrances (see above under the sub-heading '*Certificate and other statements as to the title*') and to enter 'None' when appropriate.

Signature of form The form should be signed by a partner (or other person authorised by the firm) in ink in the name of the firm. Alternatively the firm's name may be typed on the form or endorsed on it by means of a rubber stamp, provided that the name so typed or endorsed is authenticated by the ordinary signature of a partner. Facsimile signatures, whether of firms or individuals, are not acceptable to the Registry.

(b) Deeds and documents to accompany the application

The following is a summary of the deeds and documents which should be sent to the appropriate district land registry with the completed first registration application form:

(1) All the deeds and documents relating to the title which the applicant has in his possession or under his control. Deeds and documents which are in the custody of a mortgagee under a mortgage prior to the conveyance to the applicant or in respect of which, because they relate to other land or for some other reason, the applicant has only a right

to production are not regarded as being 'under the control' of the applicant. The applicant should lodge a sufficient marked abstract or certified copy of such deeds and documents and, although he has the power, the Chief Land Registrar will rarely order the originals to be produced.

Failure to send all these deeds and documents falsifies the certificate given by the applicant's solicitors on the application form. In particular it should be noted that there should be lodged:

(a) any enquiries before contract (with replies), contract for sale, requisitions on title (with replies) and any opinions of counsel;

(b) all relevant title deeds in the possession or under the control of the applicant, whether dated before or after any stipulated root of title;

(c) all abstracts and epitomes of title; and

(d) all search certificates.

The reason for requiring the production of pre-root deeds and documents is explained in note A5 in the book *Registered Land Practice Notes* (see p 16). The note also refers to the need to lodge the contract and requisitions. Not only are these material to the examination of the title, but their production may well enable the Registry to dispose of questions that would otherwise have to be the subject of requisitions. Proper attention should be given to the marking of abstracts and the verification of copies of deeds in accordance with the certificate given by the applicant's solicitors on the application form.

(2) A copy (including a copy of any plan) of the latest document of title, not being a document of record. This will usually be a copy of the conveyance, assignment, transfer or lease in favour of the applicant. A clear carbon copy of the engrossment may be used. It should be certified by the applicant's solicitors to be a true copy of the original.

(3) Sufficient particulars, by plan or otherwise, to enable the land to be fully identified on the ordnance map (particular care should be taken in certain types of case; see p 30).

(4) Any mortgage or charge by the applicant, with a certified copy if the mortgage or charge is still subsisting.

(5) In the case of a limited company or other corporate applicant, particulars of its incorporation, constitution and powers, and of any floating charges, in accordance with the

statements on the completed first registration application form. In the case of a company incorporated in England or Scotland, if the company's registered number is supplied it will be entered in the register immediately after the company's name.

(6) The lessor's land certificate, when a lease by a proprietor of registered land is to be registered, or the grantor's land certificate, when a rentcharge granted by a proprietor of registered land is to be registered. The lease or grant is a disposition of his registered land by the lessor or grantor, and must be completed by registration. Completion by registration involves the entry of notice of the lease or grant in the register of the lessor's or grantor's title as well as substantive registration of the lease or grant; and the Act requires the production of the land certificate when the notice is entered. Production of the lessor's land certificate, although desirable, is not essential in the case of a lease granted at a rent without taking a premium (*Strand Securities Ltd v Caswell* [1965] Ch 958). The land certificate is usually deposited at the appropriate district land registry to meet the application for registration. It is prudent therefore to inquire whether the lessor's or grantor's title is registered and, if so, to arrange for the deposit of the land certificate and state the deposit number on the first registration application form (the procedure for lodging documents on deposit is described on p 72). See p 94 as to the production of the charge certificate of the lessor's title; and see p 132 as to the production of the charge certificate of the grantor's title when a rentcharge created out of registered land is registered.

(7) A list in triplicate of all documents delivered. Printed form A13 (see Appendix V) may be used. Deeds and documents should be entered in the list in date order and copies should be entered as separate items. On delivery of the application, one copy of the list is returned by way of acknowledgment to the solicitors who delivered the application. On completion of the registration, another copy is issued with the deeds and documents that are not being retained in the Registry. Such deeds and documents as are being retained are marked with an asterisk on this copy. The third copy is retained and forms part of the Registry's record of the registration.

(8) Inland Revenue form L(A)451 duly completed in all appropriate cases (see p 13).

(9) A cheque for the fees payable.

5 Incorporeal and other hereditaments

Applications for registration of title to manors or other incorporeal hereditaments, mines and materials severed from the surface, tunnels and other similar hereditaments must be made and proceeded with in similar manner to the interests referred to above, subject to such modifications as the case may require and the Chief Land Registrar may approve. All necessary plans to identify such hereditaments must be furnished to the Registry. As registration of some of these interests is unusual, the applicant if in any doubt as to the correct method of preparing his application should consult the appropriate district land registry.

The provisions of the Act as to compulsory registration do not apply to incorporeal hereditaments, or to mines and minerals apart from the surface, or to corporeal hereditaments parcel of a manor and included in the sale of a manor as such.

6 Official examination of title

On receipt of the application for registration, the Registry examines the title as shown by the documents lodged and makes such searches and inquiries, and gives such notices to tenants and occupiers and other persons, as the Chief Land Registrar thinks fit. The Chief Land Registrar may, if he thinks fit, refer the whole or any part of the examination of the title to one of the special conveyancing counsel of the courts, and act on his opinion.

Section 13(c) of the Act enables the Chief Land Registrar in his discretion to grant an absolute or good leasehold title in cases where he 'is of opinion that the title is open to objection, but is nevertheless a title the holding under which will not be disturbed'.

Delay is avoided if the deeds and documents accompanying the application are presented in a way that is easy to follow and if the Registry's requisitions (if any) are answered promptly. Undue delay in dealing with requisitions may result in the cancellation of the application (see p 14).

7 Completion of registration

On completion of an application to register a freehold title, the Registry stamps the conveyance to the applicant with an official stamp showing the title number and the tenure. Where a leasehold title has been registered, the stamp is endorsed on the lease and, where the applicant is an assignee, on the assignment to him. However, the real protection of any person against possible mistake or fraud lies in a search of the public index map (see Chapter 11).

On receiving the deeds and documents back from the Registry, with the land or charge certificate, on completion of the registration, the solicitor should:
(1) carefully examine the certificate to see that it is correct; and
(2) check the deeds and documents with his receipted list to see that all except those marked with an asterisk have been returned.

If the solicitor finds a mistake in the certificate, he should return it to the Registry together with an explanatory letter and such of the deeds and documents as are necessary to show that correction is required. If the error is clerical, and is clear at a glance, eg, the wrong spelling of a name or an address, the correction will be made and the certificate returned immediately.

Deeds are occasionally retained where no abstract was lodged, and if the solicitor feels that he ought to have them back, he can usually obtain them by supplying certified copies or examined abstracts in their place. To enable the solicitor to make the copies or abstracts, the Registry will usually return the originals by post, on the receipt of a written undertaking to relodge them or furnish the copies or abstracts within a specified time, say fourteen days.

8 Acquisition of title by possession

A person claiming to have acquired a title to registered or unregistered land under the Limitation Act 1980 may apply to be registered as the proprietor of the land. Whether the land has previously been registered or not the application should take the form of an application for first registration on the appropriate application form (see Appendix V). A fee under Scale A will be payable and the applicant will commonly be called upon to pay an additional fee under article 10 of the Fees Order towards the costs of an inspection of the land. In some cases the costs of the publication of advertisements will also have to be met by the applicant.

The application should be based on the best available evidence, supported by statutory declarations. The Registry usually expects to see at least two declarations, one being by the squatter himself, and the other or others by some responsible person or persons able to declare as to the facts from his or their own knowledge.

The declarations should give a full and factual account of what has occurred. Thus it might be expected that they would establish the squatter's continuous open and exclusive possession, free from any adverse claim, for the appropriate period. The time at and the circumstances in which possession began should be stated. If there was an encroachment from the squatter's adjoining land, the nature of his ownership of that land should be shown. It must be made clear that possession was not by virtue of any rightful claim, eg, that of a tenant or licensee, and that there has been no acknowledgment of the true owner's title; and it should be established, if such be the case, that nothing is known of any lease of the land.

In considering the application, the Registry will seek to apply the principles of the general law of adverse possession.

9 Title shown procedure

The title shown procedure has been developed to simplify first registration where large building estates, the titles to which are unregistered, are about to be sold off in plots to individual purchasers who will apply for first registration. When the procedure is used, the Registry, having exhaustively examined the topography and title of the estate, issues to the owner's solicitors a letter setting out the terms on which absolute title will be granted to purchasers of individual houses or plots. The Registry is only able to apply the procedure to estates where both the topography and the title are straightforward, and where all the sales off are to take place quickly. The procedure is particularly suitable where a freehold reversioner is selling to lessees. It can also be used to enable absolute leasehold titles to be granted where a freeholder of unregistered land is granting long leases.

The procedure, which is wholly independent of the Act and Rules, has been developed to avoid the repetitive examination of a single title. It cannot be claimed as of right. Close collaboration between the Registry and the owner's solicitors is necessary, and a solicitor who wishes to avail himself of the procedure should make a preliminary inquiry of the appropriate district land registry by letter before taking any other step.

10 Public authorities: certificates of title

The Chief Land Registrar has made arrangements with a number of local and other public authorities whereby when the authority sells land it gives the purchaser a certificate as to the title in an agreed form instead of deducing title in the ordinary way. The certificate is effective at the date of the completion of the sale and it contains a statement of the incumbrances that affect the land on that day. The Registry accepts this statement, and accordingly, when the purchaser applies for the first registration of his title, he need not produce the normal conveyancing evidence of the authority's title; nor is a search in the Land Charges Department against the name of the authority required.

11 Public sector housing

Under s 154(2) of the Housing Act 1985 a landlord is obliged to give to a tenant who exercises his right to buy under that Act a certificate of title in a form approved by the Chief Land Registrar. Three such forms of certificate of title, Forms PSD1 (where the landlord conveys a freehold dwelling house), PSD2 (where the landlord owns the freehold and grants a lease) and PSD3 (where the landlord does not own the freehold and grants an underlease) have been so approved. Similarly Forms PSD 13, 14 and 15 have been approved for use in preserved right to buy cases and Form PSD16 has been approved for use in extended right to buy cases. These forms of certificate of title are only to be used in right to buy cases and they should not be used in any other circumstances. The certificate must be signed as provided and, in the case of a local authority, by the chief executive officer or by some other officer approved by the District Land Registrar.

The certificate of title procedure entirely replaces the need for the purchaser or his solicitor to examine title in the normal way, so that not only does it obviate the need for production of the title deeds but it also makes it unnecessary for a search to be made by the purchaser against the name of the vendor in the Land Charges Department. The certificate is the landlord's responsibility and he must compensate the Registry in respect of any indemnity claim arising as a result of inaccuracies in his certificate.

Under the right to buy provisions a lease (including a shared ownership lease) is registrable notwithstanding that it is granted for a term of twenty-one years or less. The possibility of such a lease being granted arises because of the delay between the tenant claiming the right to buy and completion. It is also provided that a lease (including a shared ownership lease) granted pursuant to the right to buy is compulsorily registrable whether or not the lease is granted for a term of more than twenty-one years.

Applications for first registration following the exercise of the right to buy should be lodged under cover of whichever of the first registration application forms (see p 31) is appropriate to the circumstances, but the form should be amended to show that title has not been examined and reliance has been placed on the certificate of title supplied by the landlord, which must be lodged with the application.

Where a shared ownership lease is granted under the 1985 Act, a restriction will be entered to prevent the registration of disposals of part of the land comprised in the lease, at a time when the lessee's share is less than 100 per cent, unless it is a disposal authorised by the 1985 Act. No formal procedure is laid down for evidencing the purchase of additional shares, and it is not necessary to record the purchase of an additional share on the register. However, the Registry will accept an application to enter notice of a deed recording such a purchase, if required (a fee of £35 will be payable). Where the purchase of an additional share is at a discount and a discount charge is created an application to enter notice of that charge should be made (see p 121).

The fee payable under Scale A on any application following a sale at a discount under the right to buy provisions (or under Part V of the Housing Act 1957) is assessed on the price actually paid and not on the full market value. On an application for first registration of a lease, including a shared ownership lease, made pursuant to the provisions of Part V of the Housing Act 1985 (Right to buy) or to any statutory instrument applying the same Abatement 3 reduces to one fifth the fee payable under Scale B on the largest ascertainable amount of rent. On first registration of a shared ownership lease granted under the 1985 Act, a fee under Scale A will be payable on the amount of the premium actually paid, together with a fee under Scale B on the maximum rent reserved at the time of granting the lease reduced in accordance with Abatement 3.

Where the title to a property acquired in exercise of the right to buy is already registered, the normal provisions as to registration of a disposition of registered land will apply. As such applications will not be accompanied by a certificate of title to identify them, it would assist the Registry if the application form, A4 or A5, were clearly marked 'Housing Act 1985: Right to buy case' or as appropriate.

12 Housing defects (Housing Act 1985, Part XVI)

Paragraph 17 of Schedule 20 to the Housing Act 1985 extends the provisions for compulsory registration of title to defective dwellings repurchased under that Act. It is provided that the acquiring authority must supply a certificate of title in a form approved by the Chief Land Registrar. Two such forms have been approved, PSD11 (freeholds) and PSD12 (leaseholds).

No application for the first registration of a leasehold interest is necessary where the acquiring authority is the owner of the reversion. If the title to the reversion is registered, an application should be made for cancellation of notice of the lease acquired from the reversionary title. If the reversion is not registered, the leasehold deeds should merely be placed with the title deeds to the reversion.

If the title to a repurchased dwelling is already registered, application for registration should be made in the normal way.

Chapter IV

Covenants and Other Interests

1 Covenants

(a) Burden of restrictive covenants: first registration

When the deeds and documents accompanying an application for first registration show that the land is subject to restrictive covenants (other than covenants between lessor and lessee) notice of the covenants will be entered in the register. An entry in the charges register will refer to the deed containing the covenants. Also, if the deed or a certified copy or examined abstract of it accompanies the application, the text of the covenants and stipulations (or of the abstract) will be made available. This may be done by setting out the covenants and stipulations, or the abstract, verbatim in the register or by referring to a filed document. The filed document will be the deed or a copy or abstract of it according to the circumstances of the particular registration; and when the filed document method is adopted, the deed or a copy or abstract, according to the circumstances, will be sewn up in or issued with the land or first charge certificate.

Sometimes neither the original deed nor a certified copy nor examined abstract will accompany the application. The action taken by the Registry will then depend on the circumstances. If an unverified copy or an unverified abstract of the covenants and stipulations accompanies the application, and the Registry considers the risk of its being inaccurate to be so small that it can properly be treated as though it were verified, it will be so treated and an entry will be made in the register accordingly, as explained above.

If an unverified copy or an unverified abstract of the covenants and stipulations accompanies the application but cannot properly be treated as though it were verified, and if a solicitor so requests, entries will be made in the register as follows:

[In the charges register]

'A Conveyance of the land in the title [and other land] dated   made between   contains restrictive covenants but no verified particulars of them were produced on first registration. The particulars set out in the schedule annexed of what purport to be the said covenants were provided by Messrs   solicitors acting for a vendor in [1991].'

[In the schedule of restrictive covenants]
'The following are particulars of what purport to be the covenants contained in the Conveyance dated   referred to in the charges register.'

The Registry does not consider that s 110(4) applies to these qualified entries.

If an unverified copy or an unverified abstract of the covenants and stipulations accompanies the application, but cannot be treated as verified and is not the subject of a request by solicitors as indicated in the preceding paragraph, the entry in the register will refer to the deed containing the covenants and stipulations and will state that it contains restrictive covenants but that neither the original deed nor a certified copy nor an examined abstract thereof was produced on first registration. Such an entry will be made also when no particulars, verified or unverified, of the covenants or stipulations accompany the application.

When only particulars of the restrictive stipulations, without the words of covenant, accompany an application, a normal form of entry, modified accordingly, may be used; but a full verified copy, or a full examined abstract, of the words of covenant and of the stipulations should be provided whenever possible.

The documents lodged with some applications for first registration do not contain adequate information as to whether or not restrictive covenants affect the land. These applications are of four main classes:

(1) applications to register squatters' land;
(2) 'lost deeds' applications;
(3) applications based on 'short' titles; and
(4) applications by purchasers relying on a good statutory root of title behind which there may be restrictive covenants protected by registration in the Land Charges Department but not discoverable by the purchaser.

It is the Registry's practice as regards applications of classes (1) and (2) to make an entry in the register to the effect that the land is subject to such restrictive covenants as may have been imposed thereon before a specified date so far as they are subsisting and capable of being enforced. The entry is likely to be made in cases of class (3); but in cases of class (4) it is usually dispensed with.

(b) Restrictive covenants imposed on land already registered

Restrictive covenants (other than those between lessor and lessee) imposed on land already registered must be protected by notice on the register of the burdened title (see Chapter XIV as to applications for the entry of notice). This may be done by setting out the covenants verbatim on the register, or by filing the document imposing them (or a copy of it) and sewing up an office copy of it in the land or first charge certificate. When a transfer imposing restrictive covenants is delivered for registration, a certified copy (including any plan) must accompany it as required by r 135. This copy is then available to be made an office copy and to be sewn up in the certificate.

If a transfer of part imposes restrictive covenants on the transferee's title or on the title out of which it is created, notice of these covenants is entered automatically on the register of the burdened title. However, if the transfer imposes restrictive covenants on any other title, a specific application for the entry of notice of the covenants on that title is necessary. If in a transfer of the whole of the land in a title, restrictive covenants are imposed on land in another title, a separate application to enter notice of the covenants on the register of that other title is necessary. Similarly, if restrictive covenants are imposed otherwise than in a transfer, eg, by a deed of covenant, or a deed of grant, an application must be made for notice of the instrument imposing them to be entered on the register of title to the burdened land.

It is important to identify the burdened land clearly (by plan if necessary); and of course the identity of the land intended to be benefited should not be left in doubt.

(c) Benefit of restrictive covenants

It is never possible to state on the register in unqualified terms that land has the benefit of restrictive covenants because, as a matter of general law, it can never be said that they will always remain enforceable.

In any particular case, however, the Registry will consider a special request for a note to be made in the property register to give notice that a transfer or conveyance contains covenants expressed to be imposed for the benefit of the land in the title. Such a note cannot operate as a guarantee and will not be made on a transferor's title where there are or will be many transfers of part imposing restrictive covenants.

(d) Release, waiver or modification of restrictive covenants

Rule 212 provides that any release, waiver, discharge or modification of restrictive covenants shall be noted on the register in such manner as the Chief Land Registrar may direct. It is usually extremely difficult, if not impossible, to prove that a deed purporting to release, waive, discharge or modify covenants is fully effective; and it is the practice simply to enter notice of such deeds in the register and leave the original notice of the covenants uncancelled.

When the Lands Tribunal has made an order under the Law of Property Act 1925, s 84, in relation to restrictive covenants, the entry to be made in the register will depend on the terms of the order.

(e) Indemnity and other positive covenants

The Chief Land Registrar is not required by the Act or Rules to enter indemnity or other positive covenants on the register or to give notice of their existence. However, because it is appreciated that when they are contained in a transfer or other deed which is filed in the Registry there is a tendency for them to be overlooked or for their exact nature to be forgotten, reference is made thereto on the register when they are contained in a transfer of land already registered. A vendor's solicitor will thus be reminded to take an indemnity from the purchaser on a transfer of the land.

Originally it was the Registry's practice in all these cases, unless the transfer was to be bound up in the certificate, to enter in the proprietorship register notice that the transfer contained personal covenants and to bind up in the certificate a separate document containing the actual words of covenant. In the case of applications completed after 29 February 1980 this practice has changed in relation to indemnity covenants. After that date where a transfer of registered land contains indemnity covenants in respect of restrictive or positive covenants already set out on the register or contained in a deed of which a copy is bound up in the certificate, the words of covenant are not set out (as previously) in a separately bound-up document. Instead a note is entered in the proprietorship register stating that the transfer to the proprietor contains a covenant to observe and perform the covenants in the particular deed referred to in the charges register and of indemnity in respect thereof. If the transferee has not covenanted to observe and perform the original covenants the note will merely state that the transfer to the proprietor contains a covenant of indemnity in respect thereof.

On first registration, when the original deeds are not filed in the Registry but are returned to the applicant, a note printed inside the cover of land certificates serves as a reminder about positive covenants; and when a first registered proprietor sells, his solicitor is able to consult the deeds containing any pre-registration positive covenants. This enables the solicitor to frame the requisite covenant for indemnity which will then be referred to on the register as outlined above. A first registered proprietor can be identified from the fact that the date on which he is registered as proprietor is the same as that given in the property register as the date of first registration of the land.

(f) Implied covenants

Implied covenants are considered in relation to transfers on p 87 and in relation to charges on p 113.

2 Overriding interests

The register of title is not conclusive as to matters not usually disclosed in an abstract of title. In addition to the charges and other matters set out in the charges register, registered land may (like unregistered land) be subject to 'overriding interests'. Unless the contrary is expressed on the register, all registered land is deemed to be subject to such overriding interests as may, for the time being, be subsisting in reference thereto.

A list of overriding interests is set out in s 70(1), and is as follows:
   (*a*) rights of common, drainage rights, customary rights (until extinguished), public rights, profits *à prendre*, rights of sheepwalk, rights of way, watercourses, rights of water, and other easements not being equitable easements required to be protected by notice on the register;
   (*b*) liability to repair highways by reason of tenure, quit-rents,

crown rents, heriots, and other rents and charges (until extinguished) having their origin in tenure;
(c) liability to repair the chancel of any church;
(d) liability in respect of embankments, and sea and river walls;
(e) land tax [tithe rentcharge], payments in lieu of tithe, and charges or annuities payable for the redemption of tithe rent charges; [Note: Land tax was abolished by the Finance Act 1963. The words 'tithe rentcharge' were repealed by the Tithe Act 1936 except as regards tithe rentcharges not extinguished by that Act and most tithe redemption annuities were extinguished from 2 October 1977 by the Finance Act 1977, s 556.]
(f) subject to the provisions of the Act, rights acquired or in course of being acquired under the Limitation Acts;
(g) the rights of every person in actual occupation of the land or in receipt of the rents and profits thereof, save where inquiry is made of such person and the rights are not disclosed; [Note: A spouse's rights of occupation under the Matrimonial Homes Act 1983 are not an overriding interest nor is any right of a tenant arising from a notice under the Leasehold Reform Act 1967 of his desire to have the freehold or to have an extended lease.]
(h) in the case of a possessory, qualified or good leasehold title, all estates, rights, interests and powers excepted from the effect of registration;
(i) rights under local land charges unless and until registered or protected on the register in the prescribed manner;
(j) rights of fishing and sporting, seignorial and manorial rights of all descriptions (until extinguished), and franchises;
(k) leases granted for a term not exceeding twenty-one years;
(l) in respect of land registered before 1 January 1926, rights to mines and minerals and rights of entry, search and user, and other rights and reservations incidental to or required for the purpose of giving full effect to the enjoyment of rights to mines and minerals or of property in mines or minerals, being rights which, where the title was first registered before 1 January 1898, were created before that date and, where the title was first registered after 31 December 1897, were created before the date of first registration.

The following overriding interests have been added to the list:

(*m*) adverse rights, privileges and appurtenances appertaining to other land or reputed to do so (r 258);
(*n*) redemption annuities charged on land out of which extinguished tithe rentcharge formerly issued (Tithe Act 1936, s 13(11)) (see the Note to (*e*) above);
(*o*) all rights and title conferred on the National Coal Board (Coal Act 1938, s 41; Coal Industry Nationalisation Act 1946, s 5).

Whilst some overriding interests seldom arise, others, such as rights of way and rights of drainage, are of common occurrence, and it is clearly necessary that a solicitor acting for a purchaser of registered land should have overriding interests in mind when making his inquiries before the contract is settled.

Where at the time of first registration any easement, right, privilege or benefit created by an instrument, and appearing on the title, adversely affects the land, a note thereof is usually entered in the register; but it is not the practice to enter notice of trivial or obvious liabilities or of those the entry of which would be likely to cause confusion or inconvenience (see r 199).

A number of judicial decisions have illustrated the importance of the overriding interests of persons 'in actual occupation' (sub-para (g) above). Attention is invited to the following cases:

(a) Bridges v Mees [1957] Ch 475; [1957] 3 WLR 215; [1957] 2 All ER 577, *Harman J*

Purchaser of registered land under an oral contract went into possession but neither took a transfer of the land nor protected his rights by a caution on the register of the vendor's title. He had an overriding interest under s 70(1)(*j*) and (*g*) which prevailed against a later purchaser of the same land who took a transfer and was registered as proprietor. Rectification of the register was ordered.

(b) Webb v Pollmount Ltd [1966] Ch 584; [1966] 2 WLR 543; [1966] 1 All ER 481, *Ungoed-Thomas J*

Option to purchase the freehold contained in a lease for seven years at an annual rent. Lessee in occupation as lessee. Option not protected by any entry on the register of the lessor's title. Option held to be enforceable as an overriding interest under s 70(1)(*g*).

(c) London and Cheshire Insurance Co Ltd v Laplagrene Property Co Ltd [1971] Ch 499; [1971] 2 WLR 257; [1971] 1 All ER 766, *Brightman J*

Lessee, in occupation as lessee, had a lien on the land as an unpaid vendor. Lessee found to have an overriding interest under s 70(1)(*g*) in respect of the lien which prevailed against a chargee of reversion. Lessee subsequently went out of occupation, but overriding interest not lost.

(d) Hodgson v Marks [1971] Ch 892; [1971] 2 WLR 1263; [1971] 2 All ER 684; 22 P & CR 586, *Court of Appeal*

Beneficial owner who was not the registered proprietor was held to have an overriding interest under s 70(1)(*g*) by virtue of her actual occupation as one of the persons living in the house. (The registered proprietor also was living there.) The overriding interest prevailed against a purchaser from the registered proprietor and against the purchaser's mortgagee.

(e) Williams & Glyn's Bank Limited v Boland and Another: Same v Brown and Another [1981] AC 487; [1980] 3 WLR 138; [1980] 2 All ER 408, *House of Lords*

Two appeals on similar facts. In each case the wife had contributed substantially to the purchase of a house and she and her husband were living in it as their matrimonial home. The husband was the sole registered proprietor. The wife had registered no caution, restriction or notice and the husband without her knowledge charged the land to the bank, which made no inquiry of the wife. The husband defaulted on the mortgage and the bank sought to enforce its security. Held that the wife was in actual occupation; therefore, notwithstanding the fact that her interest was also a minor interest, her equitable interest, as tenant in common, was protected as an overriding interest under s 70(1)(*g*) and prevailed against the bank.

(f) City of London Building Society v Flegg and others [1988] AC 54; [1987] 2 WLR 1266; [1987] 3 All ER 435, *House of Lords*

'Bleak House' was purchased in the joint names of Mr and Mrs Flegg. More than half the purchase money was provided by the wife's parents and the balance from a building society mortgage. Unknown to the wife's parents, who were in occupation, the Fleggs first created two further charges and then borrowed sufficient funds from the plaintiffs to pay off the original building society and two further loans. The plaintiffs sought an order for possession against the wife's parents. Held that the wife's parents' interest, as equitable tenants in common, was not an overriding interest under s 70(1)(*g*) and it was overreached under Part I of the Law of Property Act 1925 because the charge had been executed by two trustees for sale.

(g) Abbey National Building Society v Cann & another [1990] 2 WLR 832; [1990] 1 All ER 1085, *House of Lords*

A home was bought by a son, for his mother to live in, with the aid of a building society mortgage. Completion of the transfer and charge took place on 13 August 1984 and registration on 13 September 1984. The son defaulted and the building society took proceedings for possession. The mother claimed a beneficial interest protected as an overriding interest under s 70(1)(*g*) as she was in occupation at the date of registration. Held that, although the relevant date for ascertaining the existence of an overriding interest under s 23(1) and s 70(1)(*g*) was the date of registration, the date for ascertaining whether the interest was protected by occupation and had priority was the date when the estate over which priority was claimed was transferred or created not when it was registered.

(h) Lloyds Bank plc v Rosset and another [1990] 2 WLR 867; [1990] 1 All ER 1111, *House of Lords*

Property was being bought in the husband's sole name but it was agreed that the wife would have an interest. The purchasers were allowed into possession before completion to carry out renovation work and the wife spent almost every day at the property helping the builders. Without his wife's knowledge the husband borrowed money from the plaintiff. Completion of the purchase and of a charge to the plaintiff took place on the same day. The husband subsequently defaulted and the plaintiff took proceedings for possession. Held that although discussions had taken place between the husband and wife no decision had been taken that she was to have an interest in the property. The wife's actual contribution was 'de minimis'. The wife did not have a beneficial interest and the question of whether she had an overriding interest under s 70(1)(*g*) did not arise.

3 Easements

Easements as overriding interests and the Registry's practice in relation to adverse easements subsisting at the time of first registration have been referred to under the heading 'Overriding interests', above.

The effect of registration of land with an absolute freehold title is to vest in the first proprietor all rights, privileges and appurtenances belonging or appurtenant thereto (s 5), and with absolute leasehold title to vest in the first proprietor all implied or expressed rights, privileges and appurtenances attached to the leasehold interest (s 9 and see p 95 for the note entered on the property register of all modern leasehold titles in order to clarify the position as to easements). Subject to all rights affecting or in derogation of the lessor's title, registration with good leasehold title has the same effect in regard to appurtenant rights as registration with absolute leasehold title (s 10). Thus, if land to be registered has any appurtenant easements, such as rights of way, rights of drainage, etc, these will be included in the registration whether or not expressly mentioned on the register.

The Chief Land Registrar has power to enter an appurtenant right on the register on first registration, or later, where he is satisfied that it exists as a legal estate and is appurtenant to the land (r 254). Nevertheless, he has power under r 199 to decline to enter on the register appurtenant rights of an obvious nature, such as rights over made-up roads or rights of drainage thereunder.

(a) Transfers and deeds of grant

The powers of a registered proprietor of freehold or leasehold land include the power, subject to any entry in the register to the contrary, to grant or reserve any easement, right or privilege in, over or derived from the registered land or any part of it (ss 18 and 21). To be effective, a grant or reservation of an easement must not only be valid according to the general principles of land law and the state of the register but must be completed by registration so far as it affects registered land. Completion by registration involves the entry of the easement as an appurtenant right in the register of the dominant tenement if that tenement is registered and the entry of notice of the grant in the register or the servient tenement if that tenement is registered.

When a transfer of part of the land in a title grants for the land transferred an easement over land remaining in the transferor's title, the Registry as a matter of course makes appropriate entries relating to the benefit and burden of the grant in the registers of the transferee's and the transferor's titles respectively when the transfer is registered. If the transfer reserves an easement over the land transferred for the benefit of the land remaining in the title from which it is transferred, appropriate entries relating to the benefit and burden of the reservation will also be made in the registers of the transferor's and transferee's titles respectively as a matter of course when the transfer is registered. No additional fee is payable in respect of such entries relating to grants and reservations.

If, where a grant or reservation of an easement is made in a transfer of part, the dominant or servient tenement is registered but lies wholly or partly outside the land transferred and outside the remainder of the land in the title from which it is transferred, the application to register the transfer should be associated with an application to enter the benefit or burden, as the case might be, of the grant or reservation in the register of the 'outside title'. The land or charge certificate of the 'outside' title must be lodged at the appropriate district land registry to meet this application. No fee will usually be payable as the proviso to Part I(1) Schedule 3 to the Fees Order will apply.

If a transfer of whole or of part grants to the transferee an easement over unregistered land, ordinary conveyancing evidence of the transferor's title to make the grant should accompany the application to register the transfer so that the right granted may be registered as appurtenant to the land transferred. If the transfer reserves an easement over the land transferred for the benefit of unregistered land, an entry relating to the burden of the reservation will be made in the register of the title to the land transferred as a matter of course when the transfer is registered.

If a transfer of whole grants or reserves an easement over or for the benefit of land in another registered title, the application to register the transfer should be associated with an application for the burden or benefit of the grant or reservation to be entered in the register of the other title. The land or charge certificate of the other title should be delivered to the appropriate district land registry to meet this application. No fee will usually be payable as the proviso to Part I(1) Schedule 3 will apply.

When an easement is granted by a deed of grant (independently of any other transaction) the grantee should apply for the right to be registered as appurtenant to the dominant tenement, if registered, and for notice of the grant to be entered in the register of the servient tenement, if registered. The land or charge certificate(s) of the title(s) concerned must accompany the application or be delivered to the appropriate district land registry to meet it. A certified copy of the deed is required, and a fee of £35 for the first title and £20 for each subsequent title affected under Part I(1) Schedule 3 will be payable but no fee is payable if, in relation to each registered title affected, the application is accompanied by an application affecting that title upon which a scale fee (not under art 6) is payable. If the servient tenement is unregistered, ordinary conveyancing evidence of the grantor's title to make the grant should accompany the application. When both tenements are registered, care must be taken to refer to both title numbers on the application form.

When a grant or reservation of an easement cannot be fully completed by registration (for example where both the dominant and servient tenements are registered but the application is made in respect of the dominant tenement only, or where the servient tenement is unregistered and no evidence of the grantor's title to it is produced) the Registry is willing to make any entry justified by the evidence produced. Thus an entry in the register of the dominant tenement may simply record that a particular deed was 'expressed' to grant a particular right.

It must be remembered that a purchaser of registered land takes it subject only to what appears in the register and to overriding interests. Accordingly, if notice of a grant of an easement over a registered servient tenement does not appear on the register of that tenement, for example because the application for the registration of the grant was made against the title to the dominant tenement only, the grant will be ineffective against a subsequent purchaser of the servient tenement who is duly registered as its proprietor.

This will be so even though there is an entry in the register of the dominant tenement to the effect that a specified deed was 'expressed' to grant the easement. In such a case the easement will not be an overriding interest affecting the servient tenement because, not having been completed by registration, it will not be a legal easement and 'subsisting' for the purpose of s 70(1).

(b) Freehold flats

When large houses on registered land are converted into flats the Registry tries to ensure that complete particulars of the rights and easements granted and reserved on the sale of each freehold flat are referred to on the register of both the vendor's and purchaser's titles. These particulars are made available to interested persons in one of two ways according to circumstances. Either (i) they may be set out verbatim on the register, or (ii) they may be entered by reference to the documents creating them. In the latter event, wherever practicable, copies of the material documents will be bound up in the respective land or charge certificates, but where this is not so the registers will show the title numbers under which the documents are filed. In complicated cases the Registry sometimes consults the solicitors concerned in an endeavour to frame the entries in the register to meet their requirements.

4 Minor interests

Minor interests are defined in s 3(xv) as follows:

' "Minor interests" mean the interests not capable of being disposed of or created by registered dispositions and capable of being overridden (whether or not a purchaser has notice thereof) by the proprietors unless protected as provided by this Act, and all rights and interests which are not registered or protected on the register and are not overriding interests, and include—
   (a) in the case of land held on trust for sale, all interests and powers which are under the Law of Property Act 1925 capable of being overridden by the trustees for sale, whether or not such interests and powers are so protected; and
   (b) in the case of settled land, all interests and powers which are under the Settled Land Act 1925 and the Law of Property Act 1925, or either of them, capable of being overridden by the tenant for life or statutory owner, whether or not such interests and powers are so protected as aforesaid.'

By s 101(1) proprietors are empowered to create in registered land interests (eg, a life interest) not capable of subsisting as legal estates or interests and not capable of being created by means of a registered disposition under the powers expressly conferred on a registered proprietor. They may do so in the same way as if the land was unregistered. Interests created under s 101(1) take effect as minor interests (s 101(2)). They may be protected by notices, cautions, inhibitions and restrictions (see Chapter XIV).

Chapter V

Inspection, Office Copies and Searches

1 Inspection of the register

Any person may, subject to formalities and fee, inspect the register or obtain an office copy of the entries on the register and of any document other than a lease or charge referred to in the register which is in the custody of the Registrar (s 112 as substituted by the Land Registration Act 1988).

This general right to inspect does not extend to cautions against first registration, inspection of which is covered by r 70 as substituted by the Land Registration Rules 1990 (see p 166). Nor does it extend to the index of proprietors' names (see **2** below).

Except as outlined at **3** below inspection of other documents in the custody of the registrar is only at the discretion of the registrar (s 112(2) as substituted).

2 Inspection of the index of proprietors' names

The index of proprietors' names (see p 11) is not open to general inspection.

However, in addition to the special right to a search discussed at **3** below, any person may apply in Form 104 for a search to be made of the index in respect of either his own name or the name of some other person in whose property he is able to satisfy the Chief Land Registrar that he is interested generally (eg, as his trustee in bankruptcy or his personal representative). Form 104 is not available as a printed form and reference should be made to the 1976 Rules for its text. Separate applications should be made in respect of any former or alternative names, and every address which may have been used as an address for service for entry on the register should be stated.

The reply to the application will state whether or not the person named in the search appears in the index. If the person named does so appear, the reply will also state whether that person appears as the registered proprietor of land or of a registered charge and will give the relevant title number, the description of the property, whether the property is freehold or leasehold and (in the case of a registered charge) the date of the charge. When the property is leasehold, short particulars of the lease will be given. The reply constitutes an official search the accuracy of which is guaranteed.

The fee for an official search of the index of proprietors' names is £14 per name (Part II(1) of Schedule 3 to the Fee Order). It should be noted that applications for official searches of the index are to be sent to The Chief Land Registrar, HM Land Registry, Burrington Way, Plymouth, PL5 3LP, not to district land registries.

3 Inspection in the case of certain crime, receiverships and insolvency

In addition to the general right of inspection, discussed at **1** above, certain officials responsible for investigating crime, acting as receiver in special circumstances or administering the affairs of insolvent individuals or corporations have a right to inspect and obtain copies of:

(*a*) all documents which the registrar has in his custody and
(*b*) the result of a search of the index of proprietors' names (r 7 of the Land Registration (Open Register) Rules 1990) Practice Leaflet No 19 (see p 16) is available as a guide to those entitled to make such an inspection.

4 Personal inspection

District land registries are open to the public between the hours of 10 am and 4 pm Mondays to Fridays, excluding public holidays. During those hours anyone may apply on Form 111 to make a personal inspection of the register. Form 111 is available at district land registries when the visit is made or from HMSO or law stationers. Inspection by the registered proprietor is free of charge but for anyone else a fee of £21 is payable which covers inspection of the register, the filed plan and any document referred to on the register (other than a lease or charge) (Part II(2) of Schedule 3 to the Fees Order). If the title number is not known an additional fee of £7 is payable (Part II(5) of Schedule 3).

5 Office copies

(a) What can be supplied

In respect of a registered title, items can be supplied as follows:
(1) *An office copy of the entries in the register.* This will include any schedule to the register.
(2) *An office copy of the title plan.* The delay usually involved in obtaining an office copy of a large plan can commonly be avoided by means of a certificate of official inspection of the filed plan (see p 58).
(3) *An office copy of a document referred to in the register as being filed in the Registry and an office copy of any personal covenants which are referred to but not set out in the register.*

(b) What cannot be supplied

(1) *Registered leases and registered mortgages.* The originals are not filed in the Registry. The Registry holds copies of some registered leases and of most registered mortgages, office copies of these copies will not be supplied but a special request explaining why a copy cannot be obtained from the person who has the original will be considered.
(2) *Copies of documents from which extracts are taken to make entries on the register.* Where the text of a covenant, the grant of an easement or some other provision is set out verbatim on the register, an office copy of the document from which the extract is taken will not normally be supplied. The Registry is responsible for seeing that the register provides all the information it should provide, and extracts from documents are set out to avoid the expense of obtaining an office copy of the whole document. Moreover, in many cases neither the original deed on which the entry is founded nor a copy or abstract of it is held in the Registry.

(c) The application

There are two forms of application for office copies; Form 109, which is for requests for office copies of the register and title plan (or Form 102 certificate—see p 58), and Form 110, which is for requests for office copies of documents or copies of personal covenants referred to in the register as being filed. With regard to Form 110, it is essential that the deeds required be listed specifically with their nature and dates being given. The title number(s) under which the deeds are filed, as shown on the register, must be given and the number of copies required stated. Generalised requests will not be accepted.

The application should be lodged at the appropriate district registry. If the title number is not known the words 'Please supply the title number' should be written boldly at the head of Form 109 (an additional fee will then be payable—see (*d*) below).

(d) Fees for office copies

Fees are payable under Part II of Schedule 3 to the Fees Order as follows:

Office copy of the register	£7
Office copy of the title plan or a certificate of inspection in Form 102	£7
Office copy of document(s) referred to—per title	£7
Office copy of a mortgage or lease (where allowed)—per document	£14
No title number (or wrong title number) quoted	£7

A credit account (see p 15) can be used for payment of fees for office copies.

6 Certificate of official inspection of the filed plan

Instead of an office copy of the filed plan a certificate of official inspection of the filed plan may be obtained.

The application may be made either by reference to an estate layout plan approved by the Registry (see Chapter XVII) or by reference to a plan annexed to the application. The plan should be prepared on the same basis as a plan for use with a search of part discussed on p 60. The application form is Form 109. A fee of £7 is payable (Part II(8) of Schedule 3 to the Fees Order).

The certificate will be in Form 102. It will state that the land to which it relates is in the title concerned and what, if any, colour or other references shown on the filed plan and mentioned in the entries on the register affect it. The accuracy of the certificate will be guaranteed, but it will not confer on the applicant priority for the registration of any dealing.

When a transaction relates to only a part of the land in a large registered title and a certificate in Form 102 would give the applicant all the information about the filed plan that he needs, the use of such a certificate can save the additional expense and (usually) delay entailed in obtaining an office copy of the filed plan. The main use of certificates in Form 102 is in connection with developing registered building estates (see Chapter XVII) but the procedure may be used in relation to any filed plan.

7 Official searches of the register

To obtain up-to-date information as to all subsisting entries on the register of a title, it is not enough to read what appears in the land or charge certificate or in an office copy; the state of the register itself must be ascertained. The reason is that entries may have been made in the register since the date (shown on the inside cover of the certificate) on which the land or charge certificate was last officially compared with and, if necessary, made to correspond with, the register or shown on the office copy. For example, the registration of a transfer of the land subject to a registered charge would not necessarily be recorded in the charge certificate, and the registration of a second charge may not appear in the first charge certificate. A notice of deposit of land certificate may not be entered in the certificate; and cautions, creditors' notices and bankruptcy inhibitions commonly do not appear in any certificate. All these matters, however, would be the subject of entries in the register and would be revealed by an inspection of the register.

At any time, without fee, a land or charge certificate will be made to correspond with the register if lodged at the Registry for that purpose or, as explained at 5 above, an up-to-date office copy of the register may be obtained. However recent the date on which the certificate was thus 'made up' or office copy issued, it is never safe to assume that no new entry, not appearing in the certificate or office copy, has been made in the register since that date. This situation is clearly of the greatest importance to persons dealing with registered land; and to meet it a system of official searches of the register is operated under the provisions of the Land Registration (Official Searches) Rules 1990.

(a) Official searches of the register with priority by purchasers, lessees and chargees in Forms 94A and 94B

Purpose—The purpose of these searches is to enable a purchaser, lessee or chargee to obtain an official certificate as to the entries on the register of the vendor's, lessor's or chargor's title immediately before completion and to ensure that (if he complies with the procedure laid down) he will be unaffected by any entry made between the date of this certificate and the registration of his transfer, lease or charge.

Who may apply—These official searches of the register are available only to purchasers, lessees and chargees who in good faith and for valuable consideration acquire or intend to acquire a legal estate in land. Thus they are not available to a mortgagee who intends to protect the mortgage on the register by a notice under s 49 or by a caution under s 54 (a caution against dealings); nor are they available to a prospective depositee of a land or charge certificate. Such persons may, however, apply for an official search using Form 94c (see p 66). As to purchasers 'in good faith', see *Smith v Morrison, Smith v Chief Land Registrar* [1974] 1 WLR 659; [1974] 1 All ER 957.

The application—The application should be in Form 94A where the purchase, lease or charge is of all the land in the title; in Form 94B where it is of part of the land only. The form must be signed because it contains a certificate that the applicant is a person who may apply for a search with priority. It should be signed using a pen; a facsimile signature using a rubber stamp or a printed or typed signature is not acceptable.

Except as stated below, an application in Form 94B must be accompanied by a plan, in duplicate, which should be drawn to a suitable scale (generally not less than 1/2500); and, when necessary, sufficient figured dimensions must be entered on the plan to define the part affected and to tie it to the existing physical features (such as road junctions, fences or walls) shown by firm black lines on the official plan of the vendor's, lessor's or chargor's registered title. The plan should be a copy of the plan intended to be bound up in the transfer, lease or charge (see pp 87 and 198). No plan need accompany the Form 94B, however, if the part affected is:

(1) already clearly defined on the filed plan of the vendor's, lessor's or chargor's registered title by means of a colour or number reference which is referred to on the Form 94B; or

(2) a numbered plot on an estate layout plan of a registered building estate approved by the Registry as described in Chapter XVII for the purpose of official searches, provided that the plot number(s) and the date of the Registry's approval of the estate layout plan are stated on the Form 94B.

The application must be delivered to the appropriate district land registry. No fee is payable. The Registry recommends that the application be posted to reach the district registry at least five working days before the date fixed for completion of the transaction which it is sought to protect. Official search certificates are always despatched from the Registry using first class mail or document exchange.

An application which is delivered at the appropriate district land registry after 9.30 hours on one day and before or at 9.30 hours on the next day is deemed to have been delivered immediately before 9.30 hours on the second day (Land Registration (Official Searches) Rules 1990, r 2(3)). 'Day' here means a day when the Land Registry is open to the public (ibid, r 2(1)). The Land Registry is not open to the public on Saturdays, Sundays or public holidays. The rules relating to the deemed times of delivery of applications for making, rectifying or cancelling any entry in the register of a registered title (which include applications to register transfers, leases and charges of registered land) are discussed on pp 5–6 under the heading 'Delivery and priority of applications'. Rule 2(3) referred to above and r 85 as substituted by the Land Registration Rules 1990 (referred to on pp 5–6) read together make it clear that an official search in Form 94A or Form 94B will have priority over an application for registration delivered in the same 24 hour period.

If the application is in order and is deemed to have been delivered to the appropriate district land registry immediately before 9.30 hours on the particular working day, the official certificate of search in Form 94D will usually be posted back to the applicant on that day (applications in Form 94A) or on the next working day (applications in Form 94B). If, however, an application is already pending against the title (applications in Form 94A) or the part of the title affected (applications in Form 94B) the issue of the certificate will usually take longer.

The official certificate of search—The reply to an application in Form 94A or Form 94B consists of an official certificate of search. This certificate is endorsed on the back of the original Form 94A or 94B or on a separate computer printed result of search in Form 94D. The duplicate form is retained by the Registry.

The certificate gives the result of the search as at the time and date at which the application for the search is deemed to have been delivered to the appropriate district land registry. It shows, if they affect the land to which the application relates: (*a*) any adverse entries made in the register since the specified date; (*b*) any applications for registration pending but not completed by entry on the register; and (*c*) any other official search with unexpired priority. Its accuracy is guaranteed (s 83(3)).

As will be seen from the form, the application asks about adverse entries made since a specified date, being the date of the issue of an office copy of the subsisting entries on the register or the last date on which the land or charge certificate was officially examined with the register. It is in the applicant's interests that this date be as recent as possible, because the shorter the period to which the search relates, the less the likelihood that adverse entries will have been made during that period; and a 'clear' certificate of the result of the search can, of course, be given more expeditiously than a certificate into which copies of entries have to be incorporated. The Registrar may, at his discretion, show the current entries on the register by issuing an up to date office copy of the entries on the register with the result of search.

Priority conferred by the search—The official rules prescribe a priority period in relation to each properly made application in Form 94A or 94B. This period is the period beginning at the time when the application for the official search is deemed to have been delivered to the appropriate district land registry and ending immediately after 9.30 hours on the thirtieth day thereafter (Land Registration (Official Searches) Rules 1990, r 2(1)). The date of its expiry is shown on the result of search.

Any entry made in the register during the priority period will be postponed to a subsequent application to register the instrument effecting the purchase, lease or charge to which the search relates, and, if that purchase, lease or charge is dependent on a prior dealing, to a subsequent application to register the instrument effecting that dealing, provided that each such subsequent application (i) is deemed to have been delivered at the appropriate district land registry within the priority period (see p 5 under the heading 'Delivery and priority of applications'); (ii) affects the same land or charge as the postponed entry; and (iii) is in due course completed by registration.

It follows that where there is a transfer on sale, and the purchase money or part of it is being raised by a legal charge, a search on behalf of the chargee will protect both him and the transferee.

Points on the operation of priority periods—Where two or more official certificates of search relating to the same land or charge are in operation at the same time, it is commonly clear what priority the applicants for the searches intended the official certificates of search to have as between one and another. However, r 8 of the Land Registration (Official Searches) Rules 1990 provides for the determination of priorities in such situations, and in case of doubt reference should be made to that rule.

Paragraph (4) of r 8 of the Official Searches Rules provides that where an official search has been made in respect of a particular title and, by virtue of r 85 as substituted by the Land Registration Rules 1990 (see pp 5–6), an application relating to that title is deemed to have been delivered at the same time as the expiry of the priority period relating to that search, the time of delivery of the application shall be deemed to be within that priority period.

Sub-sales and re-sales—A registered proprietor (*V*) may sell part of the land in his title to a purchaser (*P*1), who agrees to sell that land to a sub-purchaser (*P*2) before the registration of the transfer by V to *P*1 has been completed. In these circumstances *P*1 will be unable to prove his title to *P*2 by producing an office copy of the register of *P*1's title because that register will not exist. However, if *P*l can supply to *P*2 an office copy of the register of *V*'s title, the following procedure can be followed.

*P*2 can apply in Form 94C for a 'non-priority' official search of the register of *V*'s title based on the office copy of that title. The official certificate of the result of the search will: (*a*) disclose any adverse entry made in *V*'s register since the date of the office copy; (*b*) reveal the presence in the Registry of the pending application to register the transfer to *P*1, stating whether or not it has been approved for entry in the register; and (*c*) reveal any other pending application for registration or for an official search affecting the land transferred to *P*1. Also *P*2 should obtain from *P*1 a copy of the transfer to *P*1.

Just before completion of the sub-sale to him, *P*2 will wish to apply for a purchaser's official search of the register, principally to obtain the statutory priority period within which to deliver his transfer for registration. If the registration of the transfer by *V* to *P*1 has by that time been completed, *P*1 will be able to provide *P*2 with an office copy of the register of Pl's title. *P*2 can apply in Form 94A for an official search in respect of the whole of the land in *P*1's title based on the office copy. If the registration of the transfer by *V* to *P*1 has not been completed, *P*2 can apply in Form 94B for an official search in respect of the relevant part of the land in *V*'s title based as before on the office copy of the register of V's title supplied to him by *P*1.

This procedure can be adapted for a chargee who proposes to lend to a sub-purchaser whose transfer has not yet been registered or where either of the two transactions is by way of lease.

(b) Official search with priority in respect of land the subject of a pending first registration application in Forms 94A and 94B(FR)

Purpose—The purpose of these searches is to enable a purchaser, lessee or chargee of land the subject of a pending first registration application to confirm that the property is, in fact, the subject of such an application lodged by a named applicant and received on a stated date, and to ascertain whether or not any applications affecting the property have been received since that date. Provided the pending first registration application is subsequently completed, the purchaser, lessee or chargee is enabled to ensure (if he complies with the procedure laid down) that he will be unaffected by an entry made between the date of his certificate and the registration of his transfer, lease or charge.

Who may apply—These official searches are available only to purchasers, lessees and chargees of land which is subject to a pending first registration application who, in good faith, and for valuable consideration, acquire, or intend to acquire, a legal estate in land. The same considerations apply as in the case of already registered titles (see p 60).

The application—The application should be in Form 94A where the purchase, lease or charge is of all the land in the pending first registration application; in Form 94B(FR) where it is of part of the land only. Both Form 94A or 94B(FR) must be signed. The remarks set out on p 60 as to signatures apply also to the signature of these forms. A copy of the plan intended to be bound up in the transfer, lease or charge, should accompany form 94B(FR).

The application must be delivered to the appropriate district land registry. No fee is payable. The Registry recommends that the application be posted to reach the district registry at least five working days before the date fixed for completion of the transaction which it is sought to protect. Official search certificates are always despatched from the Registry using first class mail or document exchange.

The same provisions apply in relation to the deemed time of delivery as are set out on p 61. If the application is in order and is deemed to have been delivered to the appropriate district land registry immediately before 9.30 hours on the particular working day, the official certificate of search in Form 94E will usually be posted back to the applicant within three working days in the case of Form 94A and within four working days in the case of Form 94B(FR). As it will be necessary for the Registry to obtain the papers relating to the pending first registration application, which may be at any stage in the course of registration, in order to complete the official search certificate, in some cases the respective periods may be longer.

The official certificate of search—The reply to an application in Form 94A or Form 94B(FR) consists of an official certificate of search. This certificate, is endorsed on the back of the original Form 94A or 94B(FR) or on a separate computer printed result of search in Form 94D. The duplicate form is retained by the Registry.

The certificate will enable the purchaser, lessee or chargee to satisfy himself that the property searched is the subject of a pending first registration application, and will state by whom the application was made and on what date the application was received. The certificate will state whether or not any applications have been received since that date which are pending, and which may affect the property, and will disclose particulars of any other official search with unexpired priority. Its accuracy is guaranteed (s 83(3)).

Priority conferred by the search—The priority period extends from the time when the application for the official search is deemed to have been delivered to the appropriate district land registry and ends immediately after 9.30 hours on the thirtieth day thereafter (Land Registration (Official Searches) Rules 1990, r 2(1)). The date of expiry is shown on the result of search.

If the application for first registration is subsequently completed by registration of all or any part of the land comprised in the purchase, lease or charge, any entry which is made in the Register during the priority period relating to the search will be postponed to a subsequent application to register the instrument affecting the purchase, lease or charge and, if the purchase, lease or charge is dependent on a prior dealing, to a subsequent application to register the instrument effecting that dealing subject to the same provisos as are set out on p 62.

It must be noted that until the pending first registration application has actually been completed, no guarantee is given that any registered title will be granted or, if granted, that it will be of the class sought. Also, no information will be provided as to the entries which may eventually be made on the Register. It is for the purchaser, lessee or chargee to satisfy himself by enquiry of the applicant for first registration that the title lodged is in order, and to identify the entries which are likely to be made. Should it be necessary, the Registry will usually be prepared to return documents lodged with an application for first registration temporarily to the solicitor or other person who originally lodged them, but the application for first registration will not proceed until they are relodged.

(c) Official searches without priority (Form 94C)

The proprietor of registered land or of a registered charge or any other person who holds the written authority of such proprietor (or of his solicitor) to inspect the register, may at any time apply in Form 94C for an official search of the register. This form of official search is available, for example, to a mortgagee who intends to protect the mortgage on the register by a notice under s 49 or by a caution under s 54 (a caution against dealings) and to a prospective depositee of a land or charge certificate.

The application (in Form 94C) must be sent to the appropriate district land registry. The position with regard to plans is as stated on p 60 for official searches in Form 94B.

A fee of £7 per title is payable under Part II(7) of Schedule 3 of the Fees Order.

If the application is in order, a certificate of the result of the search will be issued. This will show, if they affect the land in respect of which the application was made: (*a*) any adverse entries made in the register since the specified date (see p 62); (*b*) any applications for registration pending but not completed by entry on the register; and (*c*) any other applications for an official search.

The accuracy of the certificate is guaranteed; but the certificate will not confer on the applicant priority for the registration of any dealing.

(d) Official search by mortgagee in Form 106

The procedure whereby the proprietor of a registered charge or mortgagee of registered land may search the register to enable him to comply with the provisions of s 8(4) of the Matrimonial Homes Act 1983 is outlined on p 181.

(e) Searches by telephone or telex

Any credit account holder (see p 15) may apply by telephone or telex to the appropriate district land registry for details of any adverse entry made on the register since a given date and of any entry on the daylist (see p 68) or for details of a pending application for first registration. A fee of £7 is payable under Part II(6) of Schedule 3 to the Fees Order.

If the application is made by telephone, the following particulars should be given:

- A the credit account number, name, address and telephone number of the person making the application together with the name of the person on whose behalf the application is being made;
- B the title number and a short description of the property;
- C either the full name of the registered proprietor or the full name of the applicant for first registration; and
- D in the case of a search of the register the date from which the search is to be made.

If the application is made by telex, the message must be printed in the following abbreviated form:

- A the credit account number, name and telex address of the person making the application;
- B the title number;
- C a short description of the property and print 'whole search' or 'part search';
- D in the case of a search of the register the date from which the search is to be made or in the case of a pending first registration print 'First Registration';
- E the full name of the proprietor, or of the applicant for registration;
- F the name of the person on whose behalf the application is made.

Only the letters of the paragraphs and the relevant information, as indicated, need be given. The reply will be in a correspondingly abbreviated form (see below).

Whether the application is made by telephone or telex, the search will be made as soon as practicable and without regard to any pending applications not yet entered on the day list. Thus the result of the search will include any adverse entries affecting the land to which the search relates that have been made in the register since the specified date; but as regards applications for registration pending but not yet completed by entry on the register and applications for official searches, it will include only those that have been entered on the day list at the moment of search. It will confer no priority and will not be guaranteed against error.

The day list is the record of pending applications kept pursuant to r 7A (added by the Land Registration Rules 1978). It contains, in relation to the relevant title numbers, a record of the date of delivery of every pending application for first registration and every pending application for making, rectifying or cancelling any entry in the register of a registered title (r 7A). It also contains a record of applications for official searches in Forms 94A, 94B or 94B(FR) (Land Registration (Official Searches) Rules 1990 r 4(1)).

A result of search by telephone will include: (*a*) the title number; (*b*) a statement as to whether the search has extended to the whole or been limited to a part of the land in the title; (*c*) a short description of the property; (*d*) the date from which the search has been made or the date upon which the application is deemed to have been received if a pending first registration; and (*e*) the result.

A result of search given by telex will be in the following form:
- A the title number or, in the case of a pending first registration; the title number followed by 'allotted on first registration';
- B if the search was made in respect of the whole of the land in a registered title, 'Whole' will be printed. If it was in respect of a part only, the description of the property will be given;
- C the date from which the search has been made or, in the case of a pending first registration, the date upon which the application is deemed to have been received;
- D the result.

8 Searches in the Land Charges Department

A purchaser of registered land is not, by reason of any registration under the Land Charges Act 1972, affected with notice of any pending action, writ, order, deed of arrangement or land charge which can be protected under the Act by a creditors' notice, restriction, inhibition, caution or other notice, nor need he search in the Land Charges Department for such matters so far as they affect registered land. A purchaser acquiring title under a registered disposition is not concerned, subject to what is said in the next paragraph, with any pending action, writ, order, deed of arrangement, or other document, matter or claim (not being an overriding interest) not protected by a caution or other entry on the register, whether or not he has notice thereof, express, implied or constructive. (See ss 110(7) and 59(6); Land Charges Act 1972, s 14(1); Land Charges Rules 1974, r 13.)

The various means of protection prescribed by the Act exclude the Land Charges Act 1972 in relation to land registered with absolute title, and the solicitor for a purchaser (including a lessee or chargee) of such land need not search in the Land Charges Department. Where land is registered with a title less than absolute, the need for searches in the Land Charges Department falls to be considered in relation to the pre-registration title or, in the case of a qualified title, in relation to the specified qualification, as though the title were unregistered.

Although it is considered that as a matter of strict law the position is as stated, some solicitors apply for official searches in the Land Charges Department in relation to registered land because, whereas the register of title cannot provide information about the financial position of a proposing borrower who is not yet registered as proprietor, a search in the Land Charges Department will reveal any bankruptcy proceedings pending against him. A correct use of the official search machinery at the Land Registry will ensure the registration of both borrower and lender with priority over any last-minute bankruptcy proceedings, but no one wants to lend money to a potential bankrupt. For the convenience of solicitors whose sole purpose in applying for an official search in the Land Charges Department is to discover whether any proceedings in bankruptcy or a deed of arrangement have been registered, that Department operates a system of limited official searches.

9 Local land charge searches

Searches in the registers of local land charges maintained by local authorities must be made in relation to registered land exactly as though it were unregistered.

Chapter VI

Dealings Generally

1 Dealings expressly authorised by the Act

Whether registered land is freehold or leasehold, and subject to any entry in the register to the contrary, eg, a restriction, the registered proprietor may:

(1) transfer the land or any part of it (ss 18 and 21);
(2) transfer all or any mines and minerals apart from the surface, or the surface without all or any of the mines and minerals (ss 18 and 21);
(3) grant or reserve (to the extent of the registered estate and subject to the provisions of the Rentcharges Act 1977—see Chapter X) an annuity or a rentcharge in possession (either perpetual or for a term of years absolute) (ss 18 and 21);
(4) grant or reserve any easement, right or privilege in, over or derived from the registered land or any part of it (ss 18 and 21);
(5) transfer the registered land or any part of it subject to a reservation to any person of any such annuity, rentcharge, easement, right or privilege (ss 18 and 21);
(6) grant a lease of the registered land or any part of it, or of all or any mines and minerals apart from the surface, or of the surface without all or any mines and minerals, or of an easement, right or privilege in or over the land or any part thereof for any term of years absolute for any purpose, but subject, in the case of a registered leasehold estate, to the extent of that estate (ss 18 and 21);
(7) charge the land by deed (s 25);
(8) create a lien by deposit of land certificate (s 66);
(9) enter into a contract relating to the land (s 107);

(10) accept for the benefit of the land any easement, right or privilege or restrictive covenant (s 108);
(11) impose restrictive covenants on the land, and release or waive the benefit of such covenants (s 40).

All these dealings must be completed by substantive registration or by some entry or entries on the register. In many cases (notably grants of rentcharges and of certain leases) both substantive registration and some other entry or entries are needed. Souvenir land (see p 5) is an exception. Every transaction relating to registered souvenir land is to be effected and to take effect as if the title were not registered, and the Chief Land Registrar is not required to accept any application or caution relating thereto.

A person on whom the right to be registered as proprietor of land or of a charge has devolved by reason of the proprietor's death, or has been conferred by a disposition or charge, may deal with the land in the proper way before he is registered as proprietor (s 37). Thus a transferee may immediately charge or re-transfer the land.

Transfers, leases, charges and other transactions relating to registered land are discussed under their respective headings; and an attempt has been made, in Chapter I and in the chapters on specific topics, to deal with more important matters affecting registration as a whole. Some remarks on general aspects of the registration of dealings may, however, be helpful.

2 Production of certificates

The land or charge certificate must be produced to the Chief Land Registrar:
(1) on every entry in the register of a disposition by the proprietor of the registered land or charge to which it relates;
(2) on every registered transmission; and
(3) wherever notice of any estate, right or claim or a restriction is placed on the register adversely affecting the title of the registered proprietor of the land or charge except:
 (*a*) lodgment of a caution or a notice of deposit;
 (*b*) lodgment of an inhibition;
 (*c*) lodgment of a creditor's notice; or
 (*d*) entry of a notice of a lease at a rent without taking a fine.

As mentioned elsewhere, when a charge or mortgage is registered, the land certificate must be lodged and will remain in the Registry until the charge or mortgage is discharged. This must be borne in mind when considering the above rules as to the production of land certificates, since, if a charge or mortgage is registered against the title, the land certificate will already be in the Registry.

When a transfer is made by the proprietor of a registered charge in exercise of his power of sale, the land certificate will already be in the Registry. The charge certificate relating to the charge under which the power of sale is exercised must, however, be produced.

3 Documents placed on deposit

When a land or charge certificate or other document will be required at the Registry in connection with an application, but is not in the possession of the person who is to make the application, arrangements should be made for the person holding the certificate or other document to lodge it at the appropriate district land registry 'on deposit' to await the application.

The certificate or other document should be lodged under cover of a Form A15. The Registry will give this form a number, which will be notified to the depositor. The depositor should then pass on the number to the applicant, so that it can be referred to on the application form.

Documents lodged at the Registry on deposit may be returned to the depositor if no application for which they are required is lodged within two months.

If the certificate is being deposited to meet applications to register transfers or leases of part, it should be stated in the 'Why deposited' panel on the first page of Form A15 approximately how many such applications may be expected. If the certificate is being deposited for a specified purpose only pursuant to r 269, the Form A15 should be accompanied by a letter quoting the rule and stating explicitly for what purpose(s) the certificate may be used.

4 The application forms

(a) Dealings with the whole of the land in a title or titles. Application Form A4

In the space provided there must be set out in their correct priority the dealings to be registered. Thus the discharge of a charge by a vendor should appear before the transfer and any fresh charge.

If special expedition is desired, a written request should be made and the minimum expedition fee of £35 should be paid and entered in the fees panel of the application form. If the request for expedition is made by way of an endorsement on the application form, it should be made prominently; and if the request is made by letter it is advisable also to endorse the application form boldly, 'Please expedite'.

A list of the documents lodged should be set out in the space provided on the form, in the same order as the applications to which they relate, originals and copies being treated as separate items.

The following information should be supplied as indicated in the numbered panels on the Form A4:

Panel 4, p 1: The key number (if any), name, address, reference and telephone number of the solicitor to whom the acknowledgment of the application and any requisitions by the Registry, including requests for unpaid fees, are to be sent.

Panel 5, p 1: Instructions (if any) for the issue of any document to some person or firm other than that mentioned in panel 4.

Panel 6, p 4: The full name(s) and address(es) for service (including post-code) for entry in the register of any new proprietor(s) of the land. As the revised application form envisages the information supplied being copied directly from the application form to the register, particular care should be exercised in completing this panel and panel 7. In the case of a new proprietor of the land, it is important that the address in panel 6 should be the address at which he will reside on completion of the registration. Often the address in a transfer is the address of the transferee's residence at the time he contracted to purchase. If this address becomes out of date, but is nevertheless entered in the register, there is a risk that official notices sent by the Registry might not reach him. All addresses for entry in the register must be addresses in the United Kingdom (s 79) (see p 32 as to the meaning of United Kingdom in this context). Any person may have up to three addresses, including the address of his solicitors, entered in the register (r 315).

Panel 7, p 4: The full name(s) and address(es) for service (including post-code) of any new proprietor(s) of a charge. If there is more than one new charge, details should be given above the white box on the application form as directed. If the chargee is a building society, the account number should be given. The remarks at panel 6 in relation to the address for service apply also to this panel.

Panel 8, p 2: If a transfer or assent is to joint tenants, it must be stated by answering 'Yes' or 'No' in the box provided, whether or not the survivor of them can give a valid receipt for capital money arising on a disposition of the land. It is important that this panel should not be overlooked (see p 88).

Panel 9, p 2: On an application to register a company as the proprietor of land or of a charge, the specified confirmations as to the company's incorporation, powers and objects, and as to the non-contravention of its memorandum and articles of association, should be given unless it is preferred to lodge a certified copy of the memorandum and articles of association. Details of the company's registered number should also be entered here. Further discussion of the completion of this panel where a company is to be registered as proprietor of a charge is contained under 'Registered charges' (on p 115).

When the deeds delivered for registration involve a transfer to a company and a charge by that company to another company, care should be taken that, if panel 9 is used, the first set of confirmations is given by the solicitors of the transferee company and the second set by the solicitors of the chargee company.

Panel 10, p 2: If a discharge of the only remaining charge is lodged (and there is no new charge) the solicitors for the registered proprietor of the land should apply for the issue of the land certificate to them by signing the request in panel 10.

Requisitions may well be avoided by ticking the reminders at panel 11, p 2 of the form; and finally the total amount of the fees paid should be entered in the certificate and the certificate should be signed. Signature in ink in the firm's name by a partner or other authorised member of the firm is appropriate. No covering letter is necessary.

(b) Dealings with part of the land comprised in a title other than the grant of a lease. Application Form A5

Most dealings with part of the land in a title are transfers, particularly transfers of plots on registered building estates. Form A5 is, however, also the correct form for use in connection with a charge of part of the land in a title.

As is stated on the form, the application cannot be accepted for registration unless the land or charge certificate of the parent title is deposited at the appropriate district land registry or accompanies the application. Therefore, if that land or charge certificate has already been deposited at the appropriate district land registry (see p 72 as to deposits), the official reference number relating to the deposit should be entered on the form in the space provided. If, however, the certificate (or any other document relating to the parent title) accompanies the application in Form A5, it (and any such other document) should be lodged under cover of a Form A15 duly completed.

Apart from these matters, Form A5 requires completion on the same lines as Form A4. Form A5 also has a panel relating to fencing, which should not be overlooked. The total amount of the fees paid should be entered in the statement at the foot of p 4 of the form and the statement should be signed. Signature in ink in the firm's name by a partner or other authorised member of the firm is appropriate. No covering letter is necessary. Attention is invited to the reminders at the foot of p 3 of the form.

5 Acknowledgment of dealings applications

Receipt of applications for registration of dealings with the whole is not acknowledged as a matter of routine. It is hoped that such applications will only take a short time to complete and the completed application would follow close behind the acknowledgment. However the application will be acknowledged if the applicant lodges a complete acknowledgment card in Form C4B with his application.

6 Associated dealings

Where several associated dealings relating to a particular title are delivered for registration together, the application forms may be numbered consecutively (eg, when there are five applications, 1/5, 2/5, 3/5, 4/5 and 5/5) so that the Registry's staff will see readily that they should be dealt with together and in the order indicated. The appropriate number should be endorsed prominently at the top of the first page of each form. It is usually convenient, when the land or charge certificate accompanies the applications, to enclose it with the first one and to state on the others that this has been done.

7 Forms of dispositions: approval of draft instruments

Forms are prescribed for many kinds of dispositions of registered land (see Appendix V) and these forms are referred to under the relevant headings elsewhere in the text.

The Registry's approval of a draft instrument may be sought:
  (a) when it is desired to apply or adapt a prescribed or printed form to a particular transaction; or
  (b) when it is desired to effect a disposition which is within the powers conferred by the Act but for which no form is prescribed or printed. Care should be taken to see that the draft conforms generally to the Land Registration Acts and Rules (see in particular r 78 referred to below) and that it clearly identifies the land which is to be the subject of the disposition. The draft (with plan if any) and a copy (with a copy of any plan) should be sent to the appropriate district land registry. No fee is payable.

Approval will be limited to matters of form; and the person lodging the instrument for registration will be responsible for ensuring that it carries out the intention of the parties, and for all matters of substance, due execution and matters of a like nature.

If it appears to the Chief Land Registrar that any instrument is improper in form or substance, or is not clearly expressed, or does not indicate with sufficient precision the particular interest in land intended to be affected, or refers only to matters not the subject of registration under the Act, or is otherwise expressed inconsistently with the principles on which the register is to be kept, he may refuse to register it or may refuse to register it unless it is modified (r 78). In particular it is to be noted that, with the exception of settled land, references to trusts must, as far as possible, be excluded from the register (s 74).

The special procedure for the approval of draft instruments in connection with registered building estates is discussed on p 199.

8 Deeds and their execution

Section 1 of the Law of Property (Miscellaneous Provisions) Act 1989 and s 36A of the Companies Act 1985 as added by s 130(2) of the Companies Act 1989 which came into force on 31 July 1990, contain new provisions relating to the form and execution of deeds. These provisions apply to deeds executed for land registration purposes.

For an instrument to be a deed it must be in writing, it must make it clear on its face that is intended to be a deed and it must be validly executed as a deed by the person making it or one or more of the parties to it. An instrument will be accepted by the Registry as intended to be a deed if it so describes itself; or if it is expressed to be executed as a deed; or if of its nature it is required by law to be a deed, eg 'This Conveyance...' or 'This Legal Mortgage...', or it is in an appropriate form prescribed in the Rules.

Section 1 of the 1989 Act contains minimum requirements for execution by individuals. In the normal way, the individual must sign (signature includes making one's mark) and the deed and his signature must be witnessed. A seal is unnecessary. There is provision for an individual to arrange for someone else to sign on his behalf. In this case the deed must be signed in the presence of the individual whose deed it is and of two other witnesses.

Following the bringing into force of s 36A of the 1985 Act, there are two methods of execution by companies registered under the 1985 Act. First, a company may execute under its common seal in the presence of such witness(es) as are authorised by its articles of association. Alternatively, under s 36A, it may execute by the signature of a director and its secretary or of two directors. Where the first method is adopted and the witnesses are a director and the secretary in accordance with s 74(1) of the Law of Property Act 1925, no question will arise. If attestation is not in accordance with s 74(1) the Registry may call for evidence that the persons attesting the sealing are authorised by or under the company's articles of association. If the s 36A method of execution is adopted, a purchaser is entitled to assume due execution and the Registry will accept without question a deed executed in this manner and lodged by a purchaser.

Execution by an unregistered company in one of the two alternative registered company forms will normally be accepted by the Registry. Execution by foreign companies which complies with s 74(1) will be accepted without further evidence, but if any other method of execution is adopted, evidence that it is authorised will be required.

In the normal way, any deed presented for registration will be presumed to have been delivered from the fact that it has been so presented.

The Land Registration (Execution of Deeds) Rules 1990 substituted a new Form 19 in the schedule to the Rules in line with s 1 of the 1989 Act and s 36A of the 1985 Act. The new form dispenses with the need for sealing and provides alternative forms of execution by an individual or by a person signing by direction of an individual or by a company under seal or by a company not under seal. If circumstances require that the prescribed wording is not followed (eg execution by a blind or illiterate person) then the prescribed form should be followed as closely as possible and advance approval may be sought (see **7** above).

9 Execution by attorney

The method of execution by an attorney will vary according to whether the attorney is an individual or a company. If the attorney is an individual he may sign with his own signature or in the name of the donor either way in the presence of a witness. If the donor is a company the individual as attorney may sign in the company's name in the presence of a witness. If the attorney is a company it may either execute in one of the two ways outlined at **8** above or through one of its officers duly authorised by resolution execute in the name of the donor in the presence of a witness.

Rule 82(1), as substituted by the Land Registration (Powers of Attorney) Rules 1986, provides that if any instrument executed by an attorney is delivered at the Registry, there must be produced also either (*a*) the instrument creating the power of attorney, or (*b*) a copy by means of which its contents may be proved under s 3 of the Powers of Attorney Act 1971 or s 7(3) of the Enduring Powers of Attorney Act 1985, or (*c*) a document complying with s 4 of the Evidence and Powers of Attorney Act 1940. A complete copy of the power of attorney (including any explanatory notes) certified on each page as a true and complete copy by a solicitor is acceptable.

Rule 82(2), as so substituted, provides that if an order has been made pursuant to s 8 of the Enduring Powers of Attorney Act 1985 with respect to a power or the donor thereof or the attorney thereunder, the order or an office copy or certified copy (see r 309) shall be furnished to the Registrar.

Rule 82(3), as so substituted, provides that the Registry may retain any instrument creating a power of attorney or any order or any copy or document produced pursuant to the rule.

Rule 82(4), (5) and (6), as so substituted, provide that if any transaction between the donee of a power of attorney and the person dealing with him is not completed within twelve months of the date on which the power came into operation, evidence must be produced to satisfy the Registrar that the power had not been revoked at the time of the transaction. The evidence required is:

(a) when the power is in a form prescribed under the Enduring Powers of Attorney Act 1985, either a statutory declaration by the person dealing with the donee of the power that he did not, at the time of completion of the transaction know:
   (i) of any revocation of the power whether by the donor or by an order of the Court of Protection;
   (ii) of the occurrence of any event (such as the death of the donor or the bankruptcy of the donor or of any donee or a direction by the Court of Protection on exercising its powers under Pt Vll of the Mental Health Act 1983) which had the effect of revoking the power;
   (iii) that the power was not a valid enduring power of attorney and had been revoked by the donor's mental incapacity;
   or, in accordance with directions given by the Registrar on 26 April 1991, a certificate by the solicitor acting for the person dealing with the donee of the power that at the time of completion of the transaction his client did not know (i) (ii) and (iii) above;
(b) in any case to which paragraph (a) above does not apply, the evidence required is either a statutory declaration by the person dealing with the donee that he did not, at the time of the completion of the transaction know:
   (i) of any revocation of the power;
   (ii) of the occurrence of any event (such as the death, bankruptcy or other incapacity of the donor) which had the effect of revoking the power;
   or, in accordance with directions given by the Registrar on 26 April 1991, a certificate by the solicitor acting for the person dealing with the donee of the power that at the time of completion of the transaction his client did not know (a)(i)–(iii) above;

Provided that where the power is expressed in the instrument creating it to be irrevocable and to be given by way of security, any such statutory declaration must be to the effect that the declarant did not know that the power was not in fact given by way of security and did not know that the power had been revoked by the donor acting with the consent of the donee.

(a) Powers of attorney given by joint proprietors

Under section 10(2) of the Powers of Attorney Act 1971 a general power of attorney cannot be used by a trustee to delegate his power. The use by a joint proprietor of a general power of attorney pursuant to s 10 of the Act of 1971 is therefore inappropriate (see *Walia v Michael Naughton Ltd* [19851 1 WLR 1115) and a 'trustee' power must be used (see s 25 of the Trustee Act 1925 as amended by 59 of the 1971 Act). A 'trustee' power can only have effect for a maximum period of 12 months and the only other co-trustee of the donor cannot be the attorney.

(b) Powers of attorney given to receivers

The subject of powers of attorney given to receivers in debentures is discussed on pp 191–3.

10 Alteration of instruments

Rule 86 allows for an alteration to be made in an instrument after it has been delivered for registration. Such an instrument may, before any entry based on it has been made in the register and if the Registrar shall think fit, be withdrawn from registration and returned for the purpose of alteration and re-execution. This re-execution must be by all persons whose interests appear to be affected by the instrument, whether it was originally so executed by them or not. On re-delivery to the appropriate district land registry the dealing will be registered as of the date and priority of such re-delivery.

If a mistake in an instrument is found after its registration has been completed, the proper way of correcting it is by a deed of rectification. This deed should be lodged for registration (Form A4) with a certified copy, the land certificate (or the charge certificate if a charge is registered and the chargee is in any way affected) and a fee of £30 per title with a minimum fee of £600 under Part I(1) of Schedule 3 to the Fees Order. If the mistake is a minor one, however, the Chief Land Registrar may be in a position to correct it under r 13 (see p 205).

11 Change of name, address or description

A change of name of a registered proprietor or other person referred to on the register will be entered on the register, without fee, on production of the land or charge certificate and the appropriate evidence, eg, marriage certificate, deed poll or, in the case of a company, the certificate of incorporation on change of name. A certified copy of a deed poll should be lodged unless the deed has been enrolled at the Central Office. A change of a registered proprietor's address or of the description of the property will be entered on the register without fee. The land or charge certificate should be lodged. Applications may conveniently be made on Form A4.

12 Plans 'for the purpose of identification only'

Plans to instruments dealing with registered land are used (subject to r 278—general boundaries—see p 21) to define the land being dealt with; and plans 'for the purpose of identification only' are unacceptable.

13 Requisitions from the Registry

Requisitions from the Registry should be dealt with as expeditiously as possible. Undue delay may result in the cancellation of the application. See further on pp 14–15.

Chapter VII

Transfers

1 Sale of registered land

(a) Contract

When a formal contract is desired, one of the usual printed forms may be used. The contract may be protected on the register by a notice or restriction if the vendor consents and lodges his land certificate (if outstanding, ie, if there is no registered charge) at the Registry for the purpose; otherwise by a caution against dealings (see Chapter XIV). A plan will usually be necessary on a sale of part of the land in a title; see under the heading 'Transfer of part: plan' at p 87.

(b) Deduction of title

On a sale of registered land the vendor must, if required, provide the purchaser's solicitor with:
  (1) a copy of the subsisting entries on the register;
  (2) copies or abstracts of any documents referred to on the register which affect the land except those relating to incumbrances to be discharged on or before completion; and
  (3) a copy of the plan of the title (see p 58 as to the provision of an official certificate of inspection of the filed plan instead of an office copy of that plan where the disposition affects part of the land in a title) (s 110(1)).

Items (1), (2) and (3) can be prepared from the land or first charge certificate. But the certificate must first be sent to the Registry to be officially examined with and, if necessary, made to correspond with the register. It will then be returned with the date of examination stamped inside the front cover. This date must be given on the copy of the subsisting entries on the register when prepared.

A simpler time-saving and preferred method, and one that can be used when for any reason neither the land certificate nor charge certificate is available, is to obtain from the Registry an office copy of the register and of any document or plan required. These can be requested on Forms 109 and 110 (see Chapter V). Office copies do not require verification, since s 113 provides that such copies shall be admissible in evidence to the same extent as the originals would be admissible. The practice of relying on office copies is recommended by The Law Society.

Also, subject to any contrary stipulation, the vendor must provide the purchaser with such copies, abstracts and evidence (if any) as the purchaser would have been entitled to if the land had been unregistered in respect of:

(*a*) any subsisting rights and interests appurtenant to the registered land as to which the register is not conclusive; and

(*b*) any matters excepted from the effect of registration (s 110(2)).

An example of (*a*) would be a right of way as to which the register recorded merely that the proprietor claimed it. Examples of (*b*) would be weekly tenancies and local land charges. Also under these provisions, if the vendor's title is possessory or qualified he is obliged to deduce evidence of the pre-registration title or of the estate right or interest excepted from registration unless the contract provides otherwise.

Except as stated above, the vendor need not furnish the purchaser with any abstract or other written evidence of title, or any copy or abstract of the land certificate or of any charge certificate (s 110(3))

(c) Investigation of title

If office copies have been supplied as indicated above, no verification of them is necessary. However, if copies only are supplied, it is necessary to examine them against the land or first charge certificate, or against the register, filed documents and plan at the Registry.

Requisitions on title may be made but, apart from the usual common form requisitions, it is likely that very little will need to be the subject of any inquiry.

The purchaser's solicitor must, of course, consider all subsisting entries on the register. He must ensure that any restriction limiting the vendor's powers of disposition will be complied with, and that such action (if any) as may be appropriate will be taken in regard to other entries, for example that a registered charge will be discharged, or that a caution will be withdrawn, at or before completion.

Practitioners are recommended to use the prescribed forms of transfer (see below) whenever possible. When the ordinary printed form of transfer of whole is used without addition or alteration, the submission of a draft is unnecessary.

Except as discussed on p 69, there is no occasion to search the registers maintained by the Land Charges Department when investigating an absolute registered title, but the usual searches in local land charges registers and other local inquiries must be made.

Where land is registered with absolute title, a purchaser from a limited company acting in good faith and having the backing of an official search need not search in the Companies Register. However, in any case of doubt it might well be prudent for an intending chargee of a company's registered land to make a prior search in the Companies Register because, for example, the fact of the chargor company's dissolution would be discovered.

The possibility of overriding interests must be considered; and in this context judicial decisions relating to the rights of persons in actual occupation will no doubt be kept in mind (see pp 48–50).

(d) Official search of the register

Immediately before completion the practitioner must find out whether any adverse entry has been made in the register since the date of the last official examination of the land or first charge certificate against the register, or the date of the issue of the office copy of the register, depending on which of the methods of deducing title mentioned above was used.

This information is obtained by making an application for an official search of the register in Form 94A or 94B as explained in Chapter V.

In addition to disclosing the state of the register, the official certificate of search enables the purchase to be safely completed at a distance from the district land registry concerned without personal attendance there to make a last-minute search of the register. This is so because the official certificate of search gives priority to the application to register the transfer if that application is deemed to have been delivered to the appropriate district land registry within the priority period of thirty working days conferred by the official certificate of search. The official search procedure is also available to chargees and lessees; and if the transferee is to charge the land, a search on behalf of the chargee will give priority to both the application to register the transfer and an application to register the charge. These matters are more fully discussed in Chapter V.

(e) Completion

On completion of a purchase of the whole of the land comprised in a title, the purchaser's solicitor must obtain the land certificate from the vendor's solicitor, in addition to the executed transfer. If, however, the land is subject to a registered charge, the land certificate will not be in the possession of the vendor's solicitor, since it will have been retained in the Registry under s 65 when the charge was registered. If this registered charge is to be paid off at completion, the vendor's solicitor will arrange for the charge certificate to be handed over with a discharge in Form 53. The application to register the discharge and the application to register the transfer can then be made together (see Chapter VI as to the form of the application, and Chapter IX as to discharges generally).

If the land is being transferred subject to the charge, the transfer alone will need to be handed over unless the chargee is a party to the transfer, in which case the charge certificate must be lodged at the appropriate district land registry (see p 72 as to deposit of documents) to meet the application to register the transfer.

If the transfer is of part of the land in the title, the purchaser's solicitor must obtain from the vendor's solicitor an undertaking to lodge the land certificate on deposit at the Registry to meet the application to register the transfer (see p 72). If the vendor's title is subject to a registered charge which is to be discharged at completion as to the part transferred, the charge certificate must be lodged on deposit (see p 72).

It may happen that although a registered charge has been paid off, the discharge cannot be handed over at completion. Instead the vendor's solicitor undertakes that as soon as he receives it he will forward it to the purchaser's solicitor. In such a case it is unnecessary to defer lodging the application for registration until the discharge is received. Indeed, the priority secured by obtaining the official certificate of search of the register mentioned on p 62 might be lost in this way. Instead, the application should be lodged at once with an explanatory letter confirming that the chargee has been paid and that the discharge will be forwarded to the Registry as soon as it is received. In the meantime the Registry will stand the application over to await the arrival of the discharge. If after a suitable time the discharge has not been received the Registry will requisition for it.

(f) After completion: registration of the transfer

The transfer must be stamped with the appropriate Inland Revenue duty and with the particulars delivered stamp unless the provisions for lodging transfers, which require a particulars delivered stamp direct to the appropriate district land registry with Form L(A)451, apply. (See pp 13–14 as to this; and particularly as to reconciling the need for adjudication of stamp duty, when it arises, with the need to lodge the application to register the transfer within the priority of an official search.) The transfer must then be delivered to the appropriate district land registry for registration within the priority period conferred by the official search of the register in Form 94A or 94B (see Chapter V).

The application to register the transfer, which will, of course, commonly be delivered together with applications to register a discharge of a registered charge and a new charge by the transferee, should be made on a Form A4 (transfer of all land in a title) or A5 (transfer of part) as appropriate. (For points arising on these forms, see Chapter VI.)

Transfers on sale attract a fee under Scale A on the amount of the consideration. Reference should be made to article 2(5) of the Fees Order in relation to a transfer otherwise than for monetary consideration and to article 2(4) in relation to exchanges. It is important not to overlook Abatement 1 when a charge by the transferee is delivered for registration with the application to register a transfer on sale or exchange. Article 6 makes special provision for the fees to be charged on applications involving 20 or more registered titles. A statement in writing, signed by the applicant or his solicitor, of the full open market value, free from any charge or mortgage, at the date of the application, of the land must be supplied in the case of a transfer otherwise than for monetary consideration or an exchange.

2 Forms of transfers: implied covenants

The Rules prescribe various forms of transfers for use according to the circumstances; and variants of the prescribed forms have been officially approved. The forms most likely to be needed by solicitors are listed in Appendix V. Most of these have been printed and can be bought from law stationers and from HM Stationery Office. (For details see the note to Appendix V.) Others (not printed) relate to mines and minerals (Forms 25 to 30), part of the land in a lease where the rent has already been apportioned (Form 33), transfers for charitable uses (Form 36), smallholdings (Forms 37 and 38) and exchanges (Form 44). For the texts of the forms that have not been printed, reference should be made to the Schedule to the Rules.

For the purpose of introducing the covenants for title implied under ss 76 and 77 of the Law of Property Act 1925, a person may be expressed to transfer as 'beneficial owner', 'settlor', etc (see rr 76, 77, 109).

A transfer of leasehold land need not contain covenants for payment of rent, etc. In such a transfer the usual covenants are implied under s 24(1)(*a*) and (*b*). By s 24(2), on a transfer of part of the land held under a lease, the covenant by the transferee implied by s 24(1) is limited to payment of the apportioned rent (if any) and the performance and observance of such of the covenants by the lessee and conditions in the registered lease as affect the part transferred. Where the transferor remains owner of part of the land in the lease, there is implied on his part, as respects the part retained, a covenant with the transferee similar to that implied on the part of the transferee under s 24(2). On a transfer of part of the land in a lease, the covenants implied by s 24 or by s 77 of the Law of Property Act 1925 may, if desired, be modified or negatived by adding suitable words to the transfer.

3 Transfer of part: plan

It is usually necessary to have a plan for a transfer of part of the land in a title. It should be based on the filed plan of the transferor's title or be capable, in the case of new developments, of being associated therewith. If the land transferred is not physically defined other than by surveyors' pegs, the boundaries shown on the plan must be tied to permanent features by accurate measurements. (See Chapter XVII as to transfers of plots on registered building estates.) The plan must be signed by the transferor and by the transferee or by his solicitor on his behalf.

An office copy plan issued by the Land Registry may be used as the basis of a transfer plan, but it is important that a copy plan made in a solicitor's office should not be capable of being interpreted or passed off as an official plan. For this reason, it should not bear the official heading or any other official markings.

4 Easements: covenants

These matters are discussed above and in Chapter 1V. It may be noted also that in general an indemnity covenant to protect a vendor of registered land is necessary when it would be necessary if the land were unregistered.

5 Transfers to two or more transferees

A transfer to two or more persons is not required to include any special form of words on this account. If thought fit, however, a clause may be added in which it is stated that the transferees are to hold the land on trust for themselves as joint tenants beneficially, or as tenants in common, or as the case may be.

Very many owner-occupied dwellings are transferred to joint transferees, usually husband and wife, and therefore, for the convenience of applicants, the Registrar has promulgated Form 19(JP) as a printed form of transfer. This form contains a declaration as to whether or not the survivor of the transferees can give a valid receipt for capital money and makes provision for the instrument to be executed by the transferees. Completion of the declaration and execution by the transferees should not be overlooked.

Whatever form is used for a transfer to two or more persons, the solicitor lodging the application to register the transfer should complete the panel of the application form (A4 or A5) in which is asked the question whether or not the survivor of the transferees can give a valid receipt for capital money arising on a disposition of the land; and it is essential to complete the panel where the answer to the question is not apparent from the transfer or from some other document, eg, a letter, accompanying the application.

If it appears that the survivor of the transferees cannot give such a valid receipt, the Chief Land Registrar is obliged to enter the following restriction (see r 6 of the Land Registration Rules 1989) in the proprietorship register:

'RESTRICTION—No disposition by a sole proprietor of the land (not being a trust corporation) under which capital money arises is to be registered except under an order of the Registrar or of the Court.'

6 Transfers to give effect to dealings with undivided shares fees

The Fees Order contains express provisions as to the fee payable on the registration of a transfer for the purpose of giving effect to a disposition of a share in registered land or a registered charge.

If the disposition of a share is for monetary consideration (as defined in article 1 of the Fees Order) the fee is payable on the amount of the consideration in accordance with Scale A.

If the disposition of a share is otherwise than for monetary consideration the fee is payable under Scale A reduced in accordance with Abatement 2, in the case of a share in land, on the equivalent proportion of the value of the land less an equivalent proportion of the amount secured on the land by any prior charge. This can be expressed in the following formula:

[Total value of the land—Total amount secured by any prior charge] × Share disposed of.

The value of the land is the open market value free of any charge at the date of the application and a statement of such value, signed by the applicant or his solicitor, should accompany the application. In the case of a disposition of a share in a registered charge the fee is payable on the equivalent proportion of the amount thereby secured less an equivalent proportion of the amount secured on the charge by any prior charge.

So, for example, where the transfer is to give effect to a gift of a quarter share in land worth £30,000 subject to a charge securing £7,200 the Scale A fee will be payable on £5,700 calculated as follows:

[£30,000–£7,200] × 1/4 = £5,700.

7 Particular parties to transfers

(a) Corporations

In the absence of any relevant restriction in the register, no evidence of a corporation's power to transfer land of which it is the registered proprietor is required. The question as to whether a purchaser of registered land from a company should search in the Companies Register to guard against the possibility that the company may have been dissolved is considered on p 84.

When a corporation is the transferee, evidence of its incorporation, constitution and powers is usually required. In the case of a limited company transferee, the appropriate panel of the application Form A4 or A5 should be completed if applicable, otherwise certified copies of its certificate of incorporation and of its memorandum and articles of association must be produced. It is important to note that the certificates printed in the application forms will not be appropriate in every case. So, for example, they will not apply in the case of a company not trading for profit or a company incorporated outside England and Scotland. Certified copies of the constitutions of other transferee corporations should usually be produced. This does not, of course, apply to local authority transferees.

When a corporation, other than a local authority, is registered as the proprietor of land, the need for a restriction in the proprietorship register is considered in the light of the corporation's constitution and powers. Trading companies incorporated under the Companies Acts are usually registered without a restriction, but when an insurance company is registered as the proprietor of land, a restriction referring to s 29 of the Insurance Companies Act 1982 may be entered in the proprietorship register.

When a company incorporated in England or Scotland is registered as the proprietor of land or of a charge, its registered number will be entered in the register of title if this is desired and if the necessary information is furnished. Accordingly, if the company's number is provided with its name and address on the Form A4 or A5, or if the number is stated in the instrument lodged for registration, it will be entered in the register of title immediately after the company's name.

The questions of liquidation and receivership are considered in Chapter XVI.

(b) Overseas companies

Where an application is made to register an overseas company as proprietor of land or of a charge it should be accompanied by a certified copy of the equivalent of the memorandum and articles with a certified translation if not in English. The Registry will be particularly anxious to ensure that the applicant is a legal entity with power to purchase and charge or to accept a charge on English and/or Welsh land and to ascertain the formalities applicable to execution of documents by the applicant. In view of the uncertainties which may arise the Registrar will enter a restriction on the following lines in appropriate cases:

> 'RESTRICTION registered on (*date*)—Except under an order of the Registrar no disposition by the proprietor of the land is to be registered unless a certificate signed by the solicitor thereto has been furnished that the company is still registered in the country of incorporation, that it is not in receivership, liquidation or bankruptcy and that neither the constitution of the company nor its law of incorporation restrict the intended disposition.'

(c) Building, friendly, and industrial and provident societies

The rules of a building society transferee need not be lodged unless called for, but evidence is required that the land has been acquired for the purpose of the society's business. A certified copy of the rules of a friendly or industrial and provident society transferee should be produced. (Generally the rules of these societies need not be produced when they are being registered as chargees.)

When the trustees of a friendly society or of an industrial and provident society who execute a transfer of the society's registered land are different from those who are registered as the proprietors of the land, a certificate by the secretary or the solicitor of the society that the persons executing the transfer were the trustees of the society at the time of execution should accompany the application for the registration of the transfer. Usually, however, the Registry will not ask for this certificate when the trustees' signatures have been witnessed by the secretary.

(d) Personal representatives

Transfers by personal representatives are discussed in Chapter XIII.

Chapter VIII

Leases

1 Leases of registered land

(a) The lessor's title to grant and lease

An intending lessee of registered land is in the same position as an intending lessee of unregistered land as regards calling for his intending lessor's title. The lessor is not obliged to supply the evidence unless the agreement for lease so provides (s 110). However the intending lessee can, without the intending lessor's consent, obtain an office copy of the register (and plan) of the lessor's and any superior title and use the official search procedure. Inspection of the register, office copies and official searches are discussed in Chapter V.

A proprietor of registered land has full power to lease his land (or to sub-lease if it is leasehold) subject to any entry to the contrary in the register. All such entries must therefore be considered in deciding whether or not the grant of the lease will be valid. Thus a restriction may have to be complied with, or a registered chargee's consent obtained. It must be remembered, if the lessor's title is good leasehold, that a good leasehold title does not affect rights in derogation of the title of the lessor to grant the lease (s 10). It must also be remembered that a lessee who derives his title from a registered freeholder or a registered leaseholder has notice of any restrictive covenants on the lessor's register even though the covenants do not appear on the register of his own title, (s 50(2)).

(b) Form of lease

The lease may be in any form provided that it refers to the lessor's title number and, in the case of a lease of part of the land in the title, that it refers to a plan enabling the demised premises to be identified on the filed plan of the lessor's title. The subject matter of easements and like rights must be similarly clearly identifiable. See p 76 as to the execution of the lease and the signature of the lease plan, if any. In the case of a lease it is to be expected that the lessor would sign the plan to the lease and the lessee would sign the plan to the counterpart.

(c) Searches

The usual local searches and inquiries are necessary, and an official search of the public index map should be applied for (see Chapter II). An official search of the register of the lessor's title should be applied for. (The official search procedure is discussed in Chapter V.) No search in the Land Charges Department or at the Companies Registry against a lessor registered with absolute or good leasehold title is necessary.

(d) Completion

In addition to obtaining such documents and undertakings as would be necessary in unregistered conveyancing, the lessee's solicitor should obtain, if the title to the lease is to be registered or notice of it is to be entered on the lessor's title, the deposit number under which the certificate of the lessor's title has been deposited at the appropriate district land registry (or an undertaking to deposit the certificate and to inform the lessee of the deposit number) and any consents (eg, by a chargee) that the register of the lessor's title shows to be necessary. In certain events, production of the lessor's certificate cannot be insisted upon; see p 35.

(e) Registration

A lease granted by the proprietor of registered land for a term of more than twenty-one years must be completed by substantive registration, and by the entry of notice of the lease in the register of the lessor's title, if it is to be effective at law (see p 39 for leases granted pursuant to the provisions of the Housing Act 1985). This is the position whether the registered land out of which the lease is granted is freehold or leasehold. The position where only twenty-one years or less, of a term originally created for more than twenty-one years, remain unexpired at the time of the application is dealt with on p 4.

An application for substantive registration of the title to the lease must be made by the lessee's solicitors on Form 3B. The form and its completion are discussed in Chapter III. Arrangements must be made for the certificate of the lessor's title to be lodged at the Registry (but see p 35). The lessor's certificate may be lodged with the application for registration of the title to the lease, but usually will be deposited at the Registry separately by the lessor's solicitors under cover of a Form A15 (see under 'Completion' above and see p 72). When the application for substantive registration of the title to the lease is being prepared, the advantages of absolute leasehold title, discussed on pp 7–8, should be borne in mind. In particular, it is recommended that absolute leasehold title be applied for when the land demised is a plot on a registered building estate. Notice of the lease is entered on the lessor's title by the Registry as a matter of course whenever substantive registration of the title to a lease of registered land takes place.

If the lease is an overriding interest an application will be necessary if it contains an option (see p 95).

(f) Leasehold interests incapable of substantive registration

There are three cases in which leasehold interests created out of registered land are incapable of substantive registration. These are:

(1) a lease granted for a term of twenty-one years or less except for a lease granted pursuant to the provisions of the Housing Act 1985 (see pp 4 and 39);
(2) an agreement for a lease;
(3) a mortgage term where there is a subsisting right of redemption.

As regards (1), the lease will be an overriding interest not requiring protection on the register (see p 46) unless it contains an option (see p 95).

As regards (2), the agreement may be protected as an estate contract (see p 174).

In the case of (3), protection would be obtained if the mortgage were registered as a registered charge.

(g) Production of the certificate of the lessor's title

It is desirable that the land or charge certificate of the lessor's title be produced whenever notice of a lease is to be entered in the register of that title. The land certificate if outstanding (ie, if there is no registered charge) must be produced for the registration of any lease other than a lease granted at a rent without taking a premium (see s 64(1)(*c*) and p 35). The charge certificate must be produced for the registration of any lease granted with the chargee's consent. It must also be produced whenever there is an application to register a discharge of the land in the lease from a registered charge of the land in the lessor's title. There is, of course, often such a discharge when notice of a lease of part of the land in a lessor's developing title is being entered on the register of that title at the time of the substantive registration of the lease.

2 Easements and restrictive covenants in registered leases

The effect of easements granted and reserved in registered leases is covered by ss 9-12 but to remove any uncertainty the following note appears at the head of all modern registers of leasehold titles:

'Unless the contrary is indicated below, any subsisting legal easements granted by the undermentioned lease(s) for the benefit of the land in this title are included therein. The registration takes effect subject to any rights excepted and reserved by the said lease(s) so far as such rights are subsisting and affect the land in this title.'

The appurtenant easements referred to are included in the registration with the same class of title as the land itself.

If the purported grant of a particular easement by a lease registered with absolute leasehold title is not effective, an entry stating that it is not included in the title will be made in the register.

If a lease of registered land grants to the lessee an easement over land of the lessor lying in a registered title other than that out of which the lease was granted, notice of the grant must be entered in the register of the latter title if the grant is to be effective at law; and for this purpose the land or charge certificate of the latter title must be produced. Notice of restrictive covenants between lessor and lessee is not entered on any register (s 50).

3 Options in leases of registered land

Where a lease of registered land contains an option granted by the lessor that would be registered in the Land Charges Department as an estate contract if the lessor's land were unregistered, the option should be protected by an entry on the register of the lessor's title. The Registry will make such an entry automatically when notice of the lease is entered on the lessor's title, but if the lease is an overriding interest (see p 46) a separate application to protect the option on the register of the lessor's title, by means of a notice, caution or restriction, is necessary (see Chapter XIV).

4 Registered leases: endorsement of registration with lessor

Some leases require dispositions to be produced to (and in some cases to be endorsed by) the landlord or his agent. Where such a disposition is a transfer or charge of registered land r 91 allows this obligation to be complied with by production of:

either (*a*) the original transfer or charge before registration;

or (*b*) a copy of the transfer or charge (any endorsement must then be made on the copy);

or (*c*) the land or charge certificate after registration (in which case any endorsement must be made on the lease and any endorsement on the land or charge certificate is void).

5 Office copies of registered leases

Leases are not retained by the Registry on registration. If registration took place on the original grant of the lease, the Registry will have a copy of the lease; in any other cases it may have a copy. An office copy of such a copy may be supplied in special circumstances; see p 57.

6 Variation of leases

An application to register notice of a deed of variation of a registered lease or of a lease that is merely noted against the lessor's title should be made against the registered title (or, if both lease and reversion are registered, against both titles) concerned. The application may be made on Form A4 and should be accompanied by the deed, a certified copy of the deed, and a fee of £35 for the first title and £20 for each subsequent title affected under Part I(1) of Schedule 3 to the Fees Order. No fee is payable if, in relation to each registered title affected, the application is lodged with an application affecting that title on which a scale fee (not under art 6) is payable. The land certificate(s) if outstanding (ie, if there is no registered charge) of the title(s) should either accompany the application or be placed on deposit to meet it. If a title is subject to a registered charge and the proprietor of the charge is a party to the deed or concurs in the application, the charge certificate of that title must accompany the application or be placed on deposit to meet it.

Where the title of the lease itself is registered, if all persons appearing from the register to be interested in the lease are parties to the deed or have concurred in the application, and if all the land or charge certificates affected have been lodged, the entry in the register will indicate that the deed has effectively varied the lease. In any other circumstances the entry will give notice of the deed but will not guarantee its validity.

(a) Apportionment of rent by ministerial order

A proprietor's title to registered land may be affected by a ministerial order apportioning a rent either unconditionally or conditionally upon the redemption of the apportioned rent. An application should then be made to the appropriate district land registry for effect to be given to the order on the register of the title; but where the apportionment is made conditional on the redemption of the apportioned rent the application should not be made until after the redemption has taken place.

If it is not known whether the title of the land is registered, an application on Form 96 with a fee under Part II(9) of Schedule 3 to the Fees Order should be sent to the appropriate district land registry.

The application can conveniently be made on a Form A4. It should be supported by:

(1) where there is no registered charge or notice of [intended] deposit of certificate on the register of the title against which the application is made, the land certificate of that title;
(2) an official copy of the order and, in the case of a conditional order, an official copy of the certificate of redemption; and
(3) the land registration fee assessed as above for deeds of variation.

If the proprietor making the application is a lessee and he applies for the order to be registered not only on his own title but on his lessor's, there must also be lodged the lessor's consent to the application and (where there is no registered charge or notice of [intended] deposit on the register of the lessor's title) the lessor's land certificate; and this requirement applies, mutatis mutandis, where a lessor proprietor making the application applies against his own and his lessee's title.

No fee for the registration of the order in relation to a particular title will be payable where the order has been obtained with a sale of the land in that title in view and the application for the registration of the order is made together with the application for the registration of the transfer on sale.

7 Mergers and surrenders of leases

(a) Merger or surrender of a registered lease in a superior estate which is either already registered or is the subject of an application for first registration

(1) Where the same person is registered or is about to be registered in the same capacity as proprietor of both estates, the title to the inferior estate may be closed on the application of that person or his solicitor (r 206). If the superior estate is registered, the application may be made by letter. If the superior estate is the subject of an application for first registration, the application should be made by completing the relevant paragraph of the form of application for first registration (see p 33). Any incumbrance on the register of the title to the inferior estate that would prevent merger must be discharged.

(2) If the lease is to be surrendered by deed, the deed should be executed by the registered proprietor of that lease and every person appearing by the register to be interested in it (r 200), and should be in favour of the registered proprietor of the superior estate or the person entitled to be registered as proprietor of the superior estate. The deed may take the form of a transfer in Form 19 suitably adapted. For example, it may be appropriate to insert before the words of transfer: 'For the purpose of surrendering the term comprised in the registered title [and in consideration of . . .]'.

(3) If the lease has been surrendered not in writing but by operation of law, evidence must be given of the acts from which surrender is to be implied. Surrender may be implied, for example, from the grant of a new lease to the same lessee. If the new lease was granted pursuant to the Leasehold Reform Act 1967, s 14 (see pp 102–9) this fact must be disclosed. If the surrender is to be implied from the acts of the parties in giving up and accepting possession, evidence of the facts should be given in a statutory declaration by a reliable person qualified by his particular knowledge of the facts to make the declaration. Thus, if the lessee making the surrender was in actual occupation of the property and has given vacant possession to his lessor, the declaration should describe in detail when and how the premises were vacated and the keys returned to the lessor. If the lessee making the surrender was not in actual occupation because there was an underlease, the lessor must show that he is receiving the rent directly from the underlessee. He may do this by exhibiting to a statutory declaration the counterpart of the underlease and a copy of the authority

requiring the underlessee to pay the rent directly to him. If possible, the registered proprietor of the surrendered lease should be persuaded to join in the application to close his registered title. Any incumbrance on that title that would prevent merger must have been discharged. Any other available documentary evidence, such as a receipt for money paid in consideration of the surrender or an instrument of release of personal liability, should be produced.

(4) An application to register the merger or surrender of the registered lease should be supported by evidence as indicated above, by the lease and by any outstanding land certificates. If the lease cannot be produced, an explanation should be given and a certified copy or examined abstract should be lodged, if available. If there is a registered charge of the lease, the charge certificate must be produced and the charge must be discharged. Any notice of [intended] deposit or caution on the register of the title to the lease must be withdrawn. If the title to the lease is possessory, evidence sufficient for its conversion to good leasehold must be lodged, and any incumbrance that would prevent merger revealed by such evidence must be discharged before merger of the lease can be registered. If the merger or surrender requires the consent of any incumbrancer of the superior estate, that consent must, of course, be forthcoming. If the surrender is by deed for value the application should be accompanied by a completed Form L(A)451 where appropriate (see p 13).

(5) On an application for the registration of a surrender for monetary consideration other than the grant of a new lease on which a scale fee is payable a fee under Scale A is payable on the consideration—if moving from the lessor (art 2(3)(c) of the Fees Order). In the case of an application to register a surrender not for monetary consideration or where the consideration is the grant of new lease (whether effected by deed or otherwise) a fee under Scale A on the value of the land in the leasehold title is payable reduced to one fifth in accordance with Abatement 2 in Part I of Schedule 4 to the Fees Order (arts 2(5)(c) and (d) and 4) and a statement of value should accompany any such application. On an application to close or partly close a registered leasehold title other than on surrender, a fee of £35 for each title closed or partly closed is payable under Part I(2) of Schedule 3; provided that no fee is payable if the application is accompanied by an application upon which a scale fee is payable. The fee covers the cancellation of the notice of the registered lease on the register of the title to the reversion where the reversion is registered.

(6) On the completion of an application to register the merger or surrender of a registered lease, when the merger or surrender has been established, the register will be closed (and the certificate cancelled) as to that lease; if the superior title is registered, the notice of the lease in the register of that title will be cancelled; and the lease, if lodged, will be marked 'Lease determined: register closed' and issued to the applicant or as he may direct.

(b) Surrender of a registered lease where the superior estate is neither registered nor the subject of an application for first registration

(1) The determination of a registered leasehold estate may be notified on the register on the production of a surrender or other sufficient release or discharge, executed by the proprietor and every person appearing by the register to be interested (r 200). Form 19 suitably adapted may be used: see para (*a*)(2) above. If surrender by operation of law is relied on, evidence should be produced as indicated in para (*a*)(3) above.

(2) The application to register the surrender should be supported by the land certificate or charge certificate of the registered title, the lease and its counterpart, and satisfactory prima facie evidence (such as an examined abstract) of the title to the superior estate. If the lease and the counterpart cannot be produced an explanation should be given. Incumbrances must be dealt with as indicated in para (*a*)(3), (4) above. Form L(A)451 may be required (see para (*a*)(4) above).

(3) A fee of £35 for each registered title to be closed, wholly or partly, is payable unless the application is based on a surrender when a fee under Scale A is payable as in para (*a*)(5) above.

(4) On completion of the application, when surrender has been established, the lease if lodged will be marked 'Lease determined: register closed' and will be returned together with an office copy of the closed register.

(c) Merger or surrender of an unregistered lease noted on the register of a registered superior estate

(1) The application for the cancellation of the notice of the lease on the register of the superior estate must be in Form 92 and must be supported by the land certificate (if outstanding) of the superior estate and all deeds and documents relating to the title to the merged or surrendered leasehold estate (rr 201, 202). If surrender by operation of law is relied on, evidence of the kind

described in para (a)(3) above should be produced. If the merger or surrender requires the consent of any incumbrancer of the superior estate, that consent must be forthcoming. Form L(A)451 may be required (see para (a)(4) above).

(2) A fee assessed under Scale A on the value of the merged or surrendered leasehold estate at the time of its determination is payable (art 2(7) of the Fees Order).

(3) On completion of the application, when merger or surrender has been established, the lease if lodged will be returned marked 'Lease determined'.

(d) Merger of an unregistered lease on the first registration of the superior estate

(1) The relevant paragraph of the form of application for first registration (see p 35) should be completed. This asks that no note of the lease be made on the register of the title to the superior estate. There should be lodged with the application for first registration, in addition to the documents of title of the superior estate, the lease and all the deeds and documents of title relating to it. The question of merger will be considered by the Registry, in conjunction with the examination of the title to the superior estate, according to the ordinary principles of land law.

(2) The fee for first registration is assessed under Scale A on the combined value of the superior and merged estates (Fees Order, art 3(3)).

(3) On completion of the first registration, when the merger has been established, the lease if lodged will be returned marked 'Lease determined'.

(e) Assignment or surrender of an unregistered lease to the owner of the immediate reversion where that reversion is neither registered nor the subject of an application for first registration

If as a result of the assignment or surrender there is an immediate merger of the leasehold estate in the immediate reversion the assignment need not be registered even though it is for value (s 123(3); r 207).

8 Leases determined by effuxion of time: Landlord and Tenant Act 1954

Tenancies subject to the Landlord and Tenant Act 1954 can be determined only in accordance with the provisions of that Act. Therefore, the Registry will not cancel either the substantive registration of a time-expired lease or notice of the lease on the register of the lessor's title unless an express application is made. The application should be supported by a statement signed by the applicant's solicitor either certifying that the 1954 Act does not apply to the lease or stating the particular statutory provisions in accordance with which the lease has been determined. The lease need not be lodged, but if it is registered it is desirable that the land or charge certificate should be lodged for cancellation. If the lessor's title is registered, the land certificate of that title if outstanding should be lodged to meet the application for the cancellation of notice of the lease.

In the case of a registered lease, a fee of £35 is payable for each title to be closed or partly closed, provided that no such fee is payable if the application is accompanied by an application on which a scale fee is payable (Part I(2) of Schedule 3 to the Fees Order). In the case of an unregistered noted lease a fee under Scale A of the Fees Order is payable on the value of the leasehold interest at the time of its determination (Fees Order, art 2(7)). This would usually be the minimum Scale A fee of £35.

9 Agreement for lease

An agreement for a lease of registered land may be protected as an estate contract on the register of the title to the land by a notice, a caution against dealings or a restriction (see Chapter XIV).

10 Leasehold Reform Act 1967

(a) Preliminary investigations

A tenant who wishes to enfranchise or to have an extended lease may wish to find out whether his landlord's or any superior landlord's title is registered. He can do so by a search of the public index map (see Chapter II).

If superior titles are registered, the tenant may apply for office copies of the registers and of documents referred to on the registers other than leases and changes (s 112 and see Chapter V).

(b) Protecting the tenant's claim (s 5(5) of the Leasehold Reform Act)

When a tenant has given his landlord notice of his wish to enfranchise or to take an extended lease, he can protect his claim by the entry on the register(s) of the reversionary title(s) affected of a notice under s 49 or a caution against dealings under s 54. (Notices and cautions are discussed in Chapter XIV.) It should be noted that s 5(5) of the Leasehold Reform Act provides that the rights of a tenant arising from a notice under that Act do not take effect as overriding interests.

An application for the entry of a notice under s 49 should be made by letter, quoting the title number(s), and enclosing, for filing in the Registry, a certified copy of the notice served by the tenant under the Leasehold Reform Act. The land certificate(s) of the reversionary title(s) if outstanding (ie, if there is no registered charge) must be produced.

If any land certificate of the reversionary title(s) is outstanding and arrangements for its production cannot be made, an application for the entry of a caution in the register of that title should be made in Form 63. The statutory declaration on the reverse side of the form should provide details of the service of the notice by the tenant under the Leasehold Reform Act.

In either case a fee of £35 for the first title and £20 for each subsequent title affected under Part I(1) of Schedule 3 to the Fees Order will be payable.

The notice under s 49 or the caution will give notice of the tenant's claim, but will not guarantee its validity. Protection by notice under s 49 is to be preferred to protection by caution.

(c) Assignment of the rights under the Leasehold Reform Act of a tenant who has served notice of his wish to enfranchise or to have an extended lease

No entry of such an assignment can be made on the register of the tenant's title. If a transfer of a registered leasehold interest includes such an assignment, the Registry will raise no objection; but the Registry considers it desirable that the assignment should be by a separate instrument off the register.

So far as the landlord's title is concerned no action is necessary if the rights are protected by notice under s 49, but the benefit of a caution cannot be transferred, so that, if the rights assigned are protected by a caution registered against the landlord's title, the caution should be withdrawn and a new one in favour of the assignee should be registered. The statutory declaration in support of the new caution should refer both to the service of notice and to the subsequent assignment.

(d) Enfranchisement

Form of application for registration—The application will be either for first registration of a freehold estate or to register a transfer of registered freehold land, associated, in either case, perhaps, with an application relating to the merger of a registered or unregistered lease. The usual considerations will apply to these applications, but the following matters also arise.

Rights and burdens under s 10 of the Leasehold Reform Act— If the Registry is aware (see p 108 under 'Disclosure to the Registry') that a conveyance or transfer has been made under the Leasehold Reform Act, appropriate entries will be made in the register as to the benefit and burden of rights passing under s 10(2) of that Act when the conveyance or transfer is registered. If the conveyance or transfer includes new easements or restrictive covenants under s 10(3) or (4), entries will be made in the register in the ordinary way.

In some instances rights originally granted or reserved affecting the leasehold interest will, by virtue of s 10 of the Leasehold Reform Act, now affect the freehold estate. If reference to the deed which granted or reserved those rights is required to be made on the register, this should be expressly requested and the original deed, or, where appropriate, a certified copy or examined abstract of it, should be lodged.

Discharge of charges on the landlord's registered or unregistered title—The chargee may have expressly discharged the charge or released the land from it in the appropriate way according to whether the landlord's title is registered or unregistered. If not, and if the tenant claims that he has paid to the chargee enough money to discharge the land from the charge, a verified copy of the chargee's (appropriately worded) receipt must be lodged. If, however, there has been no express discharge or release, but sufficient money to discharge or release the land has been paid into court by the tenant under s 13 of the Leasehold Reform Act, there must be lodged a verified copy of the affidavit the tenant will have made under the County Court Rules 1981, Ord 49, r 8, and a verified copy of the court's official receipt.

If there has been an express discharge or release, or if, on the receipt of the appropriate evidence of payment to the chargee or into court, the Registry is satisfied that the tenant may be registered as the freeholder free from the charge, no entry of the charge will appear on the register of the tenant's freehold title. If, however, the charge certificate is not produced, notice will be served on the registered chargee explaining the nature of the transaction and inviting him to consent and to lodge the charge certificate. If in response to the notice the chargee gives prima facie grounds for objection, the application cannot proceed until the objection is disposed of either by agreement or by a judicial decision.

In the case of a floating charge by a landlord company, a certificate by the solicitor, secretary or other responsible officer of the company or of the debenture holder that the charge had not crystallised at the date of the conveyance or transfer on enfranchisement will be accepted as sufficient evidence for the registration of the tenant's freehold free from the charge.

Rentcharge on the landlord's title—Where the land has been discharged from a rentcharge and money has been paid into court under s 11(4) of the Leasehold Reform Act, the evidence of payment to be lodged at the Registry should be a verified copy of the tenant's or landlord's affidavit and a verified copy of the court's receipt (cf the discharge of a registered charge on the landlord's title, above).

(e) Extended lease

Form of application: registration of title to extended lease—An application to register the title to an extended lease should take the form of a normal application for first registration, associated, when appropriate, with an application to give effect on the register to the surrender of the tenant's existing lease, which must be taken to have been surrendered by operation of law.

When a tenant's title to his existing lease is neither registered nor noted on a landlord's registered title, the application for first registration of the title to the extended lease should be accompanied by ordinary conveyancing evidence of the tenant's title to his existing lease. This is necessary, whether absolute or good leasehold title is sought, so that appropriate entries can be made on the register of the tenant's title to the extended lease as to any rights of a mortgagee of the existing lease.

If the extended lease incorporates the terms of the existing lease, a certified copy or examined abstract of the existing lease is required for filing in the Registry.

Form of application: surrender of registered existing lease—If the title to the existing lease is registered, an application to close the title, and to cancel the notice of the lease on the register of the landlord's title if that title is registered, should be made and should be accompanied by the lease.

The tenant's land certificate, if outstanding (ie, if there is no registered charge), should also be produced; and, if there is on the tenant's register a notice of [intended] deposit of land certificate, it is helpful if this is expressly withdrawn, as it may be if, for example, a deposit of the land certificate relating to the extended lease has been arranged. (See below as to the procedure where a depositee is unwilling to lodge the land certificate.)

If a charge of the existing lease is registered and is being discharged, the charge certificate and discharge should be lodged. If the charge is not being discharged, arrangements should, if possible, be made for the charge certificate to be lodged for cancellation.

Where there is a notice of [intended] deposit of the tenant's land certificate or a registered charge of his registered existing lease and the land or charge certificate cannot be produced, the Registry will serve on the depositee or chargee a notice explaining the nature of the application and asking him to lodge the land certificate or charge certificate for cancellation. If the certificate is lodged, or if no objection is received in reply to the notice, the registered title to the existing lease will be closed. (See below as to the protection on the register of the title to the extended lease of the rights of a chargee of the existing lease whose charge has not been discharged.)

If the landlord's title is registered, his land certificate, if outstanding, should be lodged. If the landlord's title is unregistered, prima facie evidence (eg, an examined abstract) of it will be needed. The extended lease or its counterpart (or where appropriate the lodgment of an application to register the tenant's title to the extended lease) will be sufficient evidence of the surrender. On an application to close or partly close a registered leasehold title on surrender, a Scale A fee reduced in accordance with Abatement A is payable on the value of the land after deducting the amount secured on the land by any prior charge.

Form of application: surrender of noted existing lease—If the title to the existing lease is unregistered, but notice of it is entered on the landlord's registered title, an application to cancel the notice should be on Form 92. The application should be accompanied by the lease and by the other deeds and documents of the leasehold title. The landlord's land certificate, if outstanding, should be lodged. The extended lease or its counterpart (or where appropriate the lodgment of an application to register the tenant's title to the extended lease) will be sufficient evidence of the surrender. A fee assessed under Scale A on the value of the surrendered lease at the time of its determination will be payable.

The registered title to an extended lease—The ordinary considerations governing the grant of absolute or good leasehold title (see Chapter I) apply, except that for the grant of absolute title express consent to the grant of the extended lease by a landlord's chargee or mortgagee is only necessary where the existing lease was:

(1) granted after 1 January 1968; and
(2) granted after the date of the charge or mortgage; and
(3) outside the landlord's leasing powers under the charge or mortgage. (See s 14(4) of the Leasehold Reform Act.)

When a subsisting charge of the existing lease is not discharged, an entry will be made in the charges register of the title to the extended lease to the effect that the extended lease is subject to such rights as may be subsisting in favour of the persons interested in the charge of the original lease. The original charge, if lodged, will be marked 'Notice registered against title number [the number of the title to the extended lease]' and issued to the person who lodged it. If it was a registered charge, the registration markings will be cancelled. The entry will not be a registration of the charge under s 26. Where, however, a charge of the existing lease is discharged and a new legal charge of the extended lease is executed, the latter can be registered under s 26 if the title to the extended lease is registered.

If the Registry does not know whether or not an undischarged charge affects the existing lease, a suitable entry to protect any rights of any chargee of that lease will be made in the register of the title to the extended lease.

(f) Miscellaneous points

Where the landlord is a charity—Where the landlord is a charity and is obliged by the Leasehold Reform Act to convey or transfer the land on enfranchisement or to grant an extended lease, the consent of the Charity Commissioners to the conveyance, transfer or lease will not be called for notwithstanding, in the case of a landlord's registered title, any restriction on the register of that title requiring such consent. However, if in such a case the landlord's title is vested in the Official Custodian for Charities, the Official Custodian will be expected to execute the conveyance, transfer, or lease, because s 17(2)(*a*) of the Charities Act 1960 applies only to transactions authorised by order of the court or of the Charity Commissioners.

If the tenant negotiates a sale or the grant of a lease in the ordinary way instead of using the procedure of the Leasehold Reform Act, and the landlord's title is registered, any restriction in the register of that title requiring the consent of the Charity Commissioners will have to be complied with. If the landlord's title is unregistered, the need for the Commissioners' consent will be considered in the ordinary way on any application for first registration by the tenant.

Scheme under s 19 of the Leasehold Reform Act—Notice of a scheme would not be entered on a registered title. To be effective, a scheme must be registered as a local land charge, and if it had been so registered, the entry of notice on a registered title would be unnecessary. Any statutory charge imposed by the scheme would have to be registered under s 26 before it could be realised (s 59(2)). Rights under local land charges, unless and until registered or protected on the register of title in the prescribed manner, are overriding interests (see p 46).

Disclosure to the Registry—When an application to register a transfer of registered land or an application for first registration is made to give effect on the register to an enfranchisement or the grant of an extended lease under the Leasehold Reform Act, it is essential that the Registry be made aware of this fact.

In the case of an application to register a transfer of registered land, it is best that the fact be disclosed by a suitable addition (eg, 'in pursuance of the provisions of the Leasehold Reform Act 1967') to the usual form of transfer. Otherwise it should be disclosed by a letter accompanying the application. In the case of an application for first registration, it is best that there should be an appropriate recital in the conveyance or lease inducing the application. Otherwise the rights and interests, or potential rights and interests, affecting the applicant's title should be disclosed in the form of application for first registration.

Chapter IX

Charges and Liens

1 Registered charges

(a) Power to create

Section 25(1) provides that the proprietor of any registered land may by deed:
- (*a*) charge the land with the payment at an appointed time of any principal sum of money either with or without interest;
- (*b*) charge it in favour of a building society in accordance with the society's rules.

Section 25(2) provides that a charge may be in any form provided that:
- (*a*) the land is described by reference to the register or in some other way that enables the Registry to identify it without reference to any other document;
- (*b*) the charge does not refer to any other interest or charge affecting the land which:
  - (i) would have priority over the same and is not registered or protected on the register;
  - (ii) is not an overriding interest.

Section 25(3) provides that any provision in a charge which purports to:
- (i) take away from the proprietor of the charge the power of transferring it by registered disposition or of requiring its cessation to be noted on the register; or
- (ii) affect any registered land or charge other than that in respect of which the charge is to be expressly registered, shall be void.

A charge may be within s 25(1) although the 'appointed time' is the time of a future event that may or may not happen (eg, an event specified in a trust deed on the happening of which debenture trustees may enforce their security). Moreover, the principal sum may be unlimited, as in the case of a charge to secure a current account.

Where all the land in a title is being charged, s 25(2)(*a*) will be satisfied if the land is described by reference to its title number and short description. Where part only is being charged, a plan, signed by the chargor and by or on behalf of the chargee, and enabling the part charged to be clearly identified on the filed plan, is usually necessary. Where a charge is of land in a conveyance which will be the subject of an application for first registration, the land charged may be described by reference to the conveyance. Under r 72 a person entitled to apply for registration as first proprietor of land can charge the land as though he were already registered.

The exercise of the power given by s 25 is subject to any relevant entry on the register. Thus a restriction will preclude the registration of any charge by a tenant for life that is not authorised by the Settled Land Act 1925.

(b) Form

The Schedule to the Rules contains a model form of charge of registered land, Form 45, and a number of printed forms, based on it, are available (see Appendix V).

Instead of using one of these forms, the registered proprietor may execute a charge in any form complying with the provisions of s 25 provided that the charge, if it is to be a registered charge, contains either a charge of the land expressed to be by way of legal mortgage, or a demise for a term of years absolute, which, in the case of leasehold land, must be a demise for a term less than the term under which the land is held.

Where a chargee wishes to incorporate other documents in the charge by reference the Registry recommends the use of the Standard Form of Charge set out in Practice Leaflet No 20 (see p 116). A charge to a bank, a building society, a friendly society or an industrial and provident society will, of course, usually be on a pre-printed form of mortgage or charge. The Council of Mortgage Lenders recommends that the Standard Form of Charge should form the basis of such pre-printed forms.

If desired, special stipulations, eg, as to repairs, insurance or leasing, may be added to a charge in Form 45. Some suggestions are given in the notes to Form 45 in the Schedule to the Rules;

and a specimen schedule of special stipulations is to be found in Form 45A*.

(c) Incorporated documents

Rule 139, as substituted by the Land Registration (Charges) Rules 1990, requires a chargee to deliver with a charge for registration, a copy of any 'incorporated document'. 'Incorporated document' is defined as any separate document which contains provisions intended by the parties to a charge on registered land to form part of the terms and conditions of the charge, which separate document is referred to in the charge, or in another incorporated document. The obligation is fulfilled:

(1) by lodging the incorporated document with the charge; or
(2) if the incorporated document is in a standard form, eg, a mortgage condition booklet, by obtaining the Registrar's prior approval to the form and referring to it in the charge in a manner approved by the Registrar (Form 114 is to be used to apply for such approval); or
(3) if the incorporated document is of a type approved by the Registrar, ie, offer of mortgage advance, by obtaining prior approval and providing an undertaking to produce a copy of any particular document of that type if so directed (Form 114 incorporates an application for approval and form of undertaking); or
(4) in the case of a particular incorporated document, if the Registrar accepts an undertaking by the chargee to deliver a copy to the Registrar when he so directs. Examples of such documents would be debenture trust deeds and mortgage administration agreements. The Registrar will expect specific documents, such as facility letters or credit agreements, to be produced with the charge. Application for approval and the form of undertaking are incorporated in Form 115.

Normally, applications in Form 114 or Form 115 must be submitted to:

      Legal Practice Division
      HM Land Registry
      32 Lincoln's Inn Fields
      LONDON WC2A 3PH

but in the case of Form 115 relating to a charge which will be dealt with in one district land registry only, it may be sent direct to that district.

Incorporated documents will not be approved by the Registrar under r 139:

(i) where the date of the charge appears other than in the charge;
(ii) if the charging clause is not in the charge;
(iii) when an application for an obligation note (see (k) below) or for a restriction (see p 171) is contained in an unincorporated document and not in the charge.

Also, if an incorporated document is to contain information relevant to the calculation of land registration fees, the undertaking must provide for all such information to be disclosed on applications to register or note charges to which the undertaking relates.

Practice Leaflet No 20 (see p 16) explains the procedure and contains copies of the forms.

(d) Implied covenants

Where a registered charge is created on any land, unless there is an entry on the register to the contrary, s 28 implies:

(a) the usual covenants to pay the principal sum and interest; and
(b) where the charge is created out of leasehold land, covenants to pay the rent and perform the covenants and conditions in the lease, and for indemnity.

Registration of a charge containing a stipulation negativing or modifying the implied covenants is sufficient contrary entry on the register. The notes to Form 45, referred to above, contain precedents of such negativing stipulations.

(e) Completion by registration (s 26)

The charge must be completed by registration in accordance with s 26. For this purpose there should be lodged at the appropriate district land registry:

(1) the charge and a certified copy;
(2) the land certificate of the borrower's title if there is not already a registered charge;
(3) any incorporated document(s) unless this requirement has been dispensed with (see (c) above);
(4) any certificate or consent necessary to comply with any restriction on the register of the borrower's title;
(5) the appropriate application form (see below); and

(6) the fee payable (see below).

In addition, special evidence may be required in relation to particular kinds of chargors and chargees (eg, charities, as to which see Chapter XII).

The need to deliver the application for the registration of the charge to the appropriate district land registry within the priority period of the protecting official search (see Chapter V) must be kept in mind; and in connection with charges of leaseholds, the provisions of r 91, referred to on p 96, may be helpful.

If the charge is to secure further advances (see below), the register entries will show this; and if the lender is under an obligation to make further advances and application is made (see p 117) this will also be shown. The land certificate will be kept in the Registry in accordance with s 65, and a charge certificate will be issued to the lender.

If a charge accompanies an application for first registration, its existence will be disclosed on the first registration application form (see Chapter III); and no separate application for its registration will be necessary. Otherwise an application Form A4 (for the registration of a charge of all the land in a title) or A5 (for the registration of a charge of part of the land in a title) will be needed. If the application to register the charge is being made at the same time as another application affecting the title (eg, to register a transfer), one Form A4 or A5 will cover both dealings. The completion of forms of application for first registration is dealt with in Chapter III, and general points on completing forms A4 and A5 are considered in Chapter VI. Particular points relating to charges by and to trading companies are discussed below.

(f) Registration fees

Subject to Abatement 1 in Schedule 4 to the Fees Order, a fee under Scale A in Schedule 1 is payable on an application to register a charge.

Article 5 of the Fees Order contains special provisions as to the amount on which the Scale A fee is to be payable in respect of particular kinds of charges:

(1) charges to secure further advances;
(2) charges secured on registered land and on other property;
(3) charges by way of additional or substituted security or by way of guarantee;
(4) charges serving a contingent liability; and

(5) two or more changes contained in the same instrument to secure the same debt.

Special provisions are also contained in article 6 for calculating the fee payable on a charge relating to land comprised in 20 or more registered titles.

(g) Charges by companies incorporated under the Companies Acts

An application for registration of a charge by a company incorporated under the Companies Acts should be supported by a certificate by the secretary, the solicitor or a director of the chargor company that the charge does not contravene the provisions of the memorandum and articles of association of that company and, if such be the case, that the company is not an insurance company authorised to carry on long term business. This certificate can be given by completing the appropriate panel of the application form (see p 90 as to overseas companies). Registration of the charge at the Companies Registry should precede its delivery to the appropriate district land registry for registration. If a charge so delivered should have been registered at the Companies Registry but there is no evidence that it has been so registered, a note will be made on the register that it is subject to s 395 of the Companies Act 1985. It is important to bear in mind that registration of a charge of registered land at the Companies Registry is not sufficient protection. It must also be 'registered or protected by caution or otherwise' under the Act (see s 60 and p 125). A legal charge or mortgage of registered land in a debenture trust deed can be registered as a registered charge. On request, if the original trust deed and two certified copies are lodged, one copy will be filed, and the other will be sewn up in the charge certificate, and the original deed, endorsed with a registration stamp, will be returned together with the charge certificate. Charge certificates in special forms are sometimes created by arrangement between solicitors and the Registry to meet the needs of large commercial transactions.

(h) Charges to companies incorporated under the Companies Acts

If a company incorporated under the Companies Acts is to be registered as the proprietor of a charge, evidence of its incorporation, objects and powers must be provided. That evidence may take the form of a copy of its memorandum and articles of association certified as a true copy by its secretary or solicitor (see p 90 as

to overseas companies). More usually, all the evidence is provided in the form of confirmation by the solicitors to the company that:
  (a) the company is a company trading for profit and has been incorporated in England or Scotland under the Companies Acts;
  (b) the memorandum and articles of association contain provisions entitling the company to hold and sell, mortgage, lease and otherwise deal with land and to lend money on mortgage;
  (c) the company's registered number is... and the solicitors thereby apply for the entry thereof on the register.

When Form A4 or Form A5 is being used, this confirmation may be given by completing and signing the relevant parts of the form. It is important to remember to complete the chargee company's name and to strike out any inapplicable parts of the printed text. It is also important to note that the confirmation must be given by the chargee company's solicitors. Thus, when both the chargor and the chargee are companies, the application form may well have to be signed by different solicitors.

(i) Priorities

Except on first registration (see r 160) and subject to any entry to the contrary on the register (s 29), registered charges of registered land rank according to the order in which they are entered on the register. There may, of course, be an express entry to the contrary (eg, notice of a deed of variation); and where one of the charges contains a provision varying the usual rule as to priorities, registration of the charge is deemed to be sufficient entry of that provision on the register. As to charges to secure further advances, see below.

(j) Further advances

When a registered charge secures further advances, the Registry must, before making any entry on the register that would prejudice the priority of any such further advance, give the proprietor of the charge notice of the intended entry. The proprietor of the charge will not, in respect of any further advance, be affected by the entry unless the further advance is made after the date when the notice should have been received in due course of post (s 30(1)). The notice will be sent by recorded delivery post to the proprietor's registered address; and accordingly it is most important that proprietors should notify the Registry promptly of any change of address.

(k) Obligations to make further advances

When the proprietor of a registered charge is under an obligation, noted on the register, to make a further advance, a subsequent registered charge takes effect subject to any further advance made in pursuance of the obligation (s 30(3)).

If a chargee wishes such an obligation to be noted he must lodge an application in Form 113 or incorporate the operative part of Form 113 in the charge or in a deed of variation (r 139A as added by the Land Registration (Charges) Rules 1990). The operative part of Form 113 reads 'the lender is under an obligation to make further advances' and application is made to the Registrar for a note to be entered on the register to that effect.

No fee will normally be payable but if, unusually, the application is lodged on its own a fee of £35 for the first title and £20 for each subsequent title affected will be payable under Part I(1) of Schedule 3 to the Fees Order.

(l) Powers of the proprietor of the land

Subject to any express contrary intention, the proprietor of the land whilst in possession has the powers of leasing and accepting surrenders of leases given by ss 99 and 100 of the Law of Property Act 1925 as extended by the charge or any instrument varying it. All other dispositions by the proprietor of the land made without the concurrence of the proprietor of the charge take effect subject to the charge. The proprietor of the land can transfer his equity of redemption without the consent of the registered chargee provided that there is no contrary entry (eg, a restriction) on the register or in any registered charge.

(m) Powers of the proprietor of the charge

Subject to any entry on the register to the contrary, the proprietor of a registered charge has all the powers conferred by law on the owner of a legal mortgage. A contrary provision in the charge itself or in another registered charge having priority to it will constitute an entry on the register to the contrary for this purpose.

A transfer in the exercise of the chargee's power of sale should be in Form 31A or 31B which should be lodged for registration in the ordinary way together with the charge certificate and a fee under Scale A.

Subject to any entry to the contrary on the register and to the rights of any persons appearing on the register to be prior incumbrancers, the proprietor of the charge, after entry into possession and after having acquired a title under the Limitation Act 1980, can execute a declaration in Form 52. He is then entitled, subject to the production of evidence in support of the declaration, to be registered as proprietor of the land. A fee under Scale A reduced to one fifth under Abatement 2 is payable.

A foreclosure order is obtained in the same way as if the land were unregistered. An office copy of the order absolute should be lodged together with the charge certificate and a fee under Scale A reduced to one fifth under Abatement 2 so that the proprietor of the charge can be registered as proprietor of the land (subject to prior charges).

(n) Transfer of charge

A transfer of the charge is required to be in Form 54 (r 153). It should be lodged for registration, together with the charge certificate, under cover of a Form A4. The fee is payable under Scale A (transfer for monetary consideration) or Scale A reduced under Abatement 2 (transfer otherwise than for monetary consideration). Guidance on the adaptation of Form 54 for large scale mortgage transactions contained in Practice Leaflet No 20 (see p 16).

(o) Sub-charges

The proprietor of the charge can charge the debt with the payment of money in the same way as the proprietor of the land can charge the land. A charge of the debt so created is known as a sub-charge. A sub-charge is completed by registration, transferred and discharged in the same way as a charge. The charge certificate must be produced with the application to register the sub-charge; and a sub-charge certificate will be issued on completion of the registration. As s 65 does not apply to charge certificates the charge certificate will be issued with the sub-charge certificate. Subject to any entry in the register to the contrary, a sub-charge, as against the sub-chargor, implies the same covenants, and as against the sub-chargor and all persons over whose interests the charge confers power, confers the same powers and has the same effect as a charge.

Subject to any entry in the register to the contrary, registered sub-charges of the same charge, as between themselves, rank according to the order in which they are entered on the register. The fee for the registration of a sub-charge is payable under Scale A unless Abatement 1 applies and the fee for the transfer of a sub-charge is payable under Scale A (transfer for monetary consideration) or Scale A reduced by Abatement 2 (transfer otherwise than for monetary consideration).

(p) Alteration of charges

If it is desired to alter the terms of a registered charge (eg, by postponing it to a new charge or by varying the rate of interest payable) Form 51 or a deed of variation in customary conveyancing form (provided such deed identifies the property by reference to its title number) may be used (s 31 and r 150). The Form 51 or the deed of variation must be executed by the registered proprietors of the land and of the charge and of every charge of equal or inferior priority prejudicially affected by the alteration. A reduction in the interest rate or capital debt or an alteration to set out the full names of the chargors or chargees would not be considered prejudicial. An increase in the interest rate or capital sum or an extension of the charge to further advances would be prejudicial. If another chargee is not prepared to execute the Form 51 or deed of variation a letter confirming acceptance will normally be accepted. The application to register the alteration must be accompanied by the charge certificates relating to all charges affected by the alteration and the deed of variation (and a certified copy) or Form 51 (no copy). A fee of £35 for the first title and £20 for each subsequent title affected on any one application) is payable unless, in relation to each title affected, the application accompanies an application affecting that title upon which a scale fee not under art 6 is payable (Part I(1) of Schedule 3 to the Fees Order).

(q) Discharges

The discharge of a registered charge as to the whole or part of the land should be in Form 53 but the registrar may accept and act upon any proof of satisfaction which he may deem sufficient (r 151 as substituted by the Land Registration (Charges) Rules 1990). In the case of a discharge of part Form 53 must be adapted to show the extent discharged using a plan where necessary.

In the case of an individual Form 53 must be signed by the proprietor of the charge. In the case of a company registered under the Companies Act 1985 the Form 53 must be either sealed under s 74(1) of the Law of Property Act 1925 or signed as a deed, or signed and delivered, by two directors or a director and secretary under s 36A of the Companies Act 1985 or executed in some other manner authorised by the articles of association. In the case of other corporate bodies Form 53 must be either sealed under s 74(1) of the Law of Property Act 1925 or signed or executed in such a way as the Registrar is satisfied is authorised.

Prior approval of the proposed method of execution of a significant number of discharges of registered charges may be obtained by approaching the Legal Practice Division of the Registry at the address given at (c) above.

The charge certificate must always accompany an application to register a discharge, whether as to all or part of the land or as to all or part of the money. No fee is payable for the registration of a discharge of a registered charge.

If the discharged charge affects also an unregistered interest, eg, a policy of insurance, or unregistered land, and the original deed will be required after registration of the discharge, a special request for its return should be made. Where the only remaining charge of the land in a title is discharged and the solicitors for the proprietor of the land require the land certificate to be issued to them, they should complete the appropriate panel of the application Form A4.

Where it is desired to combine in one document a transfer of land with a discharge of a registered charge, Form 55 (transfer and discharge of the whole) or Form 55B (transfer and discharge of part) should be used.

If a charge (whether legal or equitable) is merely noted on the register, the devolution of its title will not appear on the register. Consequently, when it has been discharged and it is desired to have the notice cancelled, the title to the charge must be shown according to the practice of unregistered conveyancing. The discharge should be in 'unregistered' form, not in Form 53. The land certificate, if not retained in the Registry pursuant to s 65, should be produced. No fee is payable.

2 Charges subsisting at the time of first registration

Where a charge or mortgage subsists at the time of first registration, it must be disclosed in the application for first registration. If it is a legal charge or mortgage and the lender wishes (as he usually will) it can be registered in the same way as a charge of registered land created under s 25 (see r 160). Otherwise, notice of it will be entered on the register. Commonly the purchase inducing the first registration has been made with money secured by a charge created under r 72 with a view to its completion by registration. In such a case, where the borrower and the lender are separately represented, it is usual for the borrower's solicitor to prepare and sign the first registration application form, which is handed over to the lender's solicitor at completion together with the deeds. The lender's solicitor then lodges the application at the appropriate district land registry, and in due course receives the charge certificate and the deeds from that registry. In this situation it is important to make sure that the relevant address panels on the application form are correctly completed.

Where there are two or more charges created before first registration of the land their relative priorities are unaffected by the registration of some or one of them only, or by the order in which such as are registered are entered on the register (r 160).

3 Public sector housing: discount charge

(a) The discount charge

Sales under the right to buy provisions of the Housing Act 1985 (and earlier Acts) and voluntary sales under the 1985 Act and under the Housing Associations Act 1985 may allow or have allowed a discount. If so, the transfer, charge or lease must contain a covenant to repay the discount in the event of a further disposal within the statutory period. The statutory period, as provided by s 2 of the Housing and Planning Act 1986, is normally three years. 'Disposal' includes a conveyance of the freehold or the assignment of the lease or the grant of a lease for more than twenty-one years. It also includes the grant of an option to transfer or grant a lease of the property but not a mortgage. Certain disposals, including some inter-family transfers, vestings under a will or on intestacy, disposals on compulsory purchase and disposals of part of the garden or other land occupied with the dwellinghouse, are exempt from the repayment requirement.

The liability under the discount covenant is a charge on the property which takes effect as a charge by way of legal mortgage. This charge is protected by the entry of notice pursuant to s 59(2) in the following form:

'A charge having the priority specified in [eg, s 156 of the Housing Act 1985] to secure the liability under the covenant to repay discount contained in the [[conveyance][transfer][assignment] referred to in the Property Register][lease under which the land is held].'

The form of entry used in the case of a shared ownership lease is:

'A charge having the priority specified in [eg, s 156 of the Housing Act 1985] to secure the liability under the covenant to repay discount and to pay for outstanding shares contained in the lease under which the land is held.'

(b) Priority

The discount charge has priority immediately after any legal charge in favour of the vendor to secure an outstanding part of the purchase price or after any legal charge in favour of the Housing Corporation, building societies, friendly societies, the major banks, the Post Office and certain insurance and loan companies to secure an advance for the purposes of the purchase or a further advance.

As will be seen, the standard forms of entry means that the question of priority is disregarded when the entry is made. In practice the entry of the notice of the discount charge is made in the charges register before the entry of any legal charge.

The discount charge is overreached on a sale by one of the corporations or companies specified above pursuant to the power of sale in a charge having priority to the discount charge (s 24 of and para 1 of Sched 5 to the Housing and Planning Act 1986).

(c) Postponement

A discount charge may be postponed to an advance or further advance made by one of the corporations or companies referred to at *(b)* above by means of a written notice signed on behalf of the vendor or lessor to whom the covenant to repay the discount was given ('the discount chargee'). Any such postponement will be noted on the register on production of the signed notice of postponement.

(d) Cancellation of a notice of a discount charge

Where a disposal takes place within the three year period and the discount is repaid or where no disposal takes place within the three year period, application should be made to cancel the notice of a discount charge. On an application for cancellation made within the three year period, evidence will be required of the discount chargee's concurrence. A suggested form is:

HM LAND REGISTRY
LAND REGISTRATION ACTS 1925 to 1988

COUNTY AND DISTRICT
OR LONDON BOROUGH:
TITLE NUMBER:
PROPERTY:
DATE:

.... [name of discount chargee] hereby applies to the Chief Land Registrar to cancel the entry of the statutory charge under the covenant to repay discount shown as entry no......... in the Charges Register of the above title.

The form should be executed as a deed by the discount chargee except in the case of a local authority, where it may be signed by the chief executive or some other authorised official in the presence of an attesting witness.

On an application after the three year period has expired the notice will be cancelled:
(1) if there is evidence of a disposal within the three year period which may have led to discount becoming repayable, only with the concurrence of the discount chargee as above; or
(2) in certain other cases without the discount chargee's concurrence but only after service of notice by the Registry on the discount chargee.

No fee is payable for cancellation of the notice of a discount charge.

4 Equitable charges

Section 106 of the Act as substituted by s 26(1) of the Administration of Justice Act 1977 provides as follows:

'(1) The proprietor of any registered land may, subject to any

entry to the contrary on the register, mortgage, by deed or otherwise, the land or any part of it in any manner which would have been permissible if the land had not been registered and, subject to this section, with the like effect.
(2) Unless and until the mortgage becomes a registered charge,
   (a) it shall take effect only in equity, and
   (b) it shall be capable of being overridden as a minor interest (see p 54) unless it is protected as provided by sub-section (3) below.
(3) A mortgage which is not a registered charge may be protected on the register by—
   (a) a notice under section 49 of this Act,
   (b) any such other notice as may be prescribed, or
   (c) a caution under section 54 of this Act.
(4) A mortgage which is not a registered charge shall devolve and may be transferred, discharged, surrendered or otherwise dealt with by the same instruments and in the same manner as if the land had not been registered.'

Notices and cautions are discussed in Chapter XIV. In general the charge may not be protected by notice if it can be overridden by the proprietor under a trust for sale, a settlement or a statute, and can be protected by a restriction (see s 49(2)).

When a fixed equitable charge protected by notice has been paid off and cancellation of the notice is desired, any devolution of the title to the charge, and its discharge, must be proved according to unregistered conveyancing practice. A Form 53 is not appropriate for the discharge. No fee is payable. Notice of a floating charge in favour of a limited company will usually be cancelled on the production of an office copy of the memorandum of satisfaction filed at the Companies Registry. No fee is payable. The land certificate (if outstanding) of the title against which the notice is registered should be produced. The warning off and withdrawal of cautions under s 54 is discussed on pp 169–170.

Debentures

A legal charge of registered land created by a debenture trust deed can be registered as a registered charge.

If a limited company or other corporation has created debentures or debenture stock constituting a fixed equitable or floating charge on its assets, the existence of the charge must be disclosed on the application form whenever the company or corporation makes an application for the first registration of its title to land. A certified copy of the debentures, or of one of them if all are certified to be in the same terms, and of any trust deed securing them, must be lodged with the application. Notice of the charge will be entered on the register, and the copies of the debenture(s) and trust deed (if any) will be filed.

Where a company that has created debentures acquires registered land or a registered charge, or where a company that is already the registered proprietor of land or a charge creates debentures, no entry will be made in the register to protect any charge created by the debentures (whether registered in the Companies Registry or not) in the absence of a specific application for an entry to be made (s 60).

Such specific application, as regards any equitable charge created by the debentures, would commonly be for the entry of notice of the charge if the certificate could be produced or was already retained under s 65. If the certificate could not be produced and was not so retained, an application for a caution against dealings might nevertheless be made.

A purchaser taking a transfer of registered land from a limited company registered with absolute or good leasehold title is never concerned to search that company's file at the Companies Registration Office for debentures or debenture stock. If any had been created before the company became the first registered proprietor of the land, notice should appear on the register; and if the company had created debentures or debenture stock and then acquired land already registered, or had become proprietor of land already registered and then created debentures or debenture stock, a purchaser of the registered land would not be concerned with any charge created by the debentures unless it was registered or protected on the register.

Where a company is the proprietor of registered land and notice of a fixed equitable charge by the company appears on the register, any application to register a lease by the company with absolute leasehold title must be accompanied by the consent of the chargee.

Where notice of a floating charge appears on the register, and a transfer on sale of the land by the chargor company is being registered, a certificate by the solicitor or secretary of the chargor company that none of the events on the happening of which the charge would become fixed has occurred is usually accepted by the Registry as sufficient evidence for the cancellation of the notice. Alternatively a certificate to like effect from the chargee or his solicitor would usually be accepted. Where a lease by the chargor company is being registered with absolute leasehold title the consent of the chargee will be required.

The cancellation of notice of equitable charges is discussed on p 124, and the warning off and withdrawal of cautions against dealings is discussed on pp 169–170.

5 Notices of [intended] deposit

Section 66 provides that the proprietor of any registered land or charge may (subject to overriding interests, to any entry to the contrary on the register, and to any estates, interests, charges or rights registered or protected on the register) create by deposit of the land or charge certificate a lien on the land or charge which (subject as above) is equivalent to a lien created in the case of unregistered land by the deposit of title deeds or mortgage deed by an owner or mortgagee beneficially entitled.

Any person with whom a land certificate or charge certificate has been deposited as security for money may give notice of such deposit to the appropriate district land registry. Notice of the deposit will be entered in the register, without fee, and will operate as a caution against dealings (see Chapter XIV). The notice should be given in Form 85A, which may be signed by the depositee's solicitor on his behalf. The land or charge certificate **need not be** lodged.

Rule 240 provides that a person applying for registration as proprietor of land or of a charge may, whether the land or charge is already registered or not, create a lien on the land or charge equivalent to that created by a deposit of a certificate by giving notice to the appropriate district land registry that he intends to deposit the land or charge certificate, when issued, with another person as security for money. Notice of the intended deposit will be entered in the register, without fee, and will operate as a caution against dealings (see Chapter XIV). If the notice relates to a first registration, it should be in Form 85B; if it relates to a dealing with registered land, it should be in Form 85C. The notice must be signed by the depositor himself if he is an individual, and by all of several individual depositors. In the case of a corporation, signature by a director or a responsible officer of the corporation (but not by its solicitor) is accepted in place of sealing.

A notice of [intended] deposit gives the depositee protection in three ways:

(1) It is notice that the certificate is in the hands of someone as security for money.
(2) It operates as a caution against dealings. The depositee will be sent a notice of the receipt at the Registry of any application to register a dealing with the land or charge made without his consent and will have an opportunity to object to it.
(3) No transaction for which the production of the certificate is required (see pp 71–72) can take place unless the depositee releases the certificate for the purpose.

Anyone wishing to consider the degree of protection afforded by a notice of deposit in more detail should read *Re White Rose Cottage* [1965] Ch 940.

A notice of [intended] deposit cannot be entered while another such notice is on the register, nor as to part only of the land or charge to which the certificate relates.

A notice of [intended] deposit can be registered in favour of an unincorporated firm.

Forms 85A, 85B and 85C are completed in duplicate, and the duplicate is returned to the applicant by the Registry as an acknowledgement of the receipt of the original. Printed on the back of each duplicate is a Form 86, which is a form of application for the withdrawal of the notice. It is usual to use this when the notice is withdrawn. Form 86 is, however, also available as a separate form.

Form 86 may not be signed by a depositee's solicitor on his behalf. An individual depositee should sign personally (or by his attorney), and all of several individual depositees must sign. In the case of a bank, the signature of the manager or a branch manager suffices; and in the case of a joint stock bank a signature 'pro' manager or other responsible officer of head office or branch is acceptable. A responsible officer of a limited company or other corporation, or of a building, friendly or industrial and provident society may sign. Where the depositee is an unincorporated firm, a signature in the firm's name, or the manager's signature, will be accepted. A manager or other officer of a depositee should indicate the capacity in which he signs. The personal representatives of a deceased sole depositee may sign, but the grant of probate or letters of administration or an official or certified copy or examined abstract thereof must be produced.

The land or charge certificate must accompany the application to withdraw the notice. No fee is payable.

A depositee's consent to a dealing may be by way of a letter or it may be endorsed by way of reply on a notice sent by the Registry to the depositee (see (2) on p 127). A depositee's solicitor may consent on his behalf; otherwise the same conditions apply to the signature of consents as apply to the signature of withdrawals.

When there is to be a transfer of part of the land in a title, and when a lease or rentcharge is to be granted out of registered land, a depositee of the land certificate of the parent title usually provides a letter of consent, which can then be sent to the Registry together with the application to register the transfer or grant. When necessary, the consent must refer to a plan enabling the land to which it relates to be identified on the filed plan of the parent title. A transfer of whole should of course be accompanied by a withdrawal of the notice of [intended] deposit.

A notice of [intended] deposit can be 'warned off' in the same way as a caution against dealings (see Chapter XIV).

A rentcharge certificate may be deposited on the same conditions, and with the same effect, as a land certificate.

As to an official search of the register on the application of a prospective depositee of a land or charge certificate, see p 66.

Chapter X

Rentcharges

1 The Rentcharges Act 1977

The preamble of the Rentcharges Act 1977 describes it as 'An Act to prohibit the creation, and provide for the extinguishment, apportionment and redemption, of certain rentcharges.' Its main provisions, including ss 1, 2 and 3 referred to below, came into operation on 22 August 1977. The remainder came into operation on 1 February 1978.

Section 1 defines a rentcharge for the purposes of the Act as 'any annual or other periodic sum charged on or issuing out of land except (*a*) rent reserved by a lease or tenancy, or (*b*) any sum payable by way of interest'. 'Land' has the same meaning as in s 205(1) of the Law of Property Act 1925.

Section 2 prohibits the creation of any rentcharge, whether at law or in equity, after the coming into force of the section, excepting the classes specified in s 2(3). The specified classes comprise any rentcharge:

(*a*) which has the effect of making the land on which the rent is charged settled land by virtue of s 1(1)(v) of the Settled Land Act 1925;

(*b*) which would have that effect but for the fact that the land on which the rent is charged is already settled land or is held on trust for sale;

(*c*) which is an estate rentcharge;

(*d*) under any Act providing for the creation of rentcharges in connection with the execution of works on land (whether by way of improvements, repairs or otherwise) or the commutation of any obligation to do any such work; or

(*e*) by, or in accordance with the requirements of, any order of a court.

Subsections (4) and (5) of s 2 define an estate rentcharge as follows:

'(4) For the purpose of this section 'estate rentcharge' means (subject to subsection (5) below) a rentcharge created for the purpose—
- (a) of making covenants to be performed by the owner of the land affected by the rentcharge enforceable by the rent owner against the owner for the time being of the land; or
- (b) of meeting, or contributing towards, the cost of the performance by the rent owner of covenants for the provision of services, the carrying out of maintenance or repairs, the effecting of insurance or the making of any payment by him for the benefit of the land affected by the rentcharge or for the benefit of that and other land.
(5) A rentcharge of more than a nominal amount shall not be treated as an estate rentcharge for the purpose of this section unless it represents a payment for the performance by the rent owner of any such covenant as is mentioned in subsection 4(b) above which is reasonable in relation to that covenant.'

Under the transitional provisions contained in s 17 rentcharges created pursuant to agreements entered into before 22 July 1977 are excluded from the prohibition of s 2.

Section 3 of the Act of 1977, referred to in more detail on p 136, provides (subject to exceptions) for the extinguishment of rentcharges after a period of sixty years. Sections 4 to 10 deal with apportionment and redemption (see pp 135). The remaining sections deal with miscellaneous and general matters.

2 First registration of rentcharges

(a) Rentcharges capable of being registered

A rentcharge is capable of substantive registration ('first registration') if it is a legal rentcharge, ie, a rentcharge in possession issuing out of or charged on a legal freehold or leasehold estate in land and being either perpetual or for a term of years absolute (the length of the term is immaterial for this purpose), and either:
- (1) it is based on a deed dated before 22 August 1977; or
- (2) it is based on a deed dated on or after 22 August 1977

and its creation is not prohibited by s 2 of the Rentcharges Act 1977.

The fact that a rentcharge is subject to extinguishment in accordance with the provisions of the 1977 Act does not of itself prevent it from being 'perpetual' or for a term of years 'absolute' for the purposes of registration.

Rentcharges that subsist as equitable interests only, eg, because of the mode of their creation or because they are informally apportioned parts of a legal or equitable rentcharge, are incapable of substantive registration. They can be protected on the register by means of a notice: see under the heading 'Notice of rentcharge' on p 134.

(b) Rentcharges created out of unregistered land

A rentcharge created out of unregistered land is never compulsorily registrable but if otherwise registrable (see (*a*) above) it may be volutarily registered at any time.

Where a conveyance of unregistered land lodged for registration also creates a rentcharge, the Registry will take no steps to register the rentcharge substantively unless the application for registration of the land is accompanied by the appropriate form of application for first registration of the rentcharge.

The practice relating to applications for first registration is discussed in Chapter III. The forms of application for first registration of a rentcharge are listed in Appendix V. They are not available for sale but reasonable quantities can be obtained free of charge from the headquarters office of the Registry (see p 5).

The fee for first registration of title to a rentcharge is £35 under Part I(5) of Schedule 3 to the Fees Order.

It is strongly recommended that an official search of the public index map is obtained (see Chapter II) when the title to the rentcharge is being investigated.

(c) Rentcharges created out of registered land

The creation of a legal rentcharge out of registered land is a disposition of that land and accordingly must be completed by registration it if is to be fully effective. Completion by registration involves the substantive registration of the rentcharge and the entry of notice of it on the register of the title to the land out of which it issues. The entry of notice takes place as a matter of course on the substantive registration of the rentcharge.

So far only as is not prohibited by the Rentcharges Act 1977, and subject to any entry to the contrary in the register, a legal rentcharge may be created as a disposition of registered land in one of two ways. It may be the subject of a deed of grant by the proprietor of the land, in which event an application for the first registration of the title to the rentcharge must be made as described in Chapter III. The rentcharge may, however, be granted (out of the land transferred) by the transferee to the transferor in and as part of the consideration for a transfer of registered land. In this event, if an application for the registration of the transfer is made in the usual way on Form A4 (transfer of whole) or Form A5 (transfer of part) no separate application for the substantive registration of the title to the rentcharge is necessary, but the application should be accompanied by two certified copies of the transfer and, in addition to the Scale A fee, the fixed fee of £35 under Part I(5) of Schedule 3 to the Fees Order for registration of the rentcharge.

The land certificate of the grantor's title if outstanding must be produced for the substantive registration of any rentcharge created out of registered land. If the rentcharge is granted during the subsistence of a registered charge of the land in the grantor's title and more than a qualified title to the rentcharge is desired, the proprietor of the charge should join in the grant or in some other way formally consent to the postponement of his charge in favour of the rentcharge and should produce the charge certificate to meet the application for registration. Whether the certificate to be produced is a land certificate or a charge certificate, it is usual to place it on deposit to meet the application (see p 72). But when a rentcharge is granted (out of the land transferred) to a transferor of part of the land in a registered title by the transferee, in the transfer, and as part of the consideration for the transfer, the question of producing the grantor's land certificate or charge certificate does not arise because at that stage the certificate has not come into existence.

If a terminal rentcharge is granted out of leasehold land registered with good leasehold title, and more than a qualified title to the rentcharge is desired, conveyancing evidence must be produced to show that the lease (and any superior lease) was validly granted.

Every deed creating a rentcharge out of registered land must contain a reference to the title number of that land and particulars, by plan if necessary, to enable the land charged to be identified on the filed plan of the grantor's title.

The documents to accompany an application for the substantive registration of the title to a rentcharge created out of registered land are (*a*) the land or charge certificate of the grantor's title (see above); (*b*) the deed of grant or the transfer, as the case may be; (*c*) two certified copies of (*b*); (*d*) such consents as are necessary in view of the entries in the register of the grantor's title (eg, consents of a chargee, a depositee of a land certificate, or a person named in a restriction); and (*e*) where the grantor's title is good leasehold, conveyancing evidence (if available) of the superior title (see above).

The fee payable for the substantive registration of the title to a rentcharge is £35 under Part I(5) of Schedule 3 to the Fees Order.

3 The rentcharge certificate

The proprietor of a registered rentcharge receives a rentcharge certificate which contains a copy of the register of the title to the rentcharge and a plan of the land out of which the rentcharge issues. A rentcharge certificate usually also contains the original or a duplicate of the deed creating the rentcharge and, when appropriate, any deed of apportionment and abstracts of deeds creating prior rentcharges.

For reasons of brevity, other than in this Chapter, references throughout this book are to land certificates only. Where the registered interest is a rentcharge, land certificate must be read as rentcharge certificate. So, for example, as discussed on p 114, where a charge of a rentcharge has been registered the rentcharge certificate is kept in the registry and the proprietor of the charge receives a charge certificate.

4 Rentcharges incapable of substantive registration

Rentcharges subsisting as equitable interests only are incapable of substantive registration but must be appropriately protected on the register of the title to the land out of which they issue if that land is registered.

When an equitable rentcharge is created out of registered land, wherever the land is situated, notice of the rentcharge should be entered on the register of the title to the land out of which it issues. This last statement does not apply to minor interests under a settlement, as to which see s 86(2); and see p 174 for alternative ways in which a rentcharge for life, as a general equitable charge, may be protected.

If an equitable rentcharge were created (out of the land transferred) by the transferee in a transfer of registered land as the consideration or part of the consideration for the transfer, notice of it would be entered in the register of the transferee's title as a matter of course when the transfer was registered. In any other case of an equitable rentcharge created out of registered land, a separate application should be made to enter notice of the rentcharge on the register of the title out of which it issues or to enter a caution against dealings if the cooperation of the owner of the land cannot be obtained. (See paragraph 5 below and Chapter XII as to settled land and Chapter XIV as to applications for notices and cautions.)

5 Notice of rentcharge

When land is first registered, all necessary notices of subsisting rentcharges, whether legal or equitable, issuing out of the land and appearing on the title are entered in the charges register of the title to the land as a matter of course. Notices of apportionments and exonerations are also entered as appropriate.

On the substantive registration of a legal rentcharge created out of registered land, notice of the rentcharge is entered as a matter of course in the register of the title to the land out of which the rentcharge issues (see under 'First registration of rentcharges', above).

On the creation out of registered land of a rentcharge incapable of substantive registration, a specific application for the entry of notice of the rentcharge on the register of the title to the land out of which the rentcharge issues may be necessary (see under 'Rentcharges incapable of substantive registration', above).

6 Dealings with registered rentcharges

A registered rentcharge can be transferred, leased, charged, etc, in the same way and subject to the same rules as registered corporeal land, so far as the nature of a rentcharge permits; and a rentcharge certificate can be deposited as security for money in the same way and subject to the same rules as a land certificate. The advice appearing elsewhere in this guide, whilst primarily relating to registered corporeal land, applies generally to registered rentcharges.

The existence of Form 19R1 (transfer of rentcharge) should be borne in mind see Appendix V.

7 Apportionment and redemption of rentcharges

Form 20R2 (transfer of part of the land in a registered title which informally apportions an existing rentcharge) and Form 20R3 (transfer of part of the land in a registered title subject to an existing informal apportionment of a rentcharge) were designed to meet the needs of practitioners in areas where rentcharges are common.

A registered title (to corporeal land or to a rentcharge) may be affected by a ministerial order apportioning a rentcharge or a ministerial certificate that a rentcharge has been redeemed. If it is not known whether the title to the land or rentcharge is registered, an inquiry on this point, with a request for the title number if the land or rentcharge is registered, may be made on Form 96 addressed to the appropriate district land registry. A fee under Part II(9) of Schedule 3 to the Fees Order is payable. An application should then be made to the appropriate district land registry for effect to be given on the registered title to the order or the certificate; but where an apportionment is made conditional on the redemption of the rent the application should not be made until after the redemption has taken place.

The application can conveniently be made on Form A4. It should be supported by:

(1) where there is no registered charge or notice of [intended] deposit of certificate on the register of the title against which the application is made, the certificate (land certificate or rentcharge certificate) of that title;
(2) an official copy of the order and/or an official copy of the certificate of redemption as appropriate; and
(3) the land registration fee.

The fee for registering the order or the certificate of redemption is £35 for the first title and £20 for each subsequent title affected under Part I(1) of Schedule 3 to the Fees Order. No fee is payable if the application is accompanied by an application upon which a scale fee (not under art 6) is payable, so that no fee for the registration of the order or the certificate will be payable where the order or certificate has been obtained with a sale of the registered land or rentcharge in view and the application for the registration of the order or certificate is made together with the application for the registration of the transfer on sale of the land or rentcharge.

8 Extinguishment of rentcharges

Ministerial certificates of redemption of rentcharges have already been considered under the heading 'Apportionment and redemption of rentcharges', above.

Section 3(1) of the Rentcharges Act 1977 provides that, subject to exceptions, every rentcharge shall (if it has not then ceased to have effect) be extinguished at the expiry of the period of sixty years beginning:

(a) with the passing of the Act (22 July 1977), or
(b) with the date on which the rentcharge first became payable, whichever is later.

The section will not extinguish any rentcharge payable wholly or partly in lieu of tithes or of a kind referred to in s 2(3) of the Act of 1977 (disregarding s 2(5)). Variable rentcharges also are excluded from extinguishment under s 3(1) of the Act of 1977; but where a variable rentcharge ceases to be variable s 3(1) will apply as if the date on which the rentcharge first became payable were the date on which it ceased to be variable.

An application following the extinguishment of a rentcharge, other than by ministerial certificate, should be made, under cover of a Form A4, by letter supported by an appropriate evidence of extinguishment and documents as follows:

(a) Both interests registered with absolute title:

(1) land certificate;
(2) rentcharge certificate;
(3) original deed of grant or duplicate conveyance creating the rentcharge;
(4) a fixed fee of £35 for each title closed under Part I(2) of Schedule 3 to the Fees Order unless the application is accompanied by an application upon which a scale fee is payable, when no fee is payable.

(b) Land only registered:

(1) land certificate;
(2) application in form 92R;
(3) all the title deeds relating to the rentcharge (including the original deed of grant or duplicate conveyance creating it);
(4) a fixed fee of £35 for each title affected under Part I(6) of Schedule 3 to the Fees Order unless the application is

accompanied by an application upon which a scale fee is payable, when no fee is payable.

(c) Rentcharge only registered:
  (1) rentcharge certificate;
  (2) original deed of grant or duplicate conveyance creating the rentcharge;
  (3) a fee calculated as at (*a*)(4) above.

It is assumed that in each case the rentcharge and the whole of the land out of which it is payable are held by the same person(s) in the same capacity without any intervening estate.

Chapter XI

Conversion of Title

1 Conversion of good leasehold to absolute leasehold

Before a good leasehold title can be converted to an absolute leasehold title, it must be established that the lessor had power to grant the lease. Evidence of the freehold title and of any intermediate leasehold title must therefore be available (s 77(1), as substituted by the Land Registration Act 1986).

If the freehold and any superior leasehold interests are registered with an absolute title, the following points arise:

(*a*) where at the date of the grant of the lease, the title to which is to be converted, there existed a charge, mortgage or incumbrance which curtailed the lessor's power of leasing, it must be shown that there was no contravention of the curtailing provisions; and

(*b*) it must be shown that on the grant of the lease, the title to which is to be converted, the terms of any prohibition or restraint on alienation in a superior lease were complied with.

If the freehold and any superior leasehold interests are registered with titles less than absolute, evidence must be available which would enable their conversion to absolute before the good leasehold title which is the subject of the application can be converted. If the reversion is unregistered, an examined abstract of the reversionary title must be produced. The abstract must deal, in particular, with the points at (*a*) and (*b*) above in relation to the lease the title to which is being converted and any superior lease. Full verified particulars of any restrictive covenants and rentcharges affecting the land are required.

Since the effect of registration with an absolute title is to confer an absolute title to any easements granted in the lease, the title of the lessor to grant the easements should be shown. Where the Registry is not satisfied on this point, an entry may be made on the register excluding the easement concerned from the registration.

In all cases confirmation is required that the applicant is in possession of the land and that no adverse claim has been made. If any adverse claim has been made conversion cannot take place until it has been disposed of (s 77(4) as substituted).

2 Conversion of possessory titles

The Registrar may, and on application by the proprietor shall, convert a possessory title, in the case of freehold land to absolute or in the case of leasehold land to good leasehold, if:

(a) he is satisfied as to title; or
(b) the land has been registered with possessory title for at least twelve years and he is satisfied that the proprietor is in possession (s 77(2) as substituted).

If conversion is sought under (a), the application must be supported by such fresh evidence of title as is considered to justify the conversion and by all documents relating to the title as are in the proprietor's possession. In both cases (a) and (b) confirmation is required that the applicant is in possession of the land and that no adverse claim has been made. If any adverse claim has been made conversion cannot take place until it has been disposed of (s 77(4) as substituted).

There are transitional provisions relating to possessory titles registered prior to 1 January 1987. Before that date, instead of the twelve year period specified at (b) above, the relevant periods were ten years for possessory leasehold titles and fifteen years for possessory freehold titles. Where registration was effected before 1 January 1987 the proprietor is entitled to conversion either at the end of a ten or fifteen year period, as the case may be, from the date of registration or at the end of a twelve year period from 1 January 1987, whichever is the shorter (Land Registration Act 1986, s 1(2)).

3 Conversion of qualified titles

The Registrar may, and on application by the proprietor shall, convert a qualified title, in the case of freehold land to absolute and in the case of leasehold land to good leasehold if he is satisfied as to title (s 77(3) as substituted).

4 Inquiries before conversion

Before approving an application for conversion, where he is required to be satisfied as to title, the Registrar may:
- (*a*) serve notice on such persons as he considers necessary;
- (*b*) at the applicant's expense, insert notice of the application in such newspaper(s) as he directs; and
- (*c*) make such other inquiries as he considers necessary (Land Registration Rules 1986, r 5).

5 Application form and fees

All applications for conversion must be made in Form 6 as set out in the Schedule to the Land Registration Rules 1986. The fixed fee for conversion is £35, but no fee is payable where the Registrar initiates the conversion or where the application is accompanied by an application upon which a scale fee is payable (Fees Order, Schedule 3 Part I(3)).

Chapter XII
Trusts and Some Special Cases

1 Settled land

Settled land is registered in the name of the tenant for life, statutory owner or special personal representatives in whom the legal estate would be vested if the land were unregistered. The successive or other interests created by or arising under a settlement (except any legal estate which cannot be overridden under the Settled Land Act 1925 or any other statute) take effect as minor interests and therefore do not appear on the register. The rights of the persons beneficially interested in the land are, however, protected by restrictions entered in the proprietorship register.

Three restrictions are prescribed by the rules:

Restriction where the tenant for life or statutory owners who are not the trustees of the settlement are registered as proprietors (Form 9)

'RESTRICTION: No disposition by the proprietor of the land under which capital money arises is to be registered unless the money is paid to *AB* of etc, and *CD* of etc (the trustees of a settlement of whom there must not be less than two nor more than four unless a trust corporation is the sole trustee) or into court. Except under an order of the registrar no disposition by the proprietor of the land is to be registered unless authorised by the Settled Land Act 1925.'

Restriction where statutory owners who are the trustees of the settlement are registered as proprietors (Form 10)

'RESTRICTION: Except under an order of the registrar, no disposition by the proprietor of the land is to be registered unless authorised by the Settled Land Act 1925 and except where the sole proprietor is a trust corporation, no disposition under which capital money arises is to be registered unless the money is paid to at least two proprietors.'

Restriction where there are no trustees of the settlement and the tenant for life is registered as proprietor (Form 11)

'RESTRICTION: Except under an order of the registrar, no disposition under which capital money arises, or which is not authorised by the Settled Land Act 1925, is to be registered.'

For the purposes of these restrictions dispositions authorised by the Settled Land Act 1925 include dispositions in the exercise of any powers conferred by the settlement in extension of the statutory powers. Except in the instances referred to in s 86(3), the restrictions bind the proprietor in his lifetime but do not restrain or otherwise affect dispositions by his personal representatives. No fee is payable for the entry of these restrictions when, in relation to each registered title affected, their entry arises on the occasion of a registration affecting that title for which a scale fee is payable. On other occasions a fee of £35 for the first title and £20 for each subsequent title affected is payable under Part I(1) of Schedule 3 to the Fees Order. The persons interested under the settlement are at liberty to apply for any additional restriction (eg, relating to transfers of the mansion house) necessitated by the provisions of the settlement. A fee of £35 for the first title and £20 for each subsequent title affected is payable in respect of any such additional restriction unless, in relation to each registered title affected, the application for it is accompanied by an application affecting that title on which a scale fee is payable.

On the first registration of settled land, the application must include a statement in writing of the proper restriction or the information necessary to enable the Registry to frame the proper restriction.

When land already registered becomes settled land, it must be registered in the name of the tenant for life or other person in whom it would be vested if it were unregistered. Forms are prescribed by the Rules:

Form 21   Transfer (in lieu of a vesting instrument under a settlement) to a tenant for life;
Form 24   Transfer of land acquired with capital money under a settlement to a tenant for life of full age;

Form 23 Vesting declaration by a tenant for life who is already the registered proprietor;
Form 22 Transfer where trustees of the settlement are the statutory owners and are to be registered as proprietors;
Form 57 Vesting assent.

Each of these forms embodies an application for the appropriate restriction.

During a minority the personal representatives under a will or intestacy under which a settlement of registered land is created or arises must be registered as proprietors and will have all the powers conferred by the Settled Land Act 1925 on a tenant for life and on the trustees of the settlement. If and when the personal representatives would, if the minor had been of full age, have been obliged to transfer the land to him, they must (unless they are the statutory owners) thenceforth during the minority give effect on the register to the directions of the statutory owners and must apply for the registration of any prescribed restriction. They are not concerned with the propriety of any registered disposition directed by the statutory owners if it appears to be a proper one and if any capital money is paid to the settlement trustees or into court. A purchaser dealing with the personal representatives must see that any restriction on the register is complied with but need not inquire whether any directions have been given by the statutory owners (s 91(1)).

If a minor becomes entitled in possession to registered land otherwise than on a death (or will be so entitled on attaining full age) the statutory owners during the minority are entitled to have the land transferred to them (s 91(2)).

As changes take place under a settlement of registered land, the registered proprietor or his personal representatives must execute the instruments necessary to give effect to the changes on the register and must apply for any necessary changes in the restrictions appearing on the register. In general, one of the forms referred to above, modified where necessary according to the facts, will be appropriate for this purpose.

New trustees are appointed by deed in the ordinary way. Where, however, a restriction in Form 9 appears on the register, an application to modify the restriction by substituting the new names is necessary. This should be made in Form 77 signed by the registered proprietor, the retiring trustees, the continuing trustees and the new trustees or their respective solicitors. Deaths of trustees must be proved by death certificates. The land certificates (if outstanding, ie, if there is no registered charge) of all titles affected must be lodged. A fee of £35 for the first title and £20 for each subsequent title affected is payable unless subject to the proviso to Pt I(1) of Schedule 3 to the Fees Order.

When the settlement ends on the death of the tenant for life, the general personal representatives will make an assent in Form 56, and this will be lodged for registration together with the general grant. A fee under Scale A reduced to one fifth in accordance with Abatement 2 will be payable. If the settlement ends because the tenant for life becomes absolutely entitled, free from all interests under the settlement, the trustees may release the land from the minor interests under the settlement by a deed of release. If this is lodged at the Registry with a certified copy, and a request for the cancellation of the Form 9 restriction, the restriction will be cancelled. No fee is payable for the cancellation of a restriction.

2 Trusts for sale

Subject to the provisions of the Act as to settled land, neither the Chief Land Registrar nor any person dealing with a registered estate or charge is affected with notice of a trust, and references to trusts are, so far as possible, excluded from the register (s 74). It is, of course, sometimes clear from the register that proprietors are trustees. For example, where joint proprietors are registered, either with the joint proprietorship restriction set out on p 89 or without restriction, they must be trustees for sale. This fact, however, does not give notice of the trust.

As with unregistered land, the number of trustees for sale cannot exceed four, and capital money must not be paid to fewer than two trustees except where a trust corporation is the sole trustee.

Observance of this rule relating to capital money is secured by means of the joint proprietorship restriction set out on p 89 which is entered in the proprietorship register both on first registration and on dispositions of registered land where trustees for sale are registered as the proprietors of the land and the application for registration does not clearly show that a sole survivor of the proprietors will be able to give a valid receipt for capital money arising on a disposition of the land.

Subject to this restriction, and to any other entry on the register, the trustees will have full powers of disposing of the land.

Accordingly, if some further restriction is necessary to protect the interests of the beneficiaries, the trustees should apply for it to be registered. For example, in the case of partnership property, the following restriction is commonly applied for:

> 'Except under an order of the registrar no disposition by the proprietors of the land is to be registered after the death of any [either] of them without the consent of the personal representatives of the deceased proprietor.'

A disposition (off the register) of an individual share in the proceeds of sale of registered land may be followed by a transfer of the registered land designed to bring the registered ownership into line with the beneficial ownership. The assessment of the Land Registry fees payable for the registration of such transfers is considered on p 89.

The position on the death of a joint proprietor or the survivor of joint proprietors, and the cancellation of the joint proprietorship restriction in certain circumstances, are discussed in Chapter XIII.

(a) Creation of trust for sale by registered proprietor

If a registered proprietor executes a trust deed creating a trust for sale of his land and appointing trustees, he can (subject to any entry to the contrary on the register) transfer the land to the trustees by an ordinary transfer of whole (Form 19). The reference to monetary consideration may be deleted from the printed form of transfer. It is desirable, in view of s 74, that the transfer should not refer to the trust deed. However, if the transfer refers to the trust deed, it is unlikely that registration will be refused for that reason alone, provided that it is clear from the face of the transfer that the transferees are to hold the land as trustees for sale. Such a transfer will normally fall within the Stamp Duty (Exempt Instruments) Regulations 1987 and as such will be exempt from fixed duty and adjudication provided it has a certificate of exemption included or attached. If the connection between the trust deed and the transfer is not otherwise clear, an explanatory letter should accompany the application for registration.

When a transfer to trustees for sale is delivered for registration, it should be made clear, by completing the appropriate panel on the application form, whether or not the survivor of the transferees can give a valid receipt for capital money arising on a disposition of the land. The Registry will then enter the usual joint proprietorship restriction, set out on p 89, if appropriate, and the trustee should apply (in the transfer or on Form 75) for any other restriction necessary to ensure that the interest of the beneficiaries are protected and the trusts duly executed. If any special restriction based on the trust deed is needed, the deed should, strictly, be retained in the Registry (r 90); but a certified copy would usually be accepted for retention. The land certificate, if outstanding (ie, if there is no registered charge), must accompany the application to register the transfer.

The fee for registration of a transfer other than for monetary consideration is payable under Scale A reduced to one fifth under Abatement 2. No fee is payable in respect of the joint proprietorship restriction, but (subject to the proviso to Part I(1) of Schedule 3 to the Fees Order) a fee of £35 for the first title and £20 for each subsequent title affected is payable in respect of any additional restriction.

(b) Appointment of new trustees

When new or additional trustees for sale are appointed, it is necessary to give effect to the appointment on the register by securing the registration of the new body of trustees as proprietors in place of the old. There are three ways of doing this:

1 *Trusts affecting only registered land*—The registered proprietors can transfer the land to the new body of trustees by a transfer in the ordinary Form 19 prefaced by words such as 'For the purpose of effecting an appointment of new trustees...'. Supporting evidence (eg, the death certificate of a deceased proprietor or a statutory declaration of the facts relating to a proprietor who does not execute the transfer because he has remained outside the United Kingdom for over twelve months or is unfit to act) should be lodged as may be appropriate having regard to the state of the register. The Registry is not concerned with the title to make the appointment. The land certificate if outstanding (ie, if there is no registered charge) must be lodged with the application for registration. A registration fee calculated under Scale A reduced to one fifth under Abatement 2 is payable.

2 *Trusts affecting registered land and unregistered land or other property*—In such a case, there will be a deed of appointment in 'unregistered' form, which can relate to the registered land as well as to the unregistered land or other property. The proprietors of

WONTNER'S GUIDE TO LAND REGISTRY PRACTICE   147

the registered land can then transfer that land to the new body of trustees by a transfer in the ordinary Form 19 prefaced by words such as 'For the purpose of giving effect to the appointment of new trustees pursuant to the provisions of a Deed of Appointment of New Trustees of even date herewith and made between, etc. [or as the case may be] we, etc . . .'. Supporting evidence, and the land certificate if outstanding, must accompany the application, as indicated at 1 above. The Registry is not concerned with the title to make the appointment. The registration fee is payable as at 1 above.

3 *Any trust*—On the production of an ordinary deed of appointment in unregistered form, the Registry will give effect on the register to any express or implied vesting declaration in the deed (s 47). There must be lodged with the application a certified copy of the deed, the land certificate if outstanding, and the entire title to the trust. The registration fee is payable under Scale A on the value of the land after deducting the amount secured by any prior registered charge. This form of application is not to be recommended. While it does not involve the use of a transfer, it is cumbersome, and as Abatement 2 cannot be claimed will involve the payment of a higher registration fee.

In all three cases the instrument will be exempt from fixed duty under the Stamp Duty (Exempt Instruments) Regulations 1987 provided it has a certificate of exemption included or attached.

3 Sole trustees

If a sole trustee applies to be registered as proprietor of land (whether on first registration or otherwise) it is his duty to apply for a restriction or restrictions, as may be necessary, to protect the interests of the beneficiaries and to ensure that the trust is properly carried out. If he is a sole trustee for sale or the sole survivor of trustees for sale, he should apply for the entry of a restriction to prevent him from dealing with the land for value until an additional trustee has been appointed to act jointly with him. The joint proprietorship restriction set out on p 89 can be used for this purpose. The trustee should also apply for the entry of any other restriction necessary to protect the beneficiaries' interests.

For a bare trustee the following restriction is appropriate:

'Except under an order of the registrar no disposition or dealing by the proprietor of the land other than a transfer to [beneficiary] is to be registered without his consent.'

No fee will be payable for a restriction based on the joint proprietorship restriction. Subject to the proviso to Part I(1) of Schedule 3 to the Fees Order, a fee of £35 for the first title and £20 for each subsequent title affected will be payable for the entry of any additional restriction.

4 Charities

On any application for the first registration of land subject to charitable trusts, or for the registration of any transfer of registered land to be held on such trusts, the Registry must be satisfied that the charity had power to acquire the land and as to its powers of disposition.

Complete evidence of these matters is required. Thus there should be lodged certified copies of the documents forming the charity's constitution (eg, its trust deed or memorandum and articles of association) and of any approved scheme, order of the court or of the Charity Commissioners, or private Act of Parliament. In the case of a Public General Act, it is, of course, sufficient simply to cite the Act. If there is a limit on the amount of land that may be held, the secretary or solicitor to the charity should certify that the limit will not be exceeded by reason of the acquisition.

(a) Restrictions

If the evidence lodged shows that the land was properly acquired by the charity but that its powers of disposition are limited, a restriction will be entered in the proprietorship register. The form of the restriction will depend on the facts of the particular application. For example, in general, where the land is part of the permanent endowment of the charity or has at any time been occupied for the purposes of the charity, it must not be sold, leased, mortgaged or otherwise disposed of without an order of the court or of the Charity Commissioners, and accordingly the following restriction (Form 12) will be entered:

> 'No disposition or other dealing is to be registered without the consent of the Charity Commissioners or an order of the registrar.'

An appointment of new trustees is not caught by this restriction.

Also, where a charity raises part of the purchase price of a new property on mortgage, compliance with the restriction is not required before the mortgage is registered if a certificate by the charity that at the date of execution of the mortgage (which will usually be the completion date) the land was not and had not been occupied for the charity's purposes, accompanies the application.

There are exceptions to the general rule. Some charities are wholly or partially exempted (eg, by statute or by an order of the Charity Commissioners) from the control of the Charity Commissioners, and accordingly, as the case may require, the land will be registered without any restriction in favour of the Commissioners or with a restriction less comprehensive than Form 12.

Three general kinds of orders are made by the Commissioners. The first extends to all the land of the charity that is held for its general purposes and is, or has at any time been, occupied for the purposes of the charity, but does not extend to land forming part of the permanent endowment of the charity or in respect of which any special trust has been declared. Orders of this kind enable the charity without consent to enter into any transaction relating to the land to which the order applies provided that it is completed before a specified date (at present 31 December 2000).

Accordingly, when the trustees of a charity in respect of which a 2000 order is in force apply for registration as proprietors of land to which the order extends, the documents lodged should include the order or a certified copy and a certificate by the solicitor to the charity that the land is held for the general purposes of the charity and is not land forming part of the charity's permanent endowment or land in respect of which any special trust has been declared. If the application is otherwise in order, the following restriction will then be entered in the proprietorship register:

> 'No disposition or other dealing by the proprietor of the land completed after [31 December 2000 or as the case may be] is to be registered without the consent of the Charity Commissioners or an order of the registrar.'

The second general type of order, similar to a 2000 order and known as a 1992 order, covers dispositions made on or before 31 December 1992 and gives either a blanket exemption for all dispositions or an exemption for dispositions in respect of land held for specified purposes. Specific 1992 orders may also be given exempting proposed transactions with specified land. The trustees of a charity in respect of which a 1992 order is in force should lodge the order or a certified copy when applying for registration of land to which it relates. A certificate by the solicitor to the charity will be required to establish that the land is covered by the order, unless it is a blanket order. A restriction reflecting the terms of the order will be entered.

The third general kind of order made by the Charity Commissioners is the 'non-occupation' kind. Orders of this kind are made in respect of a specified property and allow the property to be dealt with without the consent of the Commissioners so long as it is not, and has not at any time been, occupied for the purposes of the charity. When an order (or certified copy) of this kind is lodged with an application to register the trustees of the charity as proprietors and the application is otherwise in order, the following restriction will be entered in the proprietorship register:

> 'Except under an order of the registrar no disposition or other dealing by the proprietor of the land is to be registered without the consent of the Charity Commissioners unless a certificate signed by the solicitor or secretary of the charity known as [name of charity] has been furnished that the land is not and has not at any time been occupied for the purposes of the charity.'

The 'non-occupation' restriction will be entered when a charity is registered as the proprietor of land if the solicitor to the charity certifies (by letter) that all the property held for the purposes of the charity may be expended for those purposes without distinction between capital and income and that the land is not and has not at any time been occupied for the purposes of the charity (see Charities Act 1960, ss 29(1), (2), 45(3)).

Statutory instruments relating to many religious bodies (eg, the Baptist, Congregational and Methodist Churches, and Diocesan Boards of the Church of England) enable those bodies in certain circumstances to dispose of land without the consent of the Charity Commissioners. If such an instrument applies in any particular case, this should be made clear in the application for registration. An appropriate restriction will then be entered in the proprietorship register.

In addition to a restriction related to the control exercised by the Charity Commissioners, it may be necessary in any particular case to enter a restriction relating to limitations imposed by the charity's constitution or by statute, eg, the Housing Associations Act 1985.

Another kind of restriction relates particularly to the trustees. When the procedure for the appointment and discharge of trustees permitted by s 35 of the Charities Act 1960 applies to a charity, the trustees may, if they wish, be registered collectively as 'The trustees of [name and charity]...' subject to the following restriction in addition to any other:

> 'Except under an order of the registrar, no disposition by the proprietors of the land following any appointment or discharge of a trustee in the manner mentioned in section 35 of the Charities Act 1960 is to be registered unless the requirements of that section have been satisfied.'

On a subsequent disposition by named trustees, there should be lodged either certified copies of the memoranda of the appointments and discharges that have taken place from time to time, to show that the persons making the disposition are the present trustees, or a letter from the secretary or solicitor to the charity certifying that the persons making the disposition are the present trustees.

(b) The Official Custodian for Charities

The registration of the Official Custodian as proprietor on first registration is considered below. He may be registered as the proprietor of registered land on behalf of a charity:

(1) on a transfer (in Form 36) to him declaring or referring to the trusts and accompanied by an official copy of the order of the court or the Charity Commissioners authorising him to accept the transfer (r 122);

(2) where the managing trustees are registered as proprietors, on production of an official copy of the order of the court or the Charity Commissioners vesting the land in him (r 128);

(3) on a transfer to the managing trustees accompanied by an official copy of the order of the court or the Charity Commissioners vesting the land in him (r 128);

(4) where the land is vested in him by statute, on production of appropriate evidence (r 128).

As to execution of deeds by or on behalf of the Official Custodian, see under the heading 'Execution of deeds', below.

When the Official Custodian is registered as the proprietor of land, the managing trustees of the charity may register an address for the service of notices.

(c) Registration of trustees collectively

Charity trustees are registered collectively as 'The trustees of [name of charity]' and not in their individual names when the procedure for the appointment and discharge of trustees permitted by s 35 of the Charities Act 1960 applies to the charity. This removes the need for an application for an entry on the register whenever there is a change of trustees. As to the restriction in such a case, and the evidence required to show who are the trustees on a subsequent disposition by named trustees, see p 151.

(d) Execution of deeds

Where land is vested in the Official Custodian for Charities in trust for a charity, the charity trustees (or the charity if it is a corporate charity) may in his name and on his behalf execute any deed which they could require him to execute:
   (1) for carrying out any transaction authorised by an order of the court or of the Charity Commissioners;
   (2) for granting a lease for a term of not more than twenty-two years from its grant, not being a lease in consideration of a fine, or for accepting a surrender of a lease (Charities Act 1960, s 17(2), (4)).

When the Official Custodian is registered as the proprietor of land and trustees of the charity execute a disposition of the land in his name and on his behalf, appropriate evidence as to who are the trustees of the charity must be produced in support of the application to register the disposition. This evidence should relate to all the trustees, whether all execute the disposition or only two or more of them execute it pursuant to s 34 of the Charities Act 1960. A certificate by the secretary or solicitor of the charity is usually accepted. See p 151 as to cases in which s 35 of the Charities Act 1960 applies. Section 34 of that Act is considered below.

When the Official Custodian is registered as the proprietor of land, he must himself execute any disposition of the land not within the provisions of s 17(2), (4) of the Charities Act 1960 referred to above (eg, a transfer on enfranchisement or the grant of an extended lease under the Leasehold Reform Act 1967).

Section 34 of the Charities Act 1960 empowers charity trustees, subject to the trusts of the charity, to confer on two or more of themselves authority to execute deeds in the names and on behalf of all of them, and, unless the contrary intention appears, such authority includes by implication authority to execute in the name and on behalf of the Official Custodian for Charities in any case in which all the trustees could do so. When a disposition of registered land is expressed to be executed pursuant to s 34, the Registry will not require evidence of the authority under which the executing trustees acted; but if the trustees of the charity are registered as proprietors collectively, evidence will be required as indicated under the heading 'Restrictions' above in relation to s 35 of the Charities Act 1960 to show that the persons executing, and those on whose behalf they execute, are the trustees of the charity.

(e) First registration

Rule 60 contains provisions relating to the first registration of charity land which cannot be sold without the consent of the Charity Commissioners.

When there are managing trustees or a committee of management, they are the persons to apply for registration, whether or not the land is vested in them. If the land is vested in the Official Custodian for Charities, they should apply for him to be registered as proprietor. If it is vested in a corporation other than the Official Custodian for Charities on trust to deal with it as directed by the managing trustees or committee of management, they should apply for the corporation to be registered as proprietor. In any other case, they should apply for the registration of themselves as proprietors.

Where there are no managing trustees or committee of management, and the land is vested in a corporation, the corporation should apply for the registration of itself as proprietor.

If the Official Custodian for Charities is to be the proprietor, there should be produced either:

(1) a conveyance to him with the original or an official copy of the order authorising him to accept the conveyance, and the disposition (if any) of the land for the benefit of the charity; or

(2) an official copy of an order, scheme or other instrument vesting the land in him, together with the disposition (if any) of the land for the benefit of the charity; or

(3) evidence that the land has become vested in him under the provisions of a statute.

(f) Transfers of registered land for charitable uses

Rule 122 provides that a transfer of land to trustees upon charitable trusts shall be made by an instrument in Form 36, a form that follows the ordinary form of transfer but also states the trusts on which the land is to be held. If the trusts are not declared by, and do not appear from, the transfer, the transfer must refer to the trust instrument, and a certified copy of that instrument must be produced.

(g) Declaration of a charitable trust of registered land

Rule 124 provides that a proprietor who declares such a trust shall forthwith produce to the Registry the land certificate and the original (or a certified copy of) the trust instrument. The appropriate restriction will then be entered on the register.

5 Minors

The position of minors under settlements of registered land has already been discussed (see under 'Settled land' above).

A purported disposition of any registered land or charge in favour of a minor will not entitle him to be registered as proprietor until he attains full age, but in the meantime will operate as a declaration of trust binding on the registered proprietor or his personal representatives (s 111).

The disposition, or a copy, or an extract therefrom, must be deposited at the Registry and must, unless and until the tenants for life (as where the minor is one of several joint tenants for life of whom some are of full age), statutory owners (as where the minor becomes entitled to settled land not on a death), personal representatives (as where the minor is entitled on a death) or trustees for sale (as where the minor is one of several joint tenants entitled absolutely some of whom are of full age) are registered as proprietors, be protected by means of a restriction or otherwise on the register.

In the case of a disposition to a minor jointly with another person of full age, the latter can be registered as proprietor.

The Registry does not ask whether any applicant for registration is of full age; and it is, of course, possible for a minor to be registered as proprietor by mistake. If such a mistake should be discovered, an application for the rectification of the register, and for the entry in the meantime of a restriction to prevent all dealings with the land, should be made at once.

When a minor who is entitled absolutely to registered land or a registered charge attains full age, the land or charge can be transferred to him by a simple transfer expressed to be made in consideration of the transferee's having become so entitled. A normal application for registration using Form A4 should be made, accompanied by the transfer, the land or charge certificate, and a fee assessed under Scale A reduced to one fifth under Abatement 2. Unless the case otherwise warrants it, there is no need to mention the minority.

6 Mental disorder

If the registered proprietor of land or of a charge is a mental patient, s 111(5) of the Act, as amended, enables his receiver, or (if there is no receiver) any person authorised in that behalf, to exercise the powers of the registered proprietor in his name and on his behalf.

A mental patient can be registered as the proprietor of land or a charge, the transaction being carried out by his receiver or an authorised person; and, by arrangement with the Court of Protection, no restriction will be entered in the register in relation to the patient's disability unless an express application is made on behalf of the patient. Where, however, a receiver is registered as proprietor, a restriction is entered in the proprietorship register as follows:

> 'RESTRICTION: Except under an order of the registrar no disposition by the proprietor of [the land][charge No] is to be registered unless made pursuant to an order of the court under the Mental Health Act 1983.'

This restriction is not entered where the mental patient was a trustee and a new trustee is to be registered in his place.

An office copy of an order of the judge or of the Court of Protection under which the receiver or authorised person acts, lodged at the Registry pursuant to s 111(5) of the Act, as amended, will not be retained in the Registry.

Where a patient recovers, an application to cancel the restriction should be accompanied by an office copy of the order of the court discharging the receiver and by the land or charge certificate. No fee is payable for the cancellation of the restriction.

Chapter XIII

Death

1 Death of sole or sole surviving proprietor

On the death of a sole or sole surviving proprietor, his personal representatives (which in this section includes a sole personal representative) are usually entitled to be registered as proprietors in his place on production of the probate or letters of administration of the estate of the sole or sole surviving proprietor (s 41). There are exceptions. Where the register states that the deceased was the administrator of the estate of a deceased person, a grant of letters of administration de bonis non to the estate of the first deceased person must be obtained, and the administrators de bonis non are then entitled to be registered as proprietors. The administrator of a person stated on the register to be an executor is not entitled to be registered in the deceased executor's place: a grant of letters of administration de bonis non to the estate of the original testator is necessary, and the administrators de bonis non will be entitled to be registered as proprietors.

If the personal representatives wish to be registered as proprietors of the land, or charge, the following evidence should be delivered to the appropriate district land registry under cover of an application Form A4:

(1) If the application relates to the proprietorship of land, the land certificate, unless it is already in the Registry because the land is subject to a registered charge. In the latter event it is desirable, though not essential, that the registered chargee should deposit his charge certificate at the district registry so that it can be made to correspond with the register. For the deposit procedure, see p 72.

(2) If the application relates to a registered charge, the charge certificate.

(3) An application for registration in Form 82.
(4) The probate or letters of administration or an official or certified copy thereof.
(5) The certificate of non-liability to inheritance tax, capital transfer tax or death duties if appropriate: see pp 161–3.
(6) A fee under Scale A reduced (subject to a minimum fee of £35) to one fifth under Abatement 2 of the Fees Order.

On the completion of the registration, the personal representatives will have full powers of disposition, subject to any entry to the contrary on the register binding them. They will not be bound by the joint proprietorship restriction referred to on p 89, and this restriction will be cancelled by the Registry as a matter of course on the registration of the personal representatives as proprietors in the place of a proprietor to whom the restriction applied. It should be noted particularly in this context that, as stated, references to 'personal representatives' in this section apply equally to a sole personal representative.

The personal representatives may, without being registered as proprietors, and subject to any entry to the contrary on the register binding them, transfer the land or charge or dispose of it by way of assent, appropriation or vesting assent (s 37). A disadvantage of this procedure is that the register remains out of date longer than it would if the personal representatives were registered as proprietors as soon as the grant of probate or letters of administration was made. Whilst the register is out of date, any notice sent by the Registry and addressed to the deceased registered proprietor may go astray, to the detriment of the interests of the beneficiaries. If the joint proprietorship restriction referred to on p 89 appears on the register in relation to the deceased proprietor when the disposition by his personal representatives is registered, it will be cancelled by the Registry as a matter of course, and the registration will take place without regard to it.

Whether the personal representatives have been registered as proprietors or not, a transfer by them will be in the usual form, and an assent, appropriation or vesting assent is required to be in Form 56 or 57 as appropriate. When an application is made to register the transfer, assent, appropriation or vesting assent, there should be delivered to the appropriate district land registry:

(a) a completed application Form A4 if the application relates to the whole of a title, or A5 if it relates to part;
(b) the land or charge certificate as indicated at (1) and (2) above;

(c) the probate or letters of administration or an official or certified copy thereof, unless they have been placed on deposit to meet applications by the personal representatives (see p 72 as to the deposit procedure) or the personal representatives are already the registered proprietors of the land or charge;
(d) the transfer, assent, appropriation or vesting assent;
(e) the certificate of non-liability to inheritance tax, capital transfer tax or death duties, if appropriate. A certificate of non-liability to death duties is not necessary on the registration of a transfer on sale because on the registration of such a transfer any existing entry in the register as to the liability of the land to the Crown for death duties will be cancelled. But notice in the register of an Inland Revenue charge in respect of inheritance tax or capital transfer tax will be cancelled only on production of a certificate in Land Registry Form 61 (CTT) given by the Commissioners of Inland Revenue. And if the certificate in Form 61 (CTT) states that it is to take effect only on the registration of a disposition to a purchaser, the notice in the register will be cancelled only when the certificate is accompanied by a proper application to register the disposition. (See also pp 161–3);
(f) in the case of a transfer for monetary consideration or of a charge by the personal representatives the appropriate fee under Scale A in Schedule 1 to the Fees Order; and in the case of a disposition otherwise than for monetary consideration, the appropriate fee under Scale A reduced to one fifth (subject to a minimum fee of £35) in accordance with Abatement 2 in Schedule 4 to the Fees Order. In the case of a disposition otherwise than for monetary consideration where the personal representatives are already registered as proprietors, no fee is payable.

A vesting assent in Form 57 is used where the land is to be vested in the tenant for life or statutory owners under a strict settlement, eg, where a settlement is created by will or arises on an intestacy, or where it continues after the death of the tenant for life. The form embodies an application for the entry of the appropriate restriction. Form 56 is the appropriate form for other assents and appropriations.

Rule 170(5) places complete responsibility on the personal representatives and their advisers in relation to registered interests forming part of the deceased's estate. It provides that 'it shall not be the duty of the Chief Land Registrar nor shall he be entitled to consider or to call for any information concerning the reason why any transfer is made, or as to the terms of the will, and, whether he has notice or not of its contents, he shall be entitled to assume that the personal representative is acting (whether by transfer, assent or appropriation or vesting assent) correctly and within his powers'.

As has been stated, Form 57 embodies an application for the appropriate restriction. In other cases of dispositions by personal representatives, it should be borne in mind that a restriction may be desirable in the interests of beneficiaries. Thus, where land is being vested in trustees to sell, subject to the consent of a beneficiary during his life, a restriction in the proprietorship register prohibiting the registration of any disposition by the proprietors of the land without the consent of the beneficiary would seem to be appropriate.

2 Death of a joint proprietor not being the survivor of joint proprietors

When one of two or more joint proprietors of a registered estate dies, the registered estate will vest by survivorship in the remaining proprietors or proprietor, who should apply for notice of the death to be entered on the register.

For this purpose there should be lodged at the appropriate district land registry:

(*a*) a completed application Form A4;
(*b*) the death certificate, or probate or letters of administration, or an official or certified copy thereof;
(*c*) the land or charge certificate, as indicated at (1) and (2) on p 157; and
(*d*) an application in Form 83.

No fee is payable.

On completion of the application, the surviving proprietors or proprietor can deal with the land or charge, subject to any entry on the register.

It often happens that a sole survivor of joint proprietors remains as proprietor of land with the joint proprietorship restriction set out on p 89. If he is a trustee for himself and/or others, (a) new trustee(s) can be appointed and registered as proprietor(s) jointly with him as indicated on pp 146–147, and the restriction will remain.

It may be, however, that the sole surviving joint proprietor has become solely and beneficially entitled to the land; and if this is

the case, he can apply for the cancellation of the restriction. The application (on Form A4) should be supported by evidence of the equitable title to the land showing that the survivor can give a valid receipt for capital money arising on a disposition of the land. Usually the Registry will accept a statutory declaration by the survivor, or a certificate by a solicitor with personal knowledge of the facts, that:
(1) in stated circumstances (eg, under the will of a deceased joint proprietor) the survivor has become legally and beneficially entitled to the whole of the land or rentcharge in the registered title;
(2) he has not incumbered his share in any way; and
(3) he has not received notice of any incumbrance of the share of any deceased proprietor.

The declaration or certificate should be accompanied by any available documentary evidence, eg, an assent relating to an undivided share. No fee is payable for the cancellation of the restriction.

The circumstances in which the joint proprietorship restriction is entered on the register are discussed on p 89 in relation to transfers of registered land. The same principles apply to first registrations.

The restriction has sometimes been entered when it did not apply, simply because solicitors did not complete the appropriate panel on the first registration application form or, in the case of a transfer of registered land, having failed to use Form A4 or A5, did not make the necessary information available in some other way. In such cases, an application for the cancellation of the restriction may be made on the lines indicated above.

3 Inheritance tax: capital transfer tax: death duties

The Finance Act 1975 (see now the Inheritance Tax Act 1984 ('IHTA 1984')—also known as the Capital Transfer Tax Act 1984—which consolidated the existing provisions) abolished estate duty in respect of deaths occurring after 12 March 1975 and (subject to exceptions) imposed a charge of capital transfer tax on lifetime transfers of capital made after 26 March 1974 and on deaths occurring after 12 March 1975. The charge on death extended to gifts inter vivos made before 27 March 1974 but within seven years of the donor's death. The Finance Act 1986 changed the name of capital transfer tax to inheritance tax (s 100) and abolished the charge on most lifetime gifts between individuals occurring at least seven years before the transferor's death (s 101).

On first registration or conversion of title the Registry will consider whether the land may be liable to an Inland Revenue charge for death duty (in practice, only estate duty), inheritance tax or capital transfer tax and will register a notice relating to such liability if appropriate. The notice will be in Form 60 of the Schedule to the Land Registration Rules 1925: the original Form 60 where the notice relates to death duties, and the Form 60 substituted by the Land Registration (Inheritance Tax) Rules 1975 where the notice relates to inheritance tax or capital transfer tax. On occasions other than first registration and conversion of title, a notice in Form 60 will be registered only on application by the Inland Revenue.

As to deaths on or before 12 March 1975, the Land Registration Act 1925 provided that a registered disposition in favour of a purchaser should operate to vest in him the estate or interest transferred or created by the disposition free from all claims of Her Majesty for death duties, notwithstanding that notice of a claim for duties might be noted on the register (s 73(1)); and that a disposition to any person other than a purchaser should take effect subject to any charge for payment of death duties and the interest thereon whether notice of a claim for the duties was entered on the register or not (s 73(2)). 'Purchaser' meant a purchaser in good faith for money or money's worth including a lessee, mortgagee or any other person who acquires any interest in the land or any charge on it.

Accordingly, a notice in the original Form 60 (death duties) will be cancelled as to the land of the disponee, without application, whenever a disposition within s 73(1) is registered. In practice such dispositions are transfers on sale; charges other than collateral, supplemental, guarantee or other contingency charges; and leases at a premium. Also, a notice in the original Form 60 will be cancelled at any time as to the whole or, where appropriate, as to a part, of the land affected thereby on the production to the appropriate district land registry of a certificate given by the Inland Revenue Department in Land Registry Form 61 (see below). No fee is payable for the cancellation of the notice.

As to inheritance tax or capital transfer tax claims on deaths after 12 March 1975 and on lifetime transfers after 26 March 1974, s 73 of the Land Registration Act 1925, as substituted by para 1 of Schedule 8 to the IHTA 1984, provides that a disposition shall

take effect subject to any subsisting Inland Revenue charge for capital transfer tax (under ss 237 and 238 of the IHTA 1984) unless:
  (a) the disposition is in favour of a purchaser within the meaning of the IHTA 1984; and
  (b) the charge is not, at the time of registration of the disposition, protected by a notice on the register.

'Purchaser' here means a purchaser in good faith for consideration in money or money's worth other than a nominal consideration and includes a lessee, mortgagee or other person who for such consideration acquires an interest in the property in question (s 272 of the IHTA 1984).

When a charge for inheritance tax or capital transfer tax is protected by notice on the register, the notice will be cancelled as to the whole or, where appropriate, as to a part, of the land affected thereby on the production to the appropriate district land registry of a certificate given by the Inland Revenue in Land Registry Form 61 (CTT) (see below), but subject to any condition specified in the certificate as to the registration of a disposition to a purchaser (r 192 as substituted by r 2 of the Land Registration (Inheritance Tax) Rules 1975). No fee is payable for the cancellation of the notice.

The statutory provisions referred to above under which a notice in relation to death duties is cancelled as a matter of course (without a certificate by the Inland Revenue in Land Registry Form 61) when a disposition in favour of a purchaser is registered do not extend to notice of a charge for inheritance tax or capital transfer tax. Accordingly, a certificate by the Inland Revenue in Land Registry Form 61 (CTT) is always necessary for the cancellation of a notice of a charge for inheritance tax or capital transfer tax.

Land Registry Forms 61 and 61 (CTT) are incorporated in Capital Taxes Office Forms 31 and 31 (CTT) respectively. An application for a certificate in one of the Land Registry forms should be made on the relevant Capital Taxes Office form, which should be sent to The Controller, Capital Taxes Office, Minford House, Rockley Road, London W14 0DF. No fee is payable for the certificates. The combined Forms 31/61 and 31 (CTT)/61(CTT) can be obtained free of charge from the Capital Taxes Office at the above address. They are also available from the bookshops of the Oyez group of companies but not from the Land Registry or HM Stationery Office.

Chapter XIV

Protection of Third Party Rights

1 Notices

The Act enables notices of many matters to be entered on the register of the title to the land affected (ss 48–52). These include land charges, until (if so registrable) the land charge is registered as a registered charge, and any right, interest or claim which it may be deemed expedient to protect by notice instead of by caution, inhibition or restriction. Other examples of the use of notices are mentioned below. The entry of a notice does not confer validity on any claim, and a disposition by the registered proprietor of the land against which a notice has been entered will take effect subject to the matter protected by the notice only if and so far as it may be valid and is not (independently of the Act) overridden by the disposition.

A contract for sale entered into by a registered proprietor of land would be registrable as a land charge of class C (iv) if the land were unregistered, and accordingly can be protected by notice on the register of the title to the land; and a grant of easements by the proprietor of registered land should be protected by the entry of notice as explained on pp 51–3. The entry of notice of other matters (eg, leases, rentcharges, restrictive covenants, rights of occupation under the Matrimonial Homes Act 1983) is referred to in other chapters. The entry of notice brings the subject-matter to the attention of anyone reading the register; but, as mentioned above, the entry will not, of itself, confer validity on the matter referred to in the notice. Except as a temporary measure pending the appointment of trustees, notice may not be entered in respect of interests that can be overridden by the proprietor under a trust for sale or strict settlement; a restriction is the appropriate form of protection for these interests. It should also be noted that, although the Charging Orders Act 1979 permits a charging order to be made in respect of an interest under a trust including a trust in respect of land, such an order can only be protected by notice if it is imposed on the registered land itself (see p 168 for protection of a charging order on the proceeds of sale by caution).

In many cases the Registry enters notice of incumbrances on the register of title of the burdened land as a matter of course. For example, on first registration notice of easements and restrictive covenants is entered as indicated in Chapter IV; on the registration of a transfer of part of the land in a title, notice of easements and restrictive covenants in the transfer will be entered as a matter of course on the registers of that title and the title to the part transferred; and on the substantive registration of a lease or rentcharge granted out of registered land, notice of the grant will be entered on the register of the grantor's title. But where notice will not be entered as a matter of course, a specific application must be made. Such an application is necessary, for example, in respect of a deed of grant of an easement (see pp 51–3); a deed of covenant imposing restrictive covenants on registered land; a contract for sale or an agreement for a lease; and an option in a lease of registered land where the lease is an overriding interest.

An application for the entry of a notice is best made on a Form A4. The document concerned and a certified copy or examined abstract of it must be lodged. The land certificate if outstanding (ie, if there is no registered charge) must be produced except in the cases of notice under the Matrimonial Homes Act 1983 (see Chapter XV) and of notice of a lease at a rent where no premium is taken (where production of the land certificate is desirable but not essential; see p 35). If a charge is registered, the land certificate will already have been retained in the Registry pursuant to s 65. In this event, production of the charge certificate is not essential unless the chargee is to be bound by the notice. The consent of any cautioner and of any depositee of the land certificate should be lodged. A fee of £35 for the first title and £20 for each subsequent title affected is payable, but no fee is payable if, in relation to each registered title affected, the application is accompanied by an application affecting that title upon which a scale fee (not under art 6) is payable (Part I(1) of Schedule 3 to the Fees Order).

An application (Form A4) to cancel a notice, when the noted interest has determined, should be accompanied by the original document and either satisfactory evidence of determination or a specific request by the incumbrancer for the notice to be cancelled.

The land certificate, if outstanding, should be lodged. No fee is payable. The register of the incumbered title will not show any devolution of the title to the noted interest that may have occurred, and therefore appropriate 'unregistered' conveyancing evidence of any such devolution should be lodged to prove either determination of the interest or the right of the applicant to apply for the notice to be cancelled. For applications to cancel notice of determined leases and rentcharges see Chapters VIII and X respectively, and for cancellation of notice of a charge under the Matrimonial Homes Act 1983 see Chapter XV.

2 Cautions

Any person claiming an interest in land not already registered can lodge a caution against first registration, and a person interested in land already registered can lodge a caution against conversion of the title or a caution against dealings with the land. A person interested in a registered charge can lodge a caution against dealings with that charge.

The benefit of a caution cannot be transferred. If the interest protected by the caution has been assigned, the assignee should register a new caution and procure the withdrawal of the old one. But when a cautioner has died, his personal representatives can exercise his rights under the caution.

(a) Cautions against first registration (s 53)

The applicant must be a person who has or claims to have such an interest in unregistered land as entitles him to object to any disposition thereof being made without his consent. The word 'disposition' is interpreted in the Registry as meaning a disposition free from incumbrances, leases and other interferences with absolute ownership. In the result, almost any person interested in the land can apply.

The caution asks that the cautioner may have notice of any application for the first registration of the land. The caution must be in Form 13 and must be supported by a statutory declaration of the cautioner's interest in Form 14. A combined form is published. The caution may be signed, and the statutory declaration made, by the cautioner or his solicitor. Three addresses for service, including the address of the cautioner's solicitor, may be given. The fee is £35 under Part I(1) of Schedule 3 to the Fees Order.

Rule 70 (as substituted by the Land Registration Rules 1990) allows any person interested in land affected by a caution against first registration to inspect the caution and the statutory declaration in support of it.

The effect of the registration of the caution is that if an application for the first registration of the land is made, a notice will be sent to the cautioner at the address(es) for service given in his application. The notice gives the cautioner an opportunity to object to the registration within fourteen days, or, if the Chief Land Registrar thinks fit, some other period not being less than seven days. If no objection is delivered to the appropriate district land registry within the time prescribed, the application proceeds.

A person who lodges a caution without reasonable cause is liable in damages to anyone injured as a result (s 56(3)).

The caution may be withdrawn (in Form 16) as to all or part of the land at any time. No fee is payable for the withdrawal.

A leaseholder contemplating a caution against first registration may wish to ensure that no one else shall be registered as the proprietor of the term, in which case he will apply accordingly (see Form 13 in the Schedule to the Rules). But he should consider whether to apply also for a caution against the first registration of the reversion, if the reversion is unregistered. Such a caution would guard against his interests being overlooked on the occasion of any application for the first registration of the reversion. This last consideration is also of concern to a person whose interest is in an agreement for a lease.

(b) Cautions against conversion (r 215)

A caution against the conversion of a title may be made in Form 69 supported by a statutory declaration in Form 14. The cautioner will be entitled to notice of any application to convert and will be able to object to the application if he wishes. The caution may be withdrawn (in Form 71) at any time. The fee in respect of the application to register the caution is £35 under Part I(1) of Schedule 3 to the Fees Order. No fee is payable for its withdrawal. A cautioner without reasonable cause is liable in damages to anyone injured as a result of the caution (s 56(3)).

(c) Cautions against dealings (s 54)

A person interested under an unregistered instrument, or interested as a judgment creditor, or otherwise howsoever, in any land or charge registered in the name of any other person may lodge a caution with the Chief Land Registrar to the effect that no dealing with such land or charge on the part of the proprietor is to be registered until notice has been served on the cautioner (s 54(1)). A person whose interest has been registered or protected by a notice or restriction on the register is not entitled to lodge a caution under s 54 in respect of such interest without the consent of the Chief Land Registrar (s 54(1), proviso).

To be properly the subject of a caution under s 54 an interest must be such as the courts would enforce against the land or charge. Examples of such interests, given in Form 14 (referred to below) as printed in the Schedule to the Rules, are: beneficial ownership of the fee simple or of a lease, and the interests of a tenant for life, a purchaser under a contract for sale, a plaintiff in an action and an equitable mortgagee under a memorandum of charge under hand; and see pp 123–4 as to the protection of mortgages by a caution under s 54. However the proviso to s 54 (1), referred to above, must be kept in mind.

A caution will not be accepted in respect of an interest in land registered with absolute or good leasehold title where the interest arose before the date of first registration of the land and was an interest from which the registered proprietor took free by virtue of registration with such a class of title. A person claiming such an interest should apply for rectification of the register.

The normal form of protection for an interest in the proceeds of sale of registered land held on trust for sale is a joint proprietorship restriction but, despite the definition of 'land' in s 3(viii), it is now established that a person claiming such an interest may protect that interest by caution under s 54 (see *Elias v Mitchell* [1972] Ch 652 and *Williams & Glyn's Bank Limited v Boland* (see p 49)). In addition, the Charging Orders Act 1979 now enables a charging order to be made in respect of the beneficial interest of a judgment debtor under a trust including a trust affecting land, thus effectively reversing the decision of the Court of Appeal in *Irani Finance Limited v Singh* [1971] Ch 59, so that a caution may be used to protect not only a charge imposed upon a registered legal estate but also a charge on a share in the proceeds of sale of land held on trust for sale.

Consent will be given, under the proviso to s 54(1), to the entry of a caution to protect an interest in the proceeds of sale, where joint proprietors are registered with a joint proprietorship restriction. A caution entered by a person claiming an interest in the proceeds of sale will not be allowed to prevent the registration of a disposition by which the protected interest would be overreached (for example, under s 27 of the Law of Property Act 1925).

In all these cases, it should be borne in mind that the cautioner cannot be one of the registered proprietors (see s 54(1)) and that the cautioner will be liable in damages to anyone injured as a result of his lodging a caution without reasonable cause (see s 56(3)).

A caution against dealings must be in Form 63 signed by the cautioner or his solicitor and supported by a statutory declaration of the cautioner's interest made in Form 14 by the cautioner or his solicitor. A combined Form 63/14 is published. The fee is £35 for the first title and £20 for each subsequent title affected but no fee is payable if, in relation to each registered title affected, the application is accompanied by an application affecting that title upon which a scale fee (not under art 6) is payable (Part I(1) of Schedule 3 to the Fees Order).

It is important to note that a caution against dealings by the proprietor of land will not affect dispositions by the proprietor of a registered charge. On registration of a transfer of the land by a registered chargee in exercise of his power of sale, any caution against dealings with the land will be cancelled automatically without the cautioner being given the opportunity to object. In appropriate cases, the cautioner should apply for a caution against dealings both with the land and with the charge. An example of such a case would be where the interest sought to be protected by the caution has priority to the charge, either because the chargee has consented to its creation or otherwise. The statutory declaration in support of an application to register a caution against dealings with the charge in such circumstances should include an explanation of why two cautions are thought to be justified.

After a caution against dealings has been lodged in respect of any registered land or charge, the Registry will not, without the cautioner's consent (signed by the cautioner or his solicitor) register any dealing with the land or charge or any notice of deposit of land or charge certificate until it has served notice on the cautioner warning him that his caution will cease to have any effect after the expiration of a period of fourteen days (or such other period not less than seven days as the Chief Land Registrar directs) unless the Chief Land Registrar makes an order to the contrary.

A caution may also be warned-off on the application at any time in writing of the proprietor of the land or charge to which the caution relates, or his solicitor (or a person entitled to be registered as proprietor or his solicitor). Notice will then be served on the cautioner that after the period limited by the notice has expired the caution will cease to have any effect unless the Chief Land Registrar makes an order to the contrary.

However, before the expiration of the period limited by the notice the cautioner can object, and show cause why the caution should continue to have effect or why the dealing or notice should not be registered. Cause may be shown either by the cautioner's appearing before the Chief Land Registrar or by means of a written statement by the cautioner or his solicitors. The Chief Land Registrar can then either order that the caution shall cease to have effect or appoint a time for all parties to appear before him so that he can hear the dispute. In the latter event, having heard the dispute and having served such notice (if any) as he thinks necessary, the Chief Land Registrar may decide the matter or he may refer it for decision by the court. Also he may at any stage refer to the court any questions arising from the dispute (r 220).

A caution against dealings may be withdrawn in Form 71 at any time, without fee, by the cautioner or his personal representatives or solicitor.

3 Restrictions

The entry of a restriction on the register is a method of limiting the powers of a registered proprietor to accord with either the general law (eg, as to charities or settled land) or particular circumstances (eg, the existence of a partnership). Some restrictions must be entered whenever the circumstances to which they apply are present. Examples of these are the joint proprietorship restriction, set out on p 89, and the restrictions relating to settled land discussed at Chapter XII. Others may be applied for voluntarily. Voluntary applications for restrictions are usually made by the proprietor himself, but exceptionally they may be made by others if they can induce the proprietor to lodge his land certificate (if outstanding) or (where he is the proprietor of a charge) his charge certificate for the purpose.

The proprietor of any registered land or charge may restrict to any extent his powers of dealing with the land or charge or of depositing the land or charge certificate by way of security. The form of the restriction must be that no transaction to which it relates is to be registered unless (*a*) notice of the application for registration is sent by post to a specified address; or (*b*) the consent of a named person or persons is given to the transaction (such consent may be given by the restrictioner or by his solicitor); or (c) some other matter or thing is done. A restriction relating to dealings with minor interests (see Chapter IV) is not permitted, however; and the Registry may refuse to enter any restriction that is unreasonable or calculated to cause inconvenience (s 58).

Some examples of voluntary restrictions are:

> (To protect partnership property) 'Except under an order of the registrar no disposition by the proprietors of the land is to be registered after the death of any (either) of them without the consent of the personal representatives of the deceased proprietor.'
>
> 'Except under an order of the registrar no disposition by the proprietor of the land is to be registered without the consent of the proprietor for the time being of Charge No
>
> 'Except under an order of the registrar no disposition by the proprietor of the land is to be registered without the consent of *AB* of etc.'

An application by a registered proprietor for the entry of a restriction may be in Form 75, signed by the applicant or his solicitor, or it may be embodied in a document lodged for registration. For example, an application for the restriction secondly set out above is commonly embodied in a charge by the proprietor of the land. The form of an application by someone other than the proprietor must be adapted to the circumstances, the grounds on which it is made must be stated, and there must be lodged such evidence as the Registry may direct. Whoever applies, the proprietor's land certificate (if outstanding) or (where he is the proprietor of a charge) his charge certificate must be lodged. Production of the land certificate will not be required where an application is made for the entry of a joint proprietorship restriction (see p 89) by someone other than the registered proprietor if the existence of the trust is not in dispute. The fee is £35 for the first title and £20 for each subsequent title affected, but no fee is payable if, in relation to each registered title affected, the application is accompanied by an application affecting that title upon which a scale fee (not under art 6) is payable (Part I(1) of Schedule 3 to the Fees Order).

An application to modify or withdraw a voluntary restriction should be in Form 77 signed by all persons for the time being appearing by the register to be interested in the restriction or their solicitors. The fee for an application to modify a restriction is assessed as above when a fee is payable. No fee is payable for the withdrawal of a restriction.

In general, a voluntary restriction cannot be cancelled as a matter of course when a dealing (even a transfer on sale) made in accordance with its provisions is registered. Therefore, if it is intended that the restriction shall not survive the registration of the dealing, it is advisable that an express withdrawal be obtained.

Compulsory restrictions cannot be modified or withdrawn merely on the application of the parties.

The joint proprietorship restriction (set out on p 89) will be cancelled without application on the registration of a transfer on sale of the whole of the land in accordance with its terms. Attention is invited to the special evidence required, as set out on p 161, for the cancellation of this restriction in certain other circumstances.

4 Inhibitions

Inhibitions are used to prohibit, wholly or partially, the exercise of a proprietor's powers of disposition. In general, restrictions are used for this purpose; and inhibitions, other than bankruptcy inhibitions (see Chapter XVI), are very uncommon. An application for an inhibition (under s 57) may be made (in accordance with r 230) to the court or to the Chief Land Registrar by any person interested in registered land or a registered charge. An application to discharge or cancel such an inhibition must be made to the court if the inhibition was originally entered pursuant to an order of the court; otherwise it must be made to the Chief Land Registrar (r 231).

A special form of inhibition is entered in the register when the incumbent of a benefice is registered as the proprietor of land in his corporate capacity (r 232).

The fee for an application to register or modify an inhibition is £35 for the first title and £20 for each subsequent title affected, but no fee is payable if, in relation to each registered title affected, the application is accompanied by an application affecting that title upon which a scale fee (not under art 6) is payable (Part I(1) of Schedule 3 to the Fees Order). No fee is payable for its withdrawal.

5 Priority notices for first registration

A person entitled to apply for first registration or his solicitor (or, with his consent in writing, any other person or his solicitor) can secure priority for the application by lodging at the appropriate district land registry a priority notice in Form 17 (in duplicate) (r 71). A fee of £35 is payable. The duplicate notice will be returned by way of acknowledgment.

If within fourteen days from the lodgment of the notice, or within such further time as the Chief Land Registrar thinks fit, application for first registration is made in accordance with the notice and accompanied by the duplicate notice, it will be dealt with in priority to any other application affecting the same land which may have been made in the meantime.

On the expiration of the period fixed for its operation, the notice will be cancelled.

6 Protection of non-local land charges, pending land actions, writs and orders, deeds of arrangement

Section 14(1) of the Land Charges Act 1972 provides that that Act shall not apply to instruments or matters required to be registered or re-registered on or after 1 January 1926 if and so far as they affect registered land and can be protected under the Land Registration Act 1925 by lodging or registering a creditor's notice, restriction, caution, inhibition or other notice. The following table indicates how such instruments and matters can be protected under the Land Registration Act 1925 so far as they affect registered land.

Classification in Land Charges Act 1972	*Protection against registered land*
Land Charge—	
class A or B	A notice or caution against dealings may be used; but usually, when the land charge takes effect as a legal charge, its substantive registration will be preferred.
class C(i)	Substantive registration is the main protection. A notice or a caution against dealings may be used.
class C(ii)	A caution against dealings or a restriction may be used.

Classification in Land Charges Act 1972 Land Charge—	Protection against registered land
class C(iii)	If the charge affects the legal estate, a notice is usual. A caution against dealings is an alternative; and it is believed that notices of [intended] deposit are used.
class C(iv)	A notice or a caution against dealings or a restriction may be used.
class D(i)	A notice (see under the sub-heading 'Inheritance tax: capital transfer tax: death duties' in Chapter XIII).
class D(ii)	Usually a notice (see Chapter IV); a caution against dealings may also be used.
class D(iii)	A notice is usual. A caution against dealings may be used.
class E	If the annuity cannot be overridden, a notice is appropriate. Alternatively, a caution against dealings or a restriction may be appropriate.
class F	A notice (see Chapter XV).
class F (renewal)	A notice or a caution against dealings (see Chapter XV).
Pending land action	A caution against dealings is usual. Exceptionally (by order of the court) an inhibition may be used. (As to bankruptcy see Chapter XVI.)
Writ or order affecting land	A caution against dealings is the usual method. (As to bankruptcy see Chapter XVI.)
Deed of arrangement affecting land	Usually the land is transferred to the trustee, who is then registered as proprietor; but a caution against dealings may be used.

7 Local land charges

Rights under local land charges affecting registered land are usually not the subject of any entry in the register of title of the land concerned; and they are then overriding interests (see p 46). They can be (but usually are not) protected by notice on the register of title. If a local land charge affecting registered land is a legal charge or a legal mortgage and is to be realised, it must be registered as a registered charge (s 59(2)).

The need to register local land charges in the registers maintained by local authorities under the Local Land Charges Act 1975 is the same whether the land is registered or not; and the charges operate in the same way against registered and unregistered land.

Searches in the registers of local land charges maintained by local authorities must be made in relation to registered land exactly as though it were unregistered.

Chapter XV

Matrimonial Homes

1 Matrimonial Homes Act 1983

A spouse's rights of occupation under the Matrimonial Homes Act 1983 are not an overriding interest, notwithstanding that the spouse is in actual occupation of the dwelling-house (see para (*g*) on p 47). They constitute a charge on the matrimonial home which, in the case of registered land, can be protected by the registration of a notice (see s 2 of the 1983 Act). Prior to 14 February 1983 such a charge could also be protected by registration of a caution against dealings. No protection under the 1983 Act is necessary when the matrimonial home is held, legally and beneficially, by husband and wife jointly.

The registration of a land charge of Class F in the Land Charges Department will afford no protection in the case of registered land. The protection of a notice (registered land) or a Class F land charge registration in the Land Charges Department (unregistered land) is only available in respect of one dwelling-house at any one time (see under the heading 'Change of matrimonial home' (below)).

In this chapter the husband is treated as the owner of the matrimonial home and the wife as the spouse whose rights are in need of protection. However, the text will apply equally when the roles are reversed.

2 Is the matrimonial home registered?

If it is not known whether the land is registered, an application for an official search of the public index map should be made on Form 96 (see 23–6). A fee under Part II(9) of Schedule 3 to the Fees Order is payable. The top of the form should be endorsed 'This search is being made solely for the purposes of the Matrimonial Homes Act 1983. Please reveal details of any registered lease.'

Provided the form is so endorsed even if no plan of the property is available, where one would normally be required, the Registry will do its best to identify the property and will not raise any point which might otherwise arise as to the precise boundaries of the property, provided that the applicant makes it clear that the search is required for the purposes of the 1983 Act. The certificate of the result of the search will reveal what interests (if any) in the land are registered including particulars of any registered lease. If any doubt remains as to whether or not the registered estate is that owned by the husband an office copy of the register can be obtained by lodging Form 109 with a fee of £7 under Part II(3)(*a*) of Schedule 3.

3 Application for notice

The application should be made to the appropriate district land registry in Form 99 which was prescribed by the Land Registration (Matrimonial Homes) Rules 1990. The land certificate is not required. If the court has made an order by virtue of s 2(4) of the 1983 Act (see below) an official copy of the order (which will be referred to on the register and retained in the Registry) should accompany the application. No fee is payable.

It is the Registry's practice not to serve notice on a husband of an application for the registration of a notice or for the renewal of registration of a notice or caution to protect his wife's rights of occupation. Notice will however be served on the proprietor of any charge which secures further advances (see pp 116 and 178) and the husband may learn of the application from such a proprietor.

4 Rights continued by order of court

A wife's rights of occupation will only continue so long as the marriage subsists, but the court may direct otherwise by an order under s 1 of the 1983 Act during the subsistence of the marriage (see s 2(4) of the 1983 Act). If the court makes an order directing that the wife's rights of occupation shall not be brought to an end by the termination of the marriage, and those rights have not already been protected on the register of title, an application for a notice should be made, as indicated above, as soon as possible (see s 5(3)(*b*) of the 1983 Act). If the court makes such an order, and the wife's rights of occupation have already been protected on the register of title, an application for renewal of the registration of the notice or caution should be made as soon as possible (see below).

5 Renewal of registration of a notice or caution

If by virtue of s 2(4) of the 1983 Act the court makes an order directing that the wife's rights of occupation shall not be brought to an end by the termination of the marriage, and those rights have already been protected on the register by a notice or, prior to 14 February 1983, by caution, an application should be made as soon as possible to renew the earlier protection (see s 5(3)(*a*) of the 1983 Act) so that the making of the order can be recorded on the register. The application should be made to the appropriate district land registry in Form 100 (also prescribed by the Land Registration (Matrimonial Homes) Rules 1990) and must be accompanied by an official copy of the court order, which will be retained in the Registry. Even if the earlier protection was by way of a notice, the land certificate need not be produced. The renewal will be effected on the register by the entry of a further notice or caution (referring to the order), as appropriate. It will not affect the priority of the wife's charge (s 5(5) of the 1983 Act). No fee is payable.

6 Change of matrimonial home

A wife may have protection in relation to only one dwellinghouse at any one time, whether the protection be the registration of a notice or caution in respect of registered land or a registration in the register of land charges of Class F at the Land Charges Department. Accordingly, any earlier subsisting registration must be disclosed on Form 99, and will be cancelled when the new registration is effected (see s 3 of the 1983 Act).

7 Charges to secure further advances

The registration of a notice or the renewal of registration of a notice or caution to protect a wife's rights of occupation under the 1983 Act is regarded as an entry that would prejudice the priority of a further advance for the purposes of s 30(1) of the Land Registration Act 1925 and as a subsequent registered charge for the purposes of s 30(3) of the latter Act. Accordingly, notice of the registration or renewal of registration of a notice or caution under the 1983 Act will be sent to the proprietor of any registered charge that secures further advances. As previously stated, notice will not be served on the registered proprietor of the land.

8 Cancellation of notice

Form 202 may be used for an application to cancel the registration or renewal of registration of a notice of a wife's rights of occupation under the 1983 Act. The application may also be made by letter. There should be produced:
  (1) the death certificate or other sufficient evidence of death of either spouse (but see (5) below); or
  (2) an official copy of a decree absolute of divorce or nullity; if a decree of divorce by an overseas court is lodged, additional evidence (eg, as to residence, domicile or nationality) may be required; and if the decree is not in English, a notarially certified translation should be provided (but see (5) below); or
  (3) an order of the court terminating the wife's rights of occupation; or
  (4) a written release of her rights by the wife; and
  (5) where the supporting evidence is evidence of the husband's death or a copy of a decree absolute produced in accordance with (1) or (2) above and:
      (*a*) by virtue of s 2(4) of the 1983 Act, the court has made an order directing that the wife's rights of occupation shall not be brought to an end by the termination of the marriage, and
      (*b*) that order is referred to on the register, satisfactory evidence that the order has ceased to have effect. (See ss 5(1), (2) and 6(1) of the 1983 Act.)

No fee is payable.

9 Cancellation of caution

An application to cancel the registration or renewal of registration of a caution protecting a wife's rights of occupation under the 1983 Act may be made in one of the following ways:
  (1) by a letter supported by (i) evidence as at (1), (2) or (3) of **8** above, and (ii) evidence as at (5) of that paragraph if such evidence would be necessary for the cancellation of the registration of a notice of the wife's rights of occupation;

(2) by withdrawal of the caution on Form 71 signed by the wife or by her solicitors;
(3) by letter, to 'warn off' the caution in accordance with r 218 of the Land Registration Rules 1925. But, in view of r 5 of the Land Registration (Matrimonial Homes) Rules 1990, no effect can be given to an application to warn off the caution(s) unless it is accompanied by either:
   (*a*) a release in writing of the rights of occupation protected by the caution, signed by the wife; or
   (*b*) a statutory declaration by the husband or by some responsible person conversant with the facts that, as to the whole or any part of the land to which the caution relates, no charge under s 2 of the 1983 Act or s 2 of the Matrimonial Homes Act 1967 has ever arisen or, if such a charge has arisen, it is no longer subsisting. The declaration should set out briefly the facts on which the declarant relies.

No fee is payable.

10 Rights of occupation of a bankrupt's spouse

A wife cannot acquire rights of occupation in the period between the presentation of a bankruptcy petition and the vesting of the bankrupt's property in a trustee (Insolvency Act 1986, s 336(1)). Any rights of occupation existing prior to the bankruptcy petition continue to subsist notwithstanding the bankruptcy (s 336(2)).

The trustee in bankruptcy may apply to the bankruptcy court at any time for an order to restrict or terminate the wife's rights. In making an order the court must have regard to all the circumstances of the case except the needs of the bankrupt. Where such an application is made one year after the date on which the bankrupt's property vested in a trustee, the court has to assume that the interests of the creditors are paramount unless there are exceptional circumstances (s 336(4) and (5)). An office copy should accompany any application based on such an order.

11 Rights of occupation of a bankrupt

Whether or not his spouse has rights of occupation, a bankrupt who:
   (*a*) is entitled to occupy a dwelling-house by virtue of a beneficial estate or interest;

(b) at some time occupied that dwelling-house with children under 18; and
(c) provided a home for those children under 18 at the time of the bankruptcy petition and at the time of the bankruptcy order;

has rights of occupation against his trustee in bankruptcy under the Matrimonial Homes Act 1983. If he is in occupation he has a right not to be evicted or excluded without leave of the bankruptcy court. If he is not in occupation he has a right, with leave of the bankruptcy court, to enter into occupation (Insolvency Act 1986, s 337).

The bankrupt's rights are a charge which has the same priority as an equitable interest created immediately before the commencement of the bankruptcy (s 337(2)(b)). Where a bankrupt has such rights, he may protect them by entry of notice under s 2(a) of the 1983 Act and he may enter such notice notwithstanding the fact that he is the registered proprietor. In his application he should state that he is applying pursuant to the provisions of the Insolvency Act 1986 and that the property is vested in his trustee in bankruptcy.

To restrict or terminate these rights, the trustee in bankruptcy must apply to the bankruptcy court which must have regard to the matters mentioned in 'Rights of occupation of a bankrupt's spouse', above (s 337(4), (5) and (6)). An office copy should accompany any application based on such an order.

12 Search by mortgagees

A mortgagee of a dwelling-house who brings an action to enforce his security is obliged, under s 8(3) of the 1983 Act, to serve notice of the action on a spouse whose rights of occupation are protected at the relevant time by notice or caution. The proprietor of a registered charge or mortgagee of registered land may apply to the appropriate district land registry on Form 106 (also prescribed by the Land Registration (Matrimonial Homes) Rules 1990) for an official certificate of the result of a search which will reveal if there is a notice or caution registered. The search will confer priority for a period of fifteen days. No fee is payable.

Chapter XVI

Insolvency

1 Bankruptcy

(a) Entry of creditors' notice and/or bankruptcy inhibition

Whenever a bankruptcy petition is presented, the officials of the court inform the Land Charges Department, and the petition is then registered in the register of pending actions kept at that Department. Details of the registration are passed from the Land Charges Department to district land registries, whose officials then enter a creditors' notice against the title of any proprietor of any registered land or charge which appears to be affected. Where it appears that the title of the proprietor of land is affected, the creditors' notice is entered in the proprietorship register as follows:

'Creditors' Notice in respect of a petition in bankruptcy presented in the   Court (Court reference No   /   ) protecting the rights of all creditors. (Land Charges Ref No PA   /   )'

Where it appears that the title of the proprietor of a registered charge is affected, the creditors' notice, in a corresponding form, is entered in the charges register.

When a bankruptcy order has been registered in the register of writs and orders affecting land kept at the Land Charges Department, details are passed to district land registries, and a bankruptcy inhibition is entered against the title of any proprietor of any registered land or charge which appears to be affected. Where it appears that the title of the proprietor of land is affected, the bankruptcy inhibition is entered in the proprietorship register as follows:

'Bankruptcy Inhibition in pursuance of a bankruptcy order made by the   Court (Court reference No   /   ). No disposition by the proprietor of the land or transmission is to be registered until a trustee in bankruptcy is registered. (Land Charges Ref No WO /)'

Where it appears that the title of the proprietor of a registered charge is affected, the bankruptcy inhibition, in a corresponding form, is entered in the charges register.

If any doubt arises as to the identity of the debtor or the bankrupt, the Registrar will make such inquiries and serve such notices as he considers necessary before deciding whether to enter a creditors' notice or bankruptcy inhibition (r 181 as substituted by the Land Registration (Companies and Insolvency) Rules 1986). In this context it is particularly important that all registered proprietors keep their address for service (see p 32) up to date.

A creditors' notice does not prevent the registered proprietor from dealing with his land or charge, but any dealing by him which is registered during the subsistence of the notice will take effect subject to the rights of the creditors protected by the notice, unless the dealing is protected by an official search of the register which gives it priority over the creditors' rights.

The entry of a bankruptcy inhibition will not prejudice dealings with or in right of interests or charges having priority over the estate or charge of the debtor. Thus the proprietor of a charge that was registered before the bankruptcy entries were made is usually in a position to sell the land.

Neither a creditors' notice nor a bankruptcy inhibition will be entered in relation to one of two or more joint proprietors. If the debtor has a beneficial interest in the land, his creditors may have the protection of the joint proprietorship restriction set out on p 89; and as to protection by a caution see s 61(10) and p 167.

(b) Registration of the official receiver or trustee in bankruptcy

All the property, including registered property, vested in the bankrupt beneficially at the date of the bankruptcy order automatically vests either in the trustee in bankruptcy when his appointment takes effect or in the official receiver on his becoming trustee (Insolvency Act 1986, s 306).

The official receiver can be registered as proprietor in place of the bankrupt on production of:

(i) an office copy or certified copy of the bankruptcy order; and

(ii) a certificate by the official receiver that the land or charge is comprised in the bankrupt's estate (r 174 as substituted by the Land Registration (Companies and Insolvency) Rules 1986).

The trustee in bankruptcy can be registered as proprietor in place of the bankrupt on production of the evidence required in the case of the official receiver specified at (i) and (ii) above (but in the case of the certificate at (ii) signed by the trustee) and either

  (a) a copy of his certificate of appointment as trustee by the meeting of the bankrupt's creditors duly certified by the trustee or his solicitor as a true copy of the original; or
  (b) a copy of his certificate of appointment as trustee by the Secretary of State; or
  (c) an office copy of the order of the court of his appointment as trustee (r 176 as substituted).

The land or charge certificate of the debtor's registered estate or interest must be lodged, and the application should be under cover of form A4. A fee under Scale A on the value of the land or charge reduced to one fifth under Abatement 2 is payable.

On the registration of the official receiver or the trustee in bankruptcy as the proprietor of the bankrupt's registered estate or interest, the creditors' notice and the bankruptcy inhibition will be cancelled.

(c) Transfer by the official receiver or trustee in bankruptcy

If the official receiver or trustee wishes to transfer the registered estate or interest without himself being registered as proprietor, the transfer must be lodged for registration accompanied by the evidence required for registration of the official receiver or trustee, as the case may be, mentioned at *(b)* above. The creditors' notice and bankruptcy inhibition are cancelled when the transfer is registered.

(d) Cancellation of the creditor's notice or bankruptcy inhibition

A creditors' notice will usually be cancelled on the production of an office copy of an order of the court authorising the cancellation of the registration of the bankruptcy petition as a pending action in the Land Charges Department; and a bankruptcy inhibition will usually be cancelled on the production of an office copy of an order of the court authorising the cancellation of the registration of the bankruptcy order in the register of writs and orders affecting land at the Land Charges Department. Authority to cancel these registrations at the Land Charges Department may be found in an order dismissing a petition or rescinding or annulling a bankruptcy order. However, if an order of the court authorises the cancellation of the registration of the bankruptcy order in the register of writs and orders affecting land but does not authorise the cancellation of the registration of the petition as a pending action, the creditors' notice will not be cancelled. In the case of a creditors' notice, if for some good reason an office copy of the relevant court order cannot be produced, a certificate of cancellation of the relevant entry in the register kept at the Land Charges Department (Form K20) will usually be accepted instead. Neither an automatic discharge under the provisions of s 279 of the Insolvency Act 1986 nor an order for discharge under s 280 of the said Act operates to revest the bankrupt's property. Production of evidence of discharge is not, therefore, sufficient to enable a creditors' notice or bankruptcy inhibition to be cancelled.

No fee is payable for the cancellation of a creditors' notice or a bankruptcy inhibition. The application for cancellation may be made under cover of a Form A4.

(e) Charge on bankrupt's home

Where a dwelling-house occupied by a bankrupt or his spouse or former spouse forms part of the bankrupt's estate and the trustee is unable to realise it, he can apply to the court for a charging order on the property. Any such order shall provide for the property to revest in the bankrupt subject to the charge (Insolvency Act 1986, s 313). Where such an order is made, an office copy or certified copy should be lodged so that the creditor's notice and/or bankruptcy inhibition can be cancelled, any other entry necessary to reflect the vesting provisions can be made and the charging order can be noted (see p 164 for entry of notice). Where there are joint proprietors a caution against dealings (see p 167) will be the appropriate method of protection.

(f) Rights of occupation of a bankrupt and of a bankrupt's spouse

The effect of bankruptcy on a spouse's statutory rights of occupation under the Matrimonial Homes Act 1983 and the rights of occupation of a bankrupt who has occupied a dwelling-house with a person under 18 are considered in Chapter XV.

2 Liquidation

The liquidator of a company may have notice of his appointment entered on the register, but the company will remain the registered proprietor. The application may be made by letter accompanied by evidence of the liquidation as follows:

(1) If the winding-up is compulsory:
EITHER:
- (*a*) a copy of the winding-up order by the court, certified by the liquidator or his solicitor as a true copy; and
- (*b*) either (i) a copy of the resolution passed at the creditors' meeting appointing a liquidator, certified as a true copy by him or his solicitor or (ii) a certificate by the liquidator (appointed at the contributories' meeting) or his solicitor that the meeting of the creditors was duly held at which either the appointment of the liquidator by the contributories' meeting was confirmed or no resolution nominating a liquidator was passed;

OR:
a copy of the order of the court appointing the liquidator; this copy should be certified by the liquidator or his solicitor as being a true copy;

OR:
a copy of the appointment by the Secretary of State of the liquidator; this copy should be certified by the liquidator or his solicitor as being a true copy;

OR:
where the official receiver is liquidator a copy of the winding-up order by the court; this copy should be certified by the official receiver or his solicitor as being a true copy.

(2) If the winding-up is a members' voluntary winding-up:
a certificate by the secretary or solicitor of the company or by the liquidator or his solicitor that a statutory declaration of solvency complying with the requirements of s 89 of the Insolvency Act 1986 has been filed with the Registrar of Companies together with a copy of the resolution appointing the liquidator, certified as a true copy by the secretary or solicitor of the company or by the liquidator or his solicitor.

(3) If the winding-up is a creditors' voluntary winding-up:
- (*a*) a copy of the resolution passed at the company's meeting

that the company be wound up, and appointing a liquidator. The copy resolution must be certified as a true copy either by the secretary or solicitor of the company or by the liquidator or his solicitor; and
(b) either:
   (i) a copy of a resolution passed at the creditors' meeting appointing a liquidator, certified as a true copy by him or his solicitor;
   or:
   (ii) a certificate by the liquidator (appointed at the company's meeting) or his solicitor that the meeting of the creditors was duly held at which either the appointment of the liquidator by the company's meeting was confirmed or no resolution nominating a liquidator was passed.

The land certificate if outstanding (ie, if there is no registered charge) or, if the company is the proprietor of a charge, the charge certificate, should be lodged. The fee is £35 for the first title and £20 for each subsequent title affected, but no fee is payable if, in relation to each registered title affected, the application is accompanied by an application affecting that title upon which a scale fee (not under art 6) is payable (Part I(1) of Schedule 3 to the Fees Order).

When notice of the appointment is entered in the register, a restriction, designed according to the facts of the particular liquidation to ensure that no disposition is registered if it is not within the liquidator's powers, will be entered.

If a transfer by a company in liquidation is lodged for registration and notice of the appointment has not previously been entered, evidence as at (1), (2) or (3) above will be required.

3 Administration orders

Where an administration order is made under the provisions of s 8 of the Insolvency Act 1986, the property of the company remains vested in the company but the administrator may have notice of the order entered on the register. Application should be by letter accompanied by an office copy of the administration order and a fee of £30 per title. There is a maximum fee of £600 on any one application, but no fee is payable if, in relation to each registered title affected, the application accompanies an application affecting that title upon which a scale fee is payable (Part I(1) of Schedule 3).

On a disposal by the administrator, the application should be accompanied by an office copy of the administration order. If the administrator disposes of a property free from a floating charge, the application should also be accompanied by a certificate from the administrator that the property has been transferred free from the floating charge pursuant to s 15 of the Insolvency Act 1986. If the disposal is made free from a fixed charge, an office copy of the court order authorising the disposal as if the property were not subject to the charge in question (Insolvency Act 1986, s 15(2)) should be lodged with the application.

Where a company subject to an administration order acquires land, the following entry will be made in the charges register:

'The land is subject to such security or securities as may exist and affect the same by virtue of the provisions of the Insolvency Act 1986, s 15(4).'

This entry will be cancelled on production of a certificate from the administrator that there are no such securities affecting the land or, on a transfer, that such securities have been discharged.

4 Company receivership

Although the court has power to appoint a receiver of a company ('a receiver') it is a power which is rarely exercised and it is not considered here. The Law of Property Act 1925 authorises the holder of a mortgage over a company's property to appoint a receiver in specified circumstances whether the mortgage contains such a power or not. These statutory powers will usually be extended by express provisions in a debenture and this section deals with the points which the Registry will need to consider in registering a disposition by a receiver appointed under a debenture. Throughout this section the word 'debenture' is used to mean the mortgage or charge, whether legal or equitable, by a company under which the receiver has been appointed.

The Insolvency Act 1986, ss 28 to 49, contains provisions which regulate the appointment and conduct of receivers generally and also designates certain receivers 'administrative receivers' with statutory powers and duties. An 'administrative receiver' is either the receiver of the whole (or substantially the whole) of a company's property appointed under a floating charge, or under such a charge and one or more other securities, or a person who would have been such a receiver but for the appointment of some other person as receiver of part of the company's property (s 29(2) of the 1986 Act). Unless otherwise stated the Registry's requirements in relation to receivers set out in this section apply equally to administrative receivers. The statutory powers of an administrative receiver are covered in Section 5 below.

(a) The debenture under which the receiver is appointed

Every application based on a disposition by a receiver should be accompanied by the original or a marked abstract or certified copy of the debenture unless it is already registered or noted against an identified registered title. The debenture must be valid and enforceable. In particular it must be duly executed and registered at the Companies Registry under s 395 of the Companies Act 1985.

(b) The appointment of the receiver

The statutory power of appointing a receiver will normally be extended by the debenture. The appointment of a receiver does not have the effect of vesting the company's property in the receiver and no note of such an appointment may be entered on the register. Evidence that the power of appointment has arisen should be lodged. A marked abstract or certified copy of the instrument of appointment should also accompany the application. Unless the debenture provides otherwise the appointment may be under hand (s 109(1) of the Law of Property Act 1925). An appointment dated prior to 19 March 1985 was required to be stamped 50p, and the stamping should be shown on the abstract or certified copy.

(c) Powers of the receiver

Whatever the nature of the transaction it must be clearly established that the receiver has power to carry it out. Unless he is an administrative receiver (see **5** below) his statutory powers are very limited (see s 109 of the Law of Property Act 1925) but they will usually be extended by the debenture. If the receiver, other than an administrative receiver, is to dispose of property then he must be given an express power to do so by the debenture. A non-administrative receiver's leasing powers, which must be given to him expressly by the debenture or be delegated to him by the chargee, give rise to complex questions which will require careful consideration if met in practice. As to execution of deeds in receivership cases see (*e*) and **5** below.

In exercising his powers the receiver will normally be acting as agent of the mortgagor and not as agent of the mortgagee. This is expressly provided in relation to the statutory powers by s 109(2) of the Law of Property Act 1925 and s 44 of the Insolvency Act 1986 and it is standard practice for a debenture to contain a statement to this effect. The receiver will not, therefore, be exercising the mortgagee's powers, and will not be in a position to release the land from the debenture. It follows that a person dealing with a receiver should obtain an express release both from the debenture and from any prior or subsequent mortgages and charges.

(d) Effect of liquidation on receiver's powers

The provisions of ss 238 to 241 and 244 and 245 of the Insolvency Act 1986 in relation to transactions at an undervalue, preferences, extortionate credit transactions and the avoidance of certain floating charges may have the effect of invalidating the debenture wholly or in part.

In appropriate cases the Registry may require evidence that the purchaser had no express notice of any pending court proceedings for the making of an administration order or for the winding-up of the company (see s 5(7) of the Land Charges Act 1972).

On the commencement of the winding-up the receiver ceases to be agent of the mortgagor but continues to have powers to act for the purposes of holding and disposing of the property comprised in the debenture including power to use the company name for that purpose (see *Sowman v David Samuel Trust Ltd* [1978]1 WLR 22; [1978] 1 All ER 616 and the authorities therein mentioned). In a winding-up by the court any disposition of the company's property made after the commencement of the winding-up is void under s 127 of the Insolvency Act 1986 unless sanctioned by an order of the court. However, where a debenture has been created prior to the winding-up, the disposition for the purposes of s 127 is the debenture, and any subsequent disposition by the debenture-holder or his receiver under powers contained in the debenture does not require an order of the court.

As to the effect of liquidation on a power of attorney given to the receiver in the debenture see below.

In appropriate cases, the Registry will serve notice of an application, based on a disposition by a receiver, on the liquidator to enable him to consider whether he accepts its validity. Applicants should therefore include details of the name and address of the liquidator in all cases where it is known that the company is being wound up.

(e) Execution of deeds in receivership cases

In all cases it appears that the receiver should personally execute the deed so as to signify that the transaction is being carried out with his authority. The deed must also be executed by or on behalf of the company and this can be done in a number of ways:

(1) By affixing the company's seal in the presence of its duly authorised officers, if available, or in the presence of the liquidator where the company is being wound up (ss 165–167 of and Sched 4, Pt III, para 7 to the Insolvency Act 1986). Unlike a liquidator, other than an administrative receiver (see **5** below), a receiver is not authorised to affix the company's seal (although it does seem theoretically possible for him to be authorised to do so by the company's articles of association).

(2) By the chargee or by the receiver as attorney for the company where so appointed by the debenture. It is usual for a debenture to appoint both the chargee and any receiver or receivers appointed by him as attorney for the company. A power of attorney must be granted by an instrument under seal (s 1 of the Powers of Attorney Act 1971). It follows that if a chargee or receiver derives his appointment as attorney from a debenture that debenture must be by deed. Since the appointment as attorney derives from the debenture, which is an instrument under seal, the fact that the instrument of appointment of the receiver by the chargee is under hand is immaterial. Where the chargee is so appointed his appointment will be a security power (see s 4(1) of the Powers of Attorney Act 1971) and will not be revoked by liquidation. However, it has been held in *Barrows v Chief Land Registrar* (reported in *The Times* on 20 October 1977) that a power of attorney given to a receiver by a company under a debenture is not a security power as it does not secure a proprietary interest of the donee or the performance of an obligation owing to him. A power of attorney given to a receiver in these circumstances would

cease on the commencement of the liquidation of the company.

If, therefore, it is sought to rely upon an instrument executed by a receiver as attorney, the application should in all cases be supported either by a statutory declaration by the applicant (or in the case of a company applicant by its director or secretary) or by a certificate by the applicant's solicitor that at the time of completion of the transaction the declarant did not know of the revocation of the power and did not know of the occurrence of any event, such as the winding-up of the donor company, which had the effect of revoking the power (r 82(6) as substituted by the Land Registration (Powers of Attorney) Rules 1986).

The form of execution pursuant to a power of attorney is provided by s 74(2)–(6) of the Law of Property Act 1925 and s 7 of the Powers of Attorney Act 1971 and is discussed in Chapter VI under **9** 'Execution by attorney'.

(3) In the case of *Barrows v Chief Land Registrar* (see (2) above) it was held that, notwithstanding the revocation of a power of attorney given in a debenture to a receiver by reason of the winding-up of the donor company, a power given to him in the same instrument to sell, convey, etc, in the name and on behalf of the company should be treated as a power in the nature of a contractual right which would survive liquidation. Such a power would have to be clearly stated in the debenture and would only be exercisable in relation to those of the receiver's powers for which it was expressly granted. The execution in such a case should clearly show that the receiver is acting in the name and on behalf of the company under powers expressly given to him for that purpose in the debenture. A suggested form of execution where the receiver is relying on his contractual powers is as follows:

```
SIGNED AS A DEED                  )
BY A LIMITED [in                  )
liquidation] by BC its receiver   )
pursuant to powers granted to him by ) A Limited
clause      of a debenture dated  ) by its receiver  (LS)
in favour of D Bank Limited in the )    BC
presence of:                      )
```

It would seem in a purchaser's interest to insist, wherever possible, upon the receiver executing a deed under a power of attorney rather than under a contractual power so as to obtain the protection of s 5 of the Powers of Attorney Act 1971.

5 Administrative receivers

Certain receivers, as defined on p 188, are designated by the Insolvency Act 1986 as administrative receivers. Unless otherwise indicated, all the requirements set out in **4** above in relation to receivers generally will apply also to administrative receivers.

The powers conferred on an administrative receiver by the debenture(s) under which he is appointed are deemed to include the statutory powers set out in Schedule 1 to the 1986 Act unless the statutory powers are inconsistent with any of the provisions of the debenture(s). The statutory powers include powers to sell, to use the company's seal, to execute in the name and on behalf of the company and to grant and accept the surrender of and to take a lease. Under s 42 of the Insolvency Act 1986, a person dealing with an administrative receiver in good faith and for value is not concerned to inquire whether the receiver is acting within his powers.

Under s 43 of the 1986 Act, the court may authorise a disposition by an administrative receiver free from a charge having priority to the charge under which the administrative receiver has been appointed. Any application based on a disposition so authorised should be supported by an office copy of the court order.

6 Inspection of the register on insolvency

In addition to their general right to inspect the register (see p 55), trustees in bankruptcy, liquidators and receivers have a right to inspect and make copies of:

(*a*) all documents which the registrar has in his custody, and

(*b*) the result of a search in the index of proprietors' names.

For (*a*) a fee of £14 per document is payable under Part II(4) of Schedule 3 to the Fees Order and for (*b*) a fee of £14 per name is payable under Part II(1) of Schedule 3.

Practice leaflet No 19 (see p 16) is available as a guide to those entitled to make such an inspection.

Chapter XVII

Building Estates

The Registry's Practice Leaflet No 7 is a general guide for solicitors acting for developers of building estates. Developers are encouraged to bring this leaflet to the attention of buyers. Any reasonable quantity is available free of charge from any office of the Registry. The leaflet indicates that the Registry is always willing to consider special circumstances relating to any particular estate and to suggest how the registration machinery may be utilised to the best advantage by developers. Practice Leaflet No 14, which is issued in conjunction with Practice Leaflet No 7, is a general guide for those involved in the surveying, setting out and preparation of layout plans of registered building estates.

The advice given below relates equally to developments by way of transfers on sale and to those by way of long leases. Where appropriate, therefore, a 'transfer' includes 'lease' and 'vendor' and 'purchaser' have corresponding meanings. 'Estate layout plan' includes a plan showing flat or maisonette development.

(a) Estate layout plans

As early as possible before the first transfer of part is likely to be lodged for registration, the developer's solicitor should send to the appropriate district land registry two copies of the estate layout plan for approval of its use in connection with official searches of the register and official certificates of inspection of the filed plan (see below). The plan must show sufficient detail to enable it to be accurately related to the filed plan of the developer's title; it must be drawn to a suitable scale, usually 1/500; its true scale and orientation must be shown and it must clearly and precisely define each plot or property and identify it by a plot number or other reference. Plans marked 'For identification only' or with some similar phrase are not acceptable. Where a property comprises more than one parcel (eg, a house and separate garage) each parcel must be distinguished on the estate layout plan by means of a separate number. If two or more floors of a purpose-built block of flats are coextensive, and the layout of the flats on each floor is identical, it is usually sufficient to lodge the plan of a single floor, but this plan must show the reference numbers distinguishing each flat on each floor. The Registry is always willing to advise as to the plan to be used for any particular estate.

When approved, one copy of the plan will be retained in the Registry. The other, marked as officially approved, will be returned to the developer's solicitor. The advantages of this approved plan are that:

(1) negotiations for the sale of individual plots can proceed without an office copy of the filed plan (see 'Verifications and searches by purchasers', below); and
(2) applications for official searches of the register and for official certificates of inspection of the filed plan may describe the land being purchased by reference to the plot number(s) on the approved plan, so avoiding the need to provide separate plans (see 'Verifications and searches by purchasers', below).

Much trouble can be avoided if, before contract, builders and surveyors check the position of fences against the approved plan. Solicitors should ask the developers to notify them immediately of any change in the layout of the estate and should return the duplicate approved plan to the Registry with a new plan (in duplicate) showing the changes. Failure to do this will probably lead to the withdrawal of approval of the obsolete part of the plan and to the cancellation of application for searches and for the registration of transfers based on the obsolete part.

The Registry should be told of the progress of the development periodically so that new surveys can be made.

(b) Surveys

Land Registry plans are based on the Ordnance Survey Map and in the case of building estates are normally drawn to a scale of 1/1250. Surveys of developing estates are made at frequent intervals and the Registry's plans are then revised to show all new buildings, fences, roads and other physical features. The registration of transfers is facilitated if the Registry is notified, when the layout plan is lodged for approval, of the areas in which new roads are being laid out and development is proceeding. The Registry should again be notified when more roads are being constructed and fences or other boundary structures are being erected.

(c) Metrication

See p 23. The Registry hopes that solicitors acting for developers will encourage their clients to use the metric system.

(d) Sales off in plots—certificate deposited at Registry

On large developing estates, the land or charge certificate usually has to be deposited at the appropriate district land registry for a long period, and to save mistakes the Registry recommends the developer to apply at the outset for an office copy of the filed plan so that he can mark off the plots as the sales take place. If the developer does this, it is unlikely that he will need to ask for the return of the land or charge certificate, made up-to-date, during the development. The return of the certificate would be likely to delay the registration of transfers of part; and a developer who contemplates asking for its return because he is concerned to avoid mistakes has the assurance that in practice any mistaken removal of land from his title, whether the result of a transfer, a release from a charge or a mistake by the Registry, is likely to be discovered quickly either through the operation of the official search system or as a result of the delivery for registration of a transfer of the land mistakenly removed.

The Registry also recommends that when a developer requires office copies of the register or certificates of inspection of the filed plan he should apply for them in batches as the development proceeds. This will avoid the disadvantages of using out-of-date office copies or certificates of inspection in the later stages of the development.

(e) Verifications and searches by purchasers

A developer can apply for office copies of the register to hand over to purchasers, or purchasers can apply for themselves. The fees payable for office copies are set out in Chapter V. Under s 113, office copies are admissible in evidence in all matters and between all parties to the same extent as the originals. Some aspects of the office copy procedure peculiar to developing leasehold building estates are dealt with in Registered Land Practice Note No B4 (see p 16 as to this book). Office copies issued on developing estates, particularly leasehold estates, are frequently backdated. This is because an office copy must be dated prior to the earliest application pending against the title. Problems should not arise as the result of an official search of part made by reference to the office copies guarantees that the plot in question remains within the title and provides details of any adverse entries made or to be made since the date of the office copies.

Where the estate layout plan has been officially approved by the Registry and the purchaser is satisfied that his plot is or will be fenced in accordance with it, it only remains for him to satisfy himself of two things. Initially he wishes to know that his plot is in the developer's title and whether any references on the filed plan affect it; and, just before completion, he wants to know that the plot is still in the title and that no adverse entry affecting it has been made in the register since the date of issue of the office copy of the register. These details are obtained as follows:

Proof that a plot being purchased is in the vendor's title— Application should be made in Form 109 to the appropriate district land registry for a certificate of official inspection of the filed plan in Form 102 (see also p 58). A fee of £7 is payable under Part II(8) of Schedule 3 to the Fees Order.

An adequate description of the property being purchased must be given in the application. This may be by reference to the plot number on the approved estate layout plan and the name of the road (or the number of the road if it has not yet been named). In the case of a property which comprises more than one parcel all relevant plot numbers must be quoted. If there is no approved estate layout plan or if there is but the applicant does not wish to rely on it, the application must be accompanied by a plan (in duplicate) of a kind that would be appropriate to an application for an official search in Form 94B (see p 60).

If the application is in order, the certificate in Form 102 will be issued without delay. It will certify that the property is in the title and whether or not it is affected by any colour or other reference shown on the filed plan and referred to in the entries in the register. The certificate's accuracy is guaranteed, but it confers no priority.

If he has this certificate, a purchaser does not need to inspect an office copy of the filed plan of the developer's title because he is given the information that he would obtain by such an inspection.

The use of certificates of official inspection of filed plans is designed to save the delay and expense of numerous applications for office copies of the filed plans of registered developing building estates.

If a draft transfer is approved for use for the estate (see (h) below) the Registry will supply a letter to the developer confirming that if easements are granted in the approved form they will be entered as appurtenant to the purchaser's title. This avoids the need to inspect the filed plan to ensure than the developer has power to grant the easements proposed. Alternatively it may be possible to arrange with the Registry to confirm on the Form 102 that a particular road, for example, over which rights of way are to be granted is within the developer's title.

Ascertaining whether any adverse entry has been made in the register affecting the plot since the date of issue of the office copy—This is done by applying for an official search of the register in Form 94B (see Chapter V).

Sometimes a plot is served by an approach road or by other easements to be granted over land owned by the same developer but in another registered title. In such a case, one Form 94B may be used for a search against both titles. The printed wording must be appropriately modified; and, in particular, if the office copies of the two registers were issued on different dates, both dates must be shown on the Form 94B.

It is unnecessary, however, to refer on the Form 94B to interests and rights to be transferred or granted over land in the same title as the corporeal land that is being transferred, because the priority under the certificate of search will extend to those interests and rights.

(f) Instrument plans

Each transfer must be accompanicd by a plan of the property concerned. Mere reference to plot numbers on the estate layout plan in a transfer of part or similar instrument is not sufficient. Transfer plans may be drawn to any suitable scale. The scales most commonly used range between 1/500 and 1/1250 but the true scale and orientation must be shown. It is recommended that an extract from the approved estate layout plan is used for thc transfer plan, but if this is not done the transfer plan should show not only the land being dealt with but also sufficient adjacent details to enable its position to be ascertained on the vendor's filed plan. These details should include figured dimensions tying the position of the land to the nearest road, corner or other physical feature and also the dimensions of the land itself. A plan for 'identification only' is unacceptable. In the case of a flat or maisonette, the transfer must identify the precise position and extent of the parcel(s) that make up the premises in the building and the floor(s) on which they are situated. Care should be taken to ensure that 'T' marks and other plan references mentioned in the body of the transfer appear on the transfer plan.

To comply with rr 79 and 113, the transfer plan must be signed by the developer and by the purchaser or the purchaser's solicitor on his behalf. If the developer is a company or corporation the plan should be executed in the same way as the transfer.

The above remarks apply, mutatis mutandis, to the plans in leases of part.

(g) Discharges

The discharge of a plot from a registered charge of the developer's title should be in Form 53. It should be accompanied by a plan of the land discharged; and the preceding remarks about transfer plans apply mutatis mutandis to discharge plans. Form 53 is not appropriate for the discharge of a noted charge. Ordinary conveyancing evidence of any devolution of the title to the charge and of its discharge as to the plot concerned is required.

When a standard form of transfer, previously approved by the Registry, is being used, the discharge need not refer to easements of the usual kinds granted by the transfer. But if the easements granted are peculiar to the particular plot, the discharge should specifically refer to them.

(h) Draft transfers

A draft of the proposed form of transfer or lease (with plan) for general use may be sent to the appropriate district land registry for approval. This will often help to avoid difficulties in connection with easements and the development generally. The draft and plan must be lodged in duplicate. No fee will be charged for the consideration and approval of the draft.

(i) Absolute leasehold title

When a developer registered with absolute title grants leases of part, lessees' solicitors are advised to apply for registration of their clients' leases with absolute leasehold title.

Chapter XVIII

Lost or Destroyed Deeds and Certificates

1 Lost or destroyed title deeds

When the title deeds of unregistered land have been lost or destroyed, an application for the first registration of the title must be supported by evidence of (*a*) the loss or destruction, (*b*) the nature of the title and (*c*) possession of the land.

(a) The loss or destruction

This is usually proved by a statutory declaration or declarations by a person or persons with first hand knowledge of the facts. The declaration(s) must show: (i) where and by whom the deeds were held immediately before their loss or destruction; (ii) whether they were held as security for money or merely for safe custody without any lien, charge or incumbrance; (iii) the full circumstances of their loss or destruction; and (iv) the efforts made to recover them or their remains if recovery was possible.

(b) Reconstruction of the title

The best available secondary evidence of the applicant's title must be produced. What it is will depend on the circumstances of the particular case and the notes under this sub-heading are offered merely as suggestions that may sometimes be useful. A completed draft of the conveyance or assignment to the applicant (and of any subsisting mortgage) should be lodged if possible, together with completed drafts or examined abstracts of as much of the earlier title as it is possible to reconstruct. These documents should if possible be exhibited to a statutory declaration by the solicitor who acted when the applicant bought, declaring that he investigated the title in the ordinary way, indicating the source from which the documents lodged with the application came, and confirming the due execution and stamping of the conveyance or assignment (and mortgage).

If all original deeds, copies, abstracts and drafts held by the applicant or his solicitor have been lost or destroyed, it is sometimes possible to obtain copies, abstracts or drafts from the solicitor who acted for the applicant's vendor. A receipted schedule of deeds, if its source and origin are proved by statutory declaration, may provide slight evidence of custody and title, and copies of particulars delivered pursuant to s 28 of the Finance Act 1931, copies of documents relating to capital transfer tax or estate duty, fire insurance policies, and receipts for rates, taxes and insurance premiums, may be useful as confirmation of ownership.

If the deeds were held by a mortgagee when they were lost or destroyed, it is useful to have a declaration by his solicitor as to his investigation of the title prior to the making of the loan. If he is in a position to do so, the solicitor should also declare that the mortgage is still subsisting or give an account of its repayment.

If the property was not in mortgage when the deeds were lost or destroyed, one or more of the statutory declarations should state explicitly that at the time of the loss or destruction the owner had not created any mortgage, charge or lien on the property and had not deposited any of his title deeds with any person, firm or body as security for money.

If the property is leasehold and the lease has been lost or destroyed, a certified copy of the counterpart can usually be obtained; and the lessor's solicitor may be able to make a declaration relating to licences to assign and production of documents by lessees for registration. In any event, the present reversioner, or his agent, will know who has paid the rent to him during the period of his ownership.

As regards land in an area formerly covered by the Middlesex or one of the Yorkshire Deeds Registries, a solicitor who has examined memorials of deeds may be able to establish or help to establish a chain of title. The records of the former deeds registries can be inspected at the addresses given in the Land Registry's Practice Leaflet No 4, as to which see p 16 and Appendix VI.

(c) Possession of the land

The applicant is usually expected to make a statutory declaration that since the date of his acquisition he has been in actual occupation of the whole of the land or in receipt of its rents and profits (particulars of which should be given) without any adverse claim against him. His declaration should, of course, extend as far as possible to other relevant facts.

(d) Generally

The application should be in the appropriate first registration form, as to which see p 31, accompanied by a Scale A fee on the current value of the land. Land Charges Searches against all known estate owners must also be lodged.

Where the title deeds have been lost, the applicant's solicitor should enclose with the application an undertaking that if all or any of the lost documents of title are recovered they will be produced to the Registry. If, after the date of first registration, further evidence of title comes to light, whether favourable or unfavourable to the registered proprietor, it should be produced to the Registry with the land or charge certificate.

Where the available evidence of title is incomplete, an applicant will not necessarily fail to obtain a registered title. Each application is considered on its merits, but absolute or good leasehold title will not be granted where the loss or destruction of the deeds cannot be adequately explained. However, if there is any risk of the non-disclosure of restrictive covenants, an entry will be made on the register to the effect that the land is subject to such restrictive covenants as may have been imposed on it before the date of the destruction or loss so far as they still subsist and are capable of being enforced. This protective entry will extend to rentcharges in areas where they are common.

2 Lost or destroyed land or charge certificates

(a) Steps to be taken on discovery of loss

When a land or charge certificate has been lost or destroyed, an application for the issue of a new certificate should be made to the appropriate district land registry as soon as possible. No application for which the production of the certificate is necessary can be completed until an application for a new certificate has been lodged and found to be in order.

As soon as the loss or destruction is discovered, an application for an office copy of the register should be made on printed Form 109. This office copy will be admissible in evidence to the same extent as the register itself and can be used until the missing certificate is replaced. It may be useful at the same time in the case of a lost certificate, and as part of the efforts to find it, to ask the Registry (by letter) to say when and to whom the certificate was last issued.

When the office copy of the register is received. the proprietor's address and the description of the property as they appear on the register should be checked. If either is out of date, the appropriate district land registry should be asked at once (by letter) to amend the register. This will ensure that any notice served by the Registry reaches the proprietor without delay and that any advertised description of the property is correct. No fee is payable for such amendments.

If it is suspected that the certificate has been stolen and may be wrongfully used, the appropriate district land registry should be consulted as to the desirability of entering an inhibition on the register by way of a safeguard against fraud.

(b) Application for new certificate

The application for a new certificate (under cover of a form A4) should be made by letter and should be supported by a statutory declaration by a responsible person who knows the facts setting out fully the time, place and circumstances of the loss or destruction of the certificate and, in the case of loss, the efforts made to find it. The declaration must establish, if such be the case, that the certificate was not deposited as security for money and that no one other than the registered proprietor has any interest in or claim to it. If the declaration is not made by the registered proprietor it should contain confirmation that the registered proprietor has specifically informed the declarant that the certificate is not in his possession. If the certificate was lost or destroyed whilst in the custody of a solicitor, the declaration should state expressly whether he held it for safe custody only, or by way of lien. In the case of a lost certificate, there should be lodged with the application an undertaking by the applicant's solicitor to surrender the certificate to the appropriate district land registry for official cancellation if it should be found at any time in the future.

The Registry may ask for additional evidence when the application is being considered and may decide to advertise the loss by means of official notices in the press. In certain circumstances the registry will serve notice of the application upon the registered proprietor and/or upon the proprietor of a registered or noted charge. Such notices will ask for information about the missing certificate and will allow for objection.

(c) Fees and advertising costs

The fee payable for an application to replace a lost or destroyed land certificate or charge certificate (in addition to the cost of any advertisement) is £35 under Part I(4) of Schedule 3 to the Fees Order.

The fee of £35 is reduced to £20 where the inability to produce the missing certificate in support of an application for registration has to be accounted for, but it is not necessary to prepare and issue a replacement certificate because the interest to which the missing certificate relates is being terminated (eg, a lost leasehold land certificate when the registered lease is merging into the reversion or a lost second or subsequent charge certificate when the registered charge is being discharged). The reduction of fee does not carry with it any relaxation of the normal requirements as to the evidence and undertaking that should support the application.

When the application is sent to the appropriate district land registry there should be sent with it:

(*a*) the fee of £35 or £20 as appropriate (see above): and

(*b*) any sum to cover advertising costs that has been notified by the district land registry in earlier correspondence.

On receipt of the application, the Registry may decide that advertising is necessary the cost of which has not been notified in earlier correspondence. In this event, the applicant will be notified of the cost before it is incurred and will be asked to pay or undertake to pay it before the application is taken further.

Chapter XIX

Rectification and Indemnity

1 Correction of minor errors

Rule 13 allows for correction of 'any clerical error or error of a like nature' either in the register or in any plan or document. The clerical error may have occurred either inside or outside the Registry. The Registrar has to be satisfied that correction under this rule is appropriate, and in order to establish this he may serve such notices and call for such evidence as he thinks fit.

Examples of such errors might be the mis-spelling of a name, the omission of a colour reference from a plan or the failure to insert the agreed terms in a standard form of charge.

2 Rectification

The Act specifically forbids rectification, except to give effect to an overriding interest (see p 46), against a proprietor in possession unless:

(1) the proprietor has caused or substantially contributed to the error or omission by fraud or lack of proper care; or
(2) for any other reason, in any particular case, it is considered that it would be unjust not to rectify the register against him (s 82(3)).

In this context possession apparently is to be construed as occupation, but the position is not clear (see *Emmet on Title* 19th ed, §20.024). The exception for overriding interests is perhaps unnecessary as registered titles are in any event subject to such interests.

Subject to this, the register (including the plan) may be rectified pursuant to an order of the court or by the Chief Land Registrar subject to an appeal to the court, in the following cases (s 82(1)):

(a) where the court has made an order for rectification;

(b) in any case and at any time with the consent of all persons interested;
(c) where an entry in the register has been obtained by fraud;
(d) where two or more persons, by mistake, are registered as proprietors of the same registered estate or charge;
(e) where a mortagagee has been registered as proprietor of the land instead of as proprietor of a charge and a right of redemption is subsisting;
(f) where a legal estate has been registered in the name of a person who, if the land had not been registered, would not have been the estate owner; and
(g) in any other case where, by reason of any error or omission in the register, or by reason of any entry made under a mistake, it may be deemed just to rectify the register.

In addition, under r 14, where the Chief Land Registrar is satisfied that all the land in a title, or too much to be dealt with as a minor correction, has been registered in error, he may enter notice of the fact on the register and either:

(i) with the consent of all persons appearing from the register to be interested; or
(ii) after notice to such persons and such inquiry (if any) as he may consider proper, and on the production of such evidence as he may deem necessary;

cancel the registration wholly or to the extent required.

3 Applications and fees for rectification

Whenever a case for rectification arises, an application should be submitted to the appropriate district land registry at the first opportunity. The application may be by letter which should set out the reason why rectification is requested and enclose all available evidence. The district land registry will seek to elucidate the full facts and, if possible, to promote an amicable solution. In the very few cases where the matter cannot be resolved locally, the papers will be forwarded to the Registry's headquarters office at Lincoln's Inn Fields for further consideration but, as stated, all applications should be submitted to the appropriate district land registry in the first instance.

The fee for rectification is calculated under Scale A, reduced in accordance with Abatement 2. The application should, however, be submitted without a fee and the Registry will requisition for payment if appropriate.

4 Indemnity

The main indemnity provisions are contained in s 83 which, subject to certain exceptions set out below, gives the right of indemnity to persons suffering loss because:
  (1) the register is rectified (including a claim in good faith following rectification as a result of forgery);
  (2) the register is not rectified;
  (3) a document lodged at the Registry is lost or destroyed; or
  (4) an error is made in an official search.

Other situations where loss gives rise to a right to indemnity are:
  (*a*) an inaccuracy in an office copy (s 113) or an error or omission in a filed abstract, copy or extract from a deed or document referred to on the register (s 110(4));
  (*b*) where a person, other than the proprietor, suffers loss as a result of the conversion of a title to absolute or good leasehold (s 77(6) as substituted by the Land Registration Act 1986 and see Chapter XI);
  (*c*) failure by the Registry to enter a creditor's notice or bankruptcy inhibition (s 61 and see Chapter XVI); and
  (*d*) failure by the Registry or the Post Office to deliver notice to a chargee, whose charge secures further advances, of a subsequent entry which prejudices the priority of a further advance (unless the chargee has not kept his address for service up to date) (s 30(2) and see p 116.

No indemnity is payable under the Act (s 83(5)):
  (i) where the claimant or a person from whom he derives title (other than under a disposition for valuable consideration which is registered or protected on the register) has caused or substantially contributed to the loss by fraud or lack of proper care;
  (ii) on account of any mines or minerals or the right to work them unless they are specifically included in the registration; and
  (iii) on account of costs incurred in taking or defending any legal proceedings without the consent of the Registrar (other than proceedings for indemnity (see s 2(2) of the Land Registration and Land Charges Act 1971)).

Indemnity arising from rectification is not to exceed the value of the property immediately before rectification. Indemnity payable where the register is not rectified is not to exceed the value of the property at the time the error or omission, which caused the loss, was made (s 83(6)).

Section 83(11) sets out the time limit for claims. This is normally six years from the date when the claimant knew or, but for his own default, might have known of his claim, but claims arising from the registration of land with an absolute or good leasehold title must normally be made within six years of the date of registration.

5 Costs and expenses

Claimants entitled to be indemnified will be paid their reasonable costs and expenses properly incurred in relation to the matter even if no other indemnity is payable (s 83(8)).

Attention is directed to the provisions of s 83(5), referred to above, which relate to situations where no indemnity is payable, and in particular s 83(5)(c) which provides that a claimant cannot be indemnified against the costs of taking or defending any legal proceedings (apart from proceedings in respect of indemnity) without the consent of the Registrar. If such consent is required, application should be made by letter to the appropriate district land registry at the earliest possible opportunity.

6 Applications for indemnity

A claim for indemnity should normally be submitted by letter to the appropriate district land registry (or to the headquarters office at Lincoln's Inn Fields if that office is dealing with the rectification out of which the claim arises). If the claim is to be based on rectification or non-rectification, it cannot be settled until the application for rectification has been disposed of.

The Chief Land Registrar is authorised to settle claims for indemnity by agreement and the overwhelming majority of claims are so settled, but if agreement cannot be reached, whether as to the right to or to the amount of indemnity, the question must be determined by the High Court (Land Registration and Land Charges Act 1971, s 2).

Appendix I
District Land Registries

Appendix I appears on page 210

APPENDIX I

Registry	Address	Telephone No	Telex No	Document Exchange No
BIRKENHEAD	The Birkenhead District Land Registry, Old Market House, Hamilton Street, Birkenhead, Merseyside L41 5FL.	051 647 2377	628475	DX 14300 Birkenhead 3
COVENTRY	The Coventry District Land Registry, Greyfriars Business Centre, 2 Eaton Road, Coventry CV1 2SD.	0203 632442	312187	DX 18900 Coventry 3
CROYDON	The Croydon District Land Registry, Sunley House, Bedford Park, Croydon CR9 3LE.	081 686 8833	917288	DX 2699 Croydon 3
DURHAM	The Durham District Land Registry, Southfield House, Southfield Way, Durham DH1 5TR.	091 386 6151	53684	DX 60200 Durham 3
GLOUCESTER	The Gloucester District Land Registry, Bruton Way, Gloucester GL1 1DQ.	0452 511111	437433	DX 7599 Gloucester 3
HARROW	The Harrow District Land Registry, Lyon House, Lyon Road, Harrow, Middlesex HA1 2EU.	081 427 8811	262476	DX4299 Harrow 4

DISTRICT LAND REGISTRIES

Registry	Address	Telephone No	Telex No	Document Exchange No
KINGSTON UPON HULL	The Kingston upon Hull District Land Registry, Earle House, Portland Street, Kingston upon Hull, Humberside HU2 8JN.	0482 223244	592818	DX 26700 Hull 4
LEICESTER	The Leicester District Land Registry, Thames Tower, 99 Burleys Way, Leicester LE1 3UB.	0533 510010	347291	DX 11900 Leicester 5
LYTHAM	The Lytham District Land Registry, Birkenhead House, East Beach, Lytham St Annes, Lancs FY8 5AB.	0253 736999	67649	DX 14500 Lytham St Annes 3
NOTTINGHAM	The Nottingham District Land Registry, Chalfont Drive, Nottingham NG8 3RN.	0602 291166	37167	DX 10298 Nottingham 3
PETERBOROUGH	The Peterborough District Land Registry, Touthill Close, City Road, Peterborough PE1 1XN.	0733 555666	32298	DX 12598 Peterborough 2

APPENDIX I

Registry	Address	Telephone No	Telex No	Document Exchange No
PLYMOUTH	The Plymouth District Land Registry, Plumer House, Tailyour Road, Crownhill, Plymouth PL6 5HY.	0752 701234	45542	DX 8299 Plymouth 4
PORTSMOUTH	The Portsmouth District Land Registry, St. Andrew's Court, St. Michael's Road, Portsmouth Hampshire PO1 2JH.	0705 865022	86165	DX 83550 Portsmouth 2
STEVENAGE	The Stevenage District Land Registry, Brickdale House, Swingate, Stevenage, Herts SG1 1XG.	0438 313003	82377	DX 6099 Stevenage 2
SWANSEA	FOR AREAS FALLING WITHIN WALES The Swansea District Land Registry, Tŷ Cwm Tawe, Phoenix Way, Llansamlet, Swansea SA7 9FQ.	0792 458877	48220	DX 82800 Swansea 2

DISTRICT LAND REGISTRIES

Registry	Address	Telephone No	Telex No	Document Exchange No
	FOR OTHER AREAS SERVED BY SWANSEA The Swansea District Land Registry, Tŷ Bryn Glas, High Street, Swansea SA1 1PW.	0792 458877	48220	DX 33700 Swansea 2
TELFORD	The Telford District Land Registry, Stafford Park 15, Telford TF3 3AL.	0952 290355	35722	DX 28100 Telford 2
TUNBRIDGE WELLS	The Tunbridge Wells District Land Registry, Tunbridge Wells, Kent TN2 5AQ.	0892 510015	95286	DX 3999 Tunbridge Wells 2
WEYMOUTH	The Weymouth District Land Registry, 1 Cumberland Drive, Weymouth, Dorset DT4 9TT.	0305 776161	418231	DX 8799 Weymouth 2

Appendix II

Areas served by District Land Registries

Set out below in column (1), in alphabetical order, is a list of all the counties and administrative areas, including London Boroughs, in England and Wales.

Column (2) indicates the District Land Registry serving each specified area.

(1) COUNTY	(2) DISTRICT LAND REGISTRY	(1) COUNTY	(2) DISTRICT LAND REGISTRY
AVON	PLYMOUTH	GREATER LONDON (London Borough)	
BEDFORDSHIRE	PETERBOROUGH		
BERKSHIRE	GLOUCESTER	Barking and Dagenham	STEVENAGE
		Barnet	HARROW
BUCKINGHAMSHIRE	LEICESTER	Bexley	CROYDON
		Brent	HARROW
CAMBRIDGESHIRE	PETERBOROUGH	Bromley	CROYDON
		Camden	HARROW
CHESHIRE	BIRKENHEAD	City of London	HARROW
CLEVELAND	DURHAM	City of Westminster	HARROW
		Croydon	CROYDON
CLWYD	SWANSEA	Ealing	SWANSEA
		Enfield	STEVENAGE
CORNWALL	PLYMOUTH	Greenwich	TELFORD
		Hackney	STEVENAGE
CUMBRIA	DURHAM	Hammersmith and Fulham	HARROW
DERBYSHIRE	NOTTINGHAM	Haringey	STEVENAGE
		Harrow	HARROW
DEVON	PLYMOUTH	Havering	STEVENAGE

AREAS SERVED BY DISTRICT LAND REGISTRIES

(1) COUNTY	(2) DISTRICT LAND REGISTRY	(1) COUNTY	(2) DISTRICT LAND REGISTRY
DORSET	WEYMOUTH	Hillingdon	SWANSEA
		Hounslow	SWANSEA
DURHAM	DURHAM	Inner and Middle Temples	HARROW
DYFED	SWANSEA	Islington	HARROW
		Kensington and Chelsea	HARROW
EAST SUSSEX	PORTSMOUTH	Kingston upon Thames	TELFORD
		Lambeth	TELFORD
ESSEX	PETERBOROUGH	Lewisham	TELFORD
		Merton	TELFORD
GLOUCESTERSHIRE	GLOUCESTER	Newham	STEVENAGE
		Redbridge	STEVENAGE
		Richmond upon Thames	TELFORD
		Southwark	TELFORD
		Sutton	CROYDON
		Tower Hamlets	STEVENAGE
		Waltham Forest	STEVENAGE
		Wandsworth	TELFORD

APPENDIX II

(1) COUNTY	(2) DISTRICT LAND REGISTRY	(1) COUNTY	(2) DISTRICT LAND REGISTRY
GREATER MANCHESTER	LYTHAM	NORTH YORKSHIRE	DURHAM
GWENT	SWANSEA	NOTTINGHAMSHIRE	NOTTINGHAM
GWYNEDD	SWANSEA	OXFORDSHIRE	GLOUCESTER
HAMPSHIRE	WEYMOUTH	POWYS	SWANSEA
HEREFORD AND WORCESTER	SWANSEA	SHROPSHIRE	TELFORD
HERTFORDSHIRE	STEVENAGE	SOMERSET	PLYMOUTH
HUMBERSIDE	KINGSTON UPON HULL	SOUTH GLAMORGAN	SWANSEA
ISLE OF WIGHT	WEYMOUTH	SOUTH YORKSHIRE	NOTTINGHAM
ISLES OF SCILLY	PLYMOUTH	STAFFORDSHIRE	BIRKENHEAD
KENT	TUNBRIDGE WELLS	SUFFOLK	KINGSTON UPON HULL
LANCASHIRE	LYTHAM	SURREY	DURHAM
LEICESTERSHIRE	LEICESTER	TYNE AND WEAR	DURHAM
LINCOLNSHIRE	KINGSTON UPON HULL	WARWICKSHIRE	GLOUCESTER
MERSEYSIDE	BIRKENHEAD	WEST GLAMORGAN	SWANSEA
MID GLAMORGAN	SWANSEA	WEST MIDLANDS	COVENTRY
NORFOLK	KINGSTON UPON HULL	WEST SUSSEX	WEYMOUTH
NORTHAMPTONSHIRE	PETERBOROUGH	WEST YORKSHIRE	NOTTINGHAM
NORTHUMBERLAND	DURHAM	WILTSHIRE	GLOUCESTER

Appendix III

Register (Non-Computerised Form)

A. PROPERTY REGISTER
containing the description of the registered land and the estate comprised in the Title
COUNTY   DISTRICT BLANKSHIRE   BROXMORE
The Freehold land shown and edged with red on the plan of the above Title filed at the Registry registered on 12 October 1934 known as 2 Moon Street.

B. PROPRIETORSHIP REGISTER	
stating nature of the Title, name, address and description of the proprietor of the land and any entries affecting the right of disposing thereof	
TITLE ABSOLUTE	
Entry number	Proprietor, etc
1	JOHN SMITH, Printer and WILLIAM BROWN, Engineer, both of 4 Moon Street, Broxmore, Blankshire, registered on 1 May 1988.
2	RESTRICTION registered on 1 May 1988:—No disposition by one proprietor of the land (being the survivor of joint proprietors and not being a trust corporation) under which capital money arises is to be registered except under an order of the registrar or of the Court.
3	CAUTION in favour of Jesse Turnbull of 30 Park Way, Newtown Blankshire, Electrical Engineer, registered on 7 October 1988.

Any entries struck through are no longer subsisting

APPENDIX III

	C. CHARGES REGISTER *containing charges, incumbrances etc, adversely affecting the land and registered dealings therewith*	
Entry number	The date at the beginning of each entry is the date on which the entry was made on this edition of the register	Remarks
1	1 May 1988 – A Conveyance of the land in this title dated 30 September 1934 and made between (1) Mary Brown (Vendor) and (2) Harold Robins (Purchaser) contains the following covenants: 'The Purchaser hereby covenants with the Vendor for the benefit of her adjoining land known as 27, 29, 31, 33 Cabot Road to observe and perform the stipulations and conditions contained in the Schedule hereto. *THE SCHEDULE before referred to* 1 No building to be erected on the land shall be other than as a private dwellinghouse. 2 No building to be erected as aforesaid shall be converted into or used as flats, maisonettes or tenements or as a boarding house. 3 The garden ground of the premises shall at all times be kept in neat and proper order and condition and shall not be converted to any other use whatsoever. 4 Nothing shall be done or permitted on the which may be a nuisance or annoyance to the adjoining houses or to the neighbourhood.'	
2	1 May 1988 – LEASE dated 25 July 1935 to Charles Jones for 99 years from 24 June 1935 at the rent of £45.	Lesser's title registered under 00003
3	1 May 1988 – NOTICE of Deposit of Land Certificate with Mid Town Bank Limited of 2 High Street, Broxmore, Blankshire, registered on 1 May 1988.	

Any entries struck through are no longer subsisting

Appendix IV

Register (Computerised Form)

Edition date: 15 July 1988

Entry No	A. PROPERTY REGISTER containing the description of the registered land and the estate comprised in the Title
1	COUNTY DISTRICT CORNSHIRE MARADON The Freehold land shown edged with red on the plan of the above Title filed at the Registry and being 9 Summers Street, Looe.
2	The mines and minerals together with ancillary rights of working are excepted.

Entry No	B. PROPRIETORSHIP REGISTER stating the nature of the Title, name, address and description of the proprietor of the land and any entnes affecting the right of disposing thereof **TITLE ABSOLUTE**
1	(2 October 1987) Proprietor(s): GROUP CAPTAIN JOSEPH ALLEN MBE of 62 Cadogan Place, London, SWI and THOMAS ALLEN of 26 Moor View, Liskeard, Cornwall.

APPENDIX IV

Entry No	**C. CHARGES REGISTER** *containing charges, incumbrances etc., adversely affecting the land and registered dealings therewith*
1	A Conveyance of the land in this title and other land dated 17 November 1975 made between (1) The National Trust for Places of Historic Interest or Natural Beauty (Vendor) and (2) John Edward Charles Brown contains covenants details of which are set out in the Schedule of restrictive covenants hereto.

Item No	**SCHEDULE OF RESTRICTIVE COVENANTS**
1	The following are details of the covenants contained in the Conveyance dated 17 November 1975 referred to in the Charges Register. 'The Purchaser with the intent that the burden shall bind the property hereby conveyed and each and every part thereof HEREBY COVENANTS with the Vendor for the benefit of adjoining land retained by the Vendor and under and by virtue of Section 8 of the National Trust Act 1937 to observe and perform the covenants and stipulations set out in the Fourth Schedule hereto FOURTH SCHEDULE RESTRICTIVE COVENANTS AND STIPULATIONS 1. Not to erect or permit to be erected any building exceeding two storeys in height nor any building having a flat roof provided that this covenant shall not prevent the erection of garages with flat roofs 2. Not to erect or permit to be erected any building having at any point a height greater than ten feet above the height of the ground on the northern boundary of the property nearest thereto 3. Not to erect any flats hotels shops or cafes on the property or use or permit the use of any buildings to be erected thereon for such purposes 4. Not to erect or permit to be erected any building other than buildings constructed of materials compatible with existing developments in the neighbourhood.'

END OF REGISTER

NOTE A: A date at the beginning of an entry is the date on which the entry was made in the Register.

NOTE B: This certificate was officially examined with the register on **15 July 1988.** This date should be stated on any application for an official search based on this certificate.

Appendix V

List of Forms

NOTE: All of these forms (except C4B, which is only available from HM Stationery Office, Nos 21, 22, 23, 24, 34, 35, 51 and 69, for the text of which reference should be made to the schedule to the Land Registration Rules 1925, No 104, for the text of which reference should be made to the Land Registration Rules 1976, and application forms for the first registration of rentcharges, which can be obtained from district registries) can be bought from HM Stationery Office and other law stationers.

Description of Form	No of Form
Acknowledgement of application	C4B
Acknowledgement card	
Application Forms	
Dealings with registered land:	
Dealing with whole	A4
Dealing with part	A5
First registrations: applications by solicitors	
freehold land	1B
leasehold land on behalf of	
other than an original lessee	2B
leasehold land on behalf of an original lessee	3B
a rentcharge	1F
First registrations: applications by owners in person (no solicitor acting)	
freehold land	1A
leasehold land (other than on the grant of a new lease)	2A
leasehold land on grant of a new lease	3A
a rentcharge	1K
Assents	
Assent or appropriation	56
Vesting assent (settled land)	57

APPENDIX V

Cautions
Caution against first registration with statutory declaration
in support   13/14
Caution against conversion of title   69
Caution against dealings with statutory declaration in
support   63/14
Renewal of caution against dealings (or notice) under
Matrimonial Homes Act 1983   100
Withdrawal of caution against first registration   16
Withdrawal of caution against dealings   71

Charges
Application to note an obligation to make
further advances   113
Application for approval of documents and
descriptions incorporated in charges   114
Application for acceptance of a particular
document incorporated in a charge   115
Charge of whole   45A
Charge accompanying a first registration   45C
Charge of whole with special stipulations   45A*
Charge of part   45B
Charge of land in a transfer of part   45D
Transfer of charge   54
Transfer and discharge of whole   55
Alteration of charge   51
Discharge of charge   53
Discharge of charge by building society or other corporate
body   53(Co)

Companies—*see* Charges; Transfers

Conversions
Application for conversion of title   6

Death—*see also* Assents; Transmissions
Certificate of non-liability to capital transfer tax
(combined with Inland Revenue 31 (CTT))   61(CTT)
Certificate of non-liability to death duty (combined with
Inland Revenue 31)   61

Deposits—*see also* Notice of [Intended] Deposit
Documents deposited at Registry to await an application
for registration   A15
Documents deposited at Registry in connection with a
pending registration   A14

Discharges—*see* Charges

Documents
Copies—*see* Office Copies

224 LIST OF FORMS

Deposit at Registry—*see* Deposits
List of documents accompanying a registration ... A13

Index Map
Application for official search ... 96

Leases—*see also* Application Forms, first registrations
Application to register notice of lease ... 84
Application for cancellation of notice of unregistered lease ... 92

Matrimonial Homes, Protection of rights of occupation
Application for registration of a notice ... 99
Application for renewal of registration of a notice or caution ... 100
Application to cancel a notice ... 202

Notice of [Intended] Deposit
Notice of deposit of land or charge certificate ... 85A
Notice of intended deposit of land certificate on first registration ... 85B
Notice of intended deposit of land certificate on a dealing ... 85C
Withdrawal of notice of deposit ... 86

Notices—*see* Leases; Matrimonial Homes; Notice of [Intended] Deposit; Priority Notice; Rentcharges

Office Copies
Application for office copies of register and plan only ... 109
Application for office copies of filed deeds ... 110

Official Searches—*see* Searches

Personal inspection of the register
Application to make a personal inspection of the register ... 111

Plans—*see also* Index Map
Application for certificate of inspection of filed plan ... 109

Priority Notice against first registration ... 17

Rentcharges—*see also* Application Forms, first registrations; Transfers
Application for cancellation of notice of an unregistered rentcharge ... 92R

Restrictions
Application to register a restriction ... 75
Application to withdraw or modify a restriction ... 77

Searches
Application by purchaser for official search with priority in respect of whole ... 94A

Application by purchaser for official search with priority in respect of part	94B
Application by purchaser for official search with priority in respect of part of the land in a pending first registration	94B(FR)
Application for official search without priority of the entries in the register	94C
Application for certificate of inspection of the filed plan	109
Application for disclosure of landlord's name and address	108
Application for official search of index map	96
Application for official search of index of proprietors' names	104
Application by mortgagee for official search under the Land Registration (Matrimonial Homes) Rules 1983	106

Settlements—*see* Assents; Transfers

Transfers

Transfer of whole (also obtainable in draft)	19
Transfer by whole by a company or corporation	19(Co)
Transfer of whole to joint proprietors	19(JP)
Transfer of part not imposing fresh restrictive covenants (also obtainable in draft)	20
Transfer imposing fresh restrictive covenants (also obtainable in draft)	43
Transfer of a rentcharge	19R1
Transfer of part informally apportioning an existing rentcharge	20R2
Transfer of part subject to an existing apportionment of a rentcharge	20R3
Transfer of part of the land comprised in a registered lease with an apportionment of rent	34
Transfer of whole in exercise of a power of sale	31
Transfer of charge	54
Transfer and discharge of whole	55
Transfer to a tenant for life (in lieu of a vesting instrument)	21
Transfer where trustees of a settlement are the statutory owners and are to be registered as proprietors	22
Transfer (vesting declaration) where tenant for life is already registered as proprietor	23
Transfer of land, acquired with capital money under a settlement, to a tenant for life of full age	24
Transfer to a company or corporation	35

Transmissions

Application to register the personal representative(s) of a deceased sole proprietor	82
Application to register the death of a joint proprietor	83

Appendix VI

Practice Leaflets Issued by HM Land Registry

1 Mergers and surrenders of leases affecting registered land.
2 Official searches of the register.
3 Land certificates and charge certificates lost or destroyed.
4 First registration of title to land where the deeds have been lost or destroyed.
5 First registration of title to land.
6 Devolution on the death of a registered proprietor.
7 Development of registered building estates.
8 Applications under the Leasehold Reform Act 1967 affecting registered land.
9 First registration of title to a rentcharge.
10 Applications to protect rights of occupation under the Matrimonial Homes Act 1983 affecting registered land.
11 Introduction of metrication.
12 Applications for office copies.
13 Surveying housing development for registration purposes.
14 Applications for official searches of the index map.
15 Boundaries in land registration.
16 Form and execution of deeds.
17 Souvenir land.
18 Guide to information held by HM Land Registry.
19 Charges and mortgages on registered land.

Appendix VII

The Land Registration Fees Order 1991 (SI 1991 No 1948)

Made   25 July 1991
Coming into force   1 November 1991

PART I

Citation, commencement and interpretation

1—(1) This Order, which supersedes the Land Registration Fees (No 2) Order 1990, may be cited as the Land Registration Fees Order 1991 and shall come into force on 1 November 1991.

(2) In this Order unless the context otherwise requires:

'account holder' means a person or firm holding a credit account;
'the Act' means the Land Registration Act 1925;
'charge' includes sub-charge;
'credit account' means an account authorised by the Registrar under article 15(1);
'Index Map section' means the document or documents comprising a single section of the Index Maps maintained by the Registrar under rule 8 of the principal rules, and the associated Parcels Index (if any) maintained by the Registrar under rule 274 of the principal rules;
'licensed conveyancer' has the same meaning as in section 11(2) of the Administration of Justice Act 1985 and includes a recognised body within the meaning of section 32(2) of that Act;
'monetary consideration' means a consideration in money or money's worth (other than a nominal consideration or a consideration solely of a covenant to pay money owing under a mortgage);
'the principal rules' means the Land Registration Rules 1925;
'scale fee' means a fee payable in accordance with a scale set out in Schedule 1 or 2;
'Schedule' means a Schedule to this Order;
'share in registered land' means a share in the proceeds of sale of registered land held on trust for sale.

Part II

SCALE AND FIXED FEES; ABATEMENTS AND EXEMPTIONS

Scale fees

2—(1) Subject to article 6, the fee for an application for the first registration of a title (other than an application by an original lessee referred to in paragraph (2) of this article or an owner of a rentcharge referred to in paragraph (5) of Part I of Schedule 3) shall be paid in accordance with Scale A in Schedule I on the value of the land determined in accordance with article 3.

(2) Subject to article 6, the fee for an application for the first registration of a title to a lease (whether or not deriving from a registered freehold or leasehold title) by the original lessee or his personal representative shall be paid in accordance with Scale A in Schedule 1 on any monetary consideration given by the lessee as part of the same transaction by way of fine, premium or otherwise and in accordance with Scale B in Schedule 2 on the largest ascertainable amount of annual rent reserved:

Provided that—

(*a*) where the amount of the rent is not ascertainable at the date of application for registration, the lease shall be treated as having been granted at a rent which attracts a fee of £35 in accordance with Scale B in Schedule 2;

(*b*) where no monetary consideration is given by the lessee as part of the same transaction by way of fine, premium or otherwise and no annual rent is reserved or the largest ascertainable amount of annual rent reserved is less than £1 a fee of £35 shall be payable.

(3) Subject to paragraph (5)(i) and to article 6, the fee for an application for the registration of:

(*a*) a transfer of registered land or of a registered charge for monetary consideration;

(*b*) a transfer for the purpose of giving effect to a disposition for monetary consideration of a share in registered land or in a registered charge;

(*c*) a surrender of a registered lease for monetary consideration (whether effected by deed or otherwise), except where the surrender is consideration or part consideration for the grant of a new lease to the registered proprietor for the registration of which a scale fee is paid;

shall be paid in accordance with Scale A in Schedule 1 on the amount or value of the consideration:

Provided that:

(*a*) where a sale and sub-sale of land are effected by separate instruments of transfer, a separate fee shall be payable under this paragraph in respect of each transfer;

(b) where a sale and sub-sale are effected by one instrument of transfer, the fee shall be assessed upon the monetary consideration given by the sub-purchaser in respect of that land.

(4) The fee for an application in relation to registered land for the registration of:

(a) an exchange (whether or not money is paid for equality);
(b) a vesting order or declaration made under section 47 of the Act;

shall be paid in accordance with Scale A in Schedule 1 on the value of the land which is the subject of the dealing, determined in accordance with article 4, but after deducting therefrom the amount secured upon the land by any prior charge.

(5) Subject to paragraph (7) of Part II of Schedule 4, the fee for an application for the registration of:

(a) a transfer of registered land otherwise than for monetary consideration;
(b) a transfer for the purpose of giving effect to the disposition otherwise than for monetary consideration of a share in registered land;
(c) a surrender of a registered lease (whether effected by deed or otherwise) where the surrender is consideration or part consideration for the grant of a new lease to the registered proprietor for the registration of which a scale fee is paid;
(d) a surrender of a registered lease otherwise than for monetary consideration (whether effected by deed or otherwise);
(e) a transmission of registered land on death or bankruptcy;
(f) an assent of registered land (including a vesting assent);
(g) an appropriation of registered land;
(h) a rectification of the register;
(i) a transfer of a matrimonial home (being registered land) made pursuant to an order of the Court

shall be paid in accordance with Scale A in Schedule 1, reduced in accordance with Abatement 2 in Part I of Schedule 4, on the value of the land in each registered title which is the subject of the dealing, determined in accordance with article 4, but after deducting therefrom the amount secured upon the land by any prior charge:

Provided that—

(a) in the case of a disposition of a share only in registered land the fee shall be paid in accordance with Scale A in Schedule 1, reduced in accordance with Abatement 2 in Part I of Schedule 4, on the equivalent proportion of the value of the land in each registered title which is the subject of the dealing but after deducting therefrom an equivalent proportion of the amount secured on the land by any prior charge;

(b) where, in the case of rectification of the register, the fee appears to the Registrar to be unreasonable or excessive he may reduce or waive it.

(6) Subject to article 6 and paragraph (7) of Part II of Schedule 4, the fee for an application for the registration of:

(a) a charge;
(b) the transfer of a charge otherwise than for monetary consideration;
(c) a transfer for the purpose of giving effect to the disposition otherwise than for monetary consideration of a share in a registered charge;

shall be paid in accordance with Scale A in Schedule 1, reduced where applicable in accordance with Abatement 2 in Part I of Schedule 4, on the amount of the charge determined in accordance with article 5:

Provided that in the case of a disposition of a share only in a registered charge the fee shall be paid in accordance with Scale A in Schedule 1 on the equivalent proportion of the amount of each registered charge which is the subject of the dealing.

(7) The fee for an application to cancel an entry in the register of notice of an unregistered lease which has determined on merger, surrender or otherwise shall be paid in accordance with Scale A in Schedule 1 on the value thereof at the time of its determination.

Valuation (first registration)

3—(1) In the case of an application by a purchaser for the first registration of title to land made within one year of a sale (other than an exchange, whether or not money is paid for equality, or the sale of a share only in the proceeds of sale of such land) the value of the land shall be taken as the amount of the monetary consideration given together with the amount outstanding at the time of the purchase under any charge or mortgage subject to which the land was purchased.

(2) In the case of an application for first registration not falling within paragraph (1), the value of the land shall be ascertained by the Registrar at such sum as in his opinion the land would fetch if sold in the open market at the date of the application free from any charge or mortgage; and as evidence of such value the Registrar may require a statement in writing, signed by the applicant or his solicitor or licensed conveyancer or by any other person who, in the Registrar's opinion, is competent to make such a statement.

(3) Where an application for first registration is made on the purchase of a leasehold estate by the reversioner or of a reversion by the leaseholder or on any other like occasion and determination of an unregistered interest, by way of merger, surrender or otherwise, takes place, the value of the land shall be the combined value of the reversionary and determined interests assessed in accordance with paragraphs (1) and (2).

Valuation (registered land)

4—(1) Where the value of the land in a registered title falls to be determined under this Order it shall be ascertained by the Registrar at such sum as in his opinion the land would fetch if sold in the open market free from any charge or mortgage:

(*a*) in the case of a surrender at a date immediately prior to the surrender;

(*b*) in any other case at the date of the application.

(2) As evidence of such value the Registrar may require a statement in writing, signed by the applicant or his solicitor or licensed conveyancer or by any other person who, in the Registrar's opinion, is competent to make such a statement.

Valuation (charges)

5—(1) Subject to paragraph (5), where the amount of a charge falls to be determined under this Order it shall be taken to be:

(*a*) in the case of a fixed charge, the amount secured by the charge;

(*b*) in the case of a charge to secure further advances, where the total amount of the advances or of the money to be owing at any one time is in any way limited, the amount so limited;

(*c*) in the case of a charge to secure further advances, where the total amount of the advances or of the money to be owing at any one time is in no way limited, an amount equal to the value of the registered land comprised in the charge after deducting therefrom the amount secured on it by any prior registered charge.

(2) Where a charge of a kind referred to in paragraph (1)(a) or (1)(b) is secured on unregistered land or other property as well as on registered land, the fee in accordance with article 2(6) shall be payable on an amount calculated in accordance with the following formula:

$$\frac{\text{Value of registered land}}{\text{Value of whole security}} \times \text{Amount of the charge}$$

(3) The fee in accordance with Scale A in Schedule 1 for the registration of a charge by way of additional or substituted security or by way of guarantee shall be payable on the lesser of:

(*a*) the amount secured or guaranteed; or

(*b*) the value of the land after deducting the amount secured on the land by any prior registered charge.

(4) The fee in accordance with Scale A in Schedule 1 for the registration of a charge (not falling within paragraph (3)) to secure an obligation or liability which is contingent upon the happening of a future event shall be payable on the value of the land after deducting the amount secured on the land by any prior registered charge:

Provided that if the maximum amount or value of the obligation or liability which may arise is in any way limited under the charge and is capable of being ascertained at the time of the application to register the charge then the fee shall be payable on that amount or value, if less than the value of the land after deducting the amount secured on the land by any prior registered charge.

(5) For the purpose of this Order, where two or more charges are contained in the same instrument and secure the same debt, the chargor, or each of the several chargors if more than one, shall be treated as having effected a single charge the amount of which is equal to the lesser of:

- (*a*) the whole debt; or
- (*b*) the value of the registered land charged by the chargor after deducting therefrom the amount secured on it by any prior registered charge.

Large scale applications
  6—(1) In this article:

- (*a*) 'large scale application' means an application to which this article applies and which relates to not fewer than 20 units of land as defined in sub-paragraph (*b*); and
- (*b*) 'unit of land' means:
    - (i) where the land is unregistered, a separate area of land not adjoining any other unregistered land comprised in the same application;
    - (ii) where the land is registered, the land registered under a single title number.

(2) This article applies to applications for:

- (*a*) first registration of title to land;
- (*b*) first registration of title to a lease;
- (*c*) registration of a transfer of registered land for monetary consideration;
- (*d*) registration of a transfer of a registered charge for monetary consideration;
- (*e*) registration of a transfer for the purpose of giving effect to the disposition for monetary consideration of a share in registered land or a share in a registered charge;
- (*f*) registration of a charge.

(3) The fee for a large scale application shall be:

- (*a*) £20 in respect of each unit of land to which the application relates; or
- (*b*) the amount payable in respect of the application under article 2;

whichever is the greater.

APPENDIX VII 233

Fixed fees
7—(1) Subject to paragraphs (3) and (4), the fees for the applications and services specified in Schedule 3 shall be those set out in that schedule.

(2) The fee for an application in Form 112A or Form 112B in Schedule 1 to the Land Registration (Open Register) Rules 1990 shall be the aggregate of the fees payable for the services provided, save that the maximum fee for any one application shall be £175.

(3) The Registrar may, if he thinks fit, waive any fee or part of a fee or any category of fee payable under this article.

(4) If, having regard to the extent of the land to which an application for a search of the index map relates, the Registrar considers that the cost of the work involved in dealing with that application would substantially exceed any fee otherwise payable under this Order, such additional fee shall be payable as the Registrar shall direct as appropriate to cover the excess cost of the work involved.

(5) Notification of the additional fee shall be given to the applicant and, if he then elects to withdraw his application, no fee shall be payable.

Abatements and exemptions
8—(1) The abatements set out in Part I of Schedule 4 shall apply in respect of the applications therein mentioned.

(2) No fee shall be payable in respect of any of the applications and services specified in Part II of Schedule 4.

PART III
GENERAL AND ADMINISTRATIVE PROVISIONS

Refund of fees
9—(1) Where an amount exceeding the prescribed fee has been paid, there shall be refunded any excess remaining after the deduction, if the Registrar so directs, of an amount not exceeding £10 in respect of **the cost of** repayment.

(2) Where the person or firm lodging the application is an account holder, any amount to be refunded under paragraph (1) may at the discretion of the Registrar be repaid to the account holder by crediting the amount to the account holder's credit account.

(3) Subject to article 7(5), if any application is cancelled or withdrawn no part of the fee therefor shall be refunded unless the Registrar so directs.

Cost of advertisements and special enquiries
10 If in the course of dealing with any application, the Registrar directs publication of an advertisement or any special enquiry, the costs so incurred shall be defrayed by the applicant unless the Registrar directs to the contrary.

Fixed boundaries
11 Where application is made for the boundaries of land to be noted

on the register as fixed under rule 277 of the principal rules such fee shall be charged as the Registrar may consider necessary to cover the cost of any examination of title, enquiries, mapping, surveying, notices or other work involved.

Special expedition

12 Where application for special expedition in connection with an application is granted, such further fee, being not less than £35, shall be payable as the Registrar shall direct having regard to the special work involved.

Application not otherwise referred to

13 Upon an application for which no other fee is payable under this Order and which is not exempt from payment, there shall be paid such fee (if any) not exceeding a fee in accordance with Scale A in Schedule 1 on the value of the land or on the amount of the charge as the Registrar shall direct having regard to the work involved.

Method of payment

14 Subject to article 15:

(*a*) every fee shall be paid by means of a cheque or postal order crossed and made payable to H.M. Land Registry;

(*b*) where the amount of a fee payable on an application is immediately ascertainable, the fee shall be paid on delivery of the application;

(*c*) where the amount of a fee payable on an application is not immediately ascertainable, on delivery of the application there shall be paid on account of the fee such sum, being not less than the minimum fee payable in accordance with Scale A in Schedule 1, as the applicant may reasonably estimate to be the fee payable and there shall be lodged therewith an undertaking to pay on demand the balance of the fee due, if any.

Credit accounts

15—(1) Any person or firm may, if authorised by the Registrar, use a credit account in accordance with this article for the purpose of the payment of fees for applications and services of such kind as the Registrar shall from time to time direct.

(2) Where an account holder makes an application in respect of which credit facilities are available, he may make a request, in such manner as the Registrar shall direct, for the appropriate fee to be debited to the account holder's credit account.

(3) When a person or firm having a credit account makes a written application in respect of which credit facilities are available but which is not accompanied by any fee and does not contain a request for the fee to be debited to that account, the Registrar may, if he thinks fit, nevertheless accept the application and debit the fee to that person's or that firm's account.

(4) A statement of account shall be sent by the Registrar to each account

holder at the end of each calendar month or such other period as the Registrar shall direct either in any particular case or generally.

(5) On receipt of the statement and if no question arises thereon the account holder shall pay by cheque any sum due on his account forthwith.

(6) Cheques shall be crossed and made payable to H.M. Land Registry and sent to the Accounts Section, H.M. Land Registry, Burrington Way, Plymouth, PL5 3LP or at such other address as the Registrar shall direct.

(7) The Registrar may at any time and without giving reasons terminate or suspend any or all authorisations given under paragraph (1).

SCHEDULE 1   Article 2

SCALE A

APPLICATIONS FALLING UNDER ARTICLE 2

NOTE 1: On application for registration of title by an original lessee, fees are payable under this scale on the amount or value of any monetary consideration given by way of fine, premium or otherwise and also in accordance with Scale B in Schedule 2 on the amount of any annual rent.

NOTE 2: For abatement of the fee for registration of a charge accompanying an application to register a transaction for monetary consideration upon which a scale fee is payable see Abatement 1 in Part 1 of Schedule 4.

NOTE 3: For abatement of the fee in respect of certain transactions with registered land see Abatement 2 in Part 1 of Schedule 4.

NOTE 4: Where the amount of the value is a figure which includes pence, the value may be rounded down to the nearest £1.

Value £	Fee £	Value £	Fee £
0–25,000	35	100,001–200,000	250
25,001–30,000	40	200,001–300,000	300
30,001–35,000	50	300,001–400,000	350
35,001–40,000	60	400,001–600,000	400
40,001–45,000	70	600,001–800,000	450
45,001–50,000	80	800,001–1,000,000	500
50,001–60,000	100	1,000,001–2,000,000	600
60,001–70,000	120	2,000,001–3,000,000	700
70,001–80,000	140	3,000,001–4,000,000	800
80,001–90,000	160	4,000,001–5,000,000	900
90,001–100,000	200	5,000,001–10,000,000	1,000
		10,000,001 and over	1,200

SCHEDULE 2

Article 7

Scale B

First Registration by Original Lessee

NOTE 1: On application for registration of title by an original lessee, fees are payable under this scale on the amount of the annual rent and also, if there is monetary consideration given by way of fine, premium or otherwise in accordance with Scale A in Schedule 1 on the amount or value of such consideration.

NOTE 2: For abatement of the fee for registration of a charge accompanying an application to register a transaction for monetary consideration upon which a scale fee is payable, see Abatement 1 in Part 1 of Schedule 4.

NOTE 3: For abatement of the fee for registration of a 'Right to Buy' lease, see Abatement 3 in Part 1 of Schedule 4.

NOTE 4: Where the amount of the rent is a figure which includes pence, the rent may be rounded down to the nearest £1.

Annual Rent £	Fee £	Annual Rent £	Fee £
Under 1	0	10,001–20,000	240
1–2,500	35	20,001–30,000	350
2,501–5,000	60	30,001–40,000	450
5,001–7,500	90	40,001–50,000	550
7,501–10,000	130	50,001 and over	650

SCHEDULE 3

Article 7

Part I

Applications

Fee

(1) To register or modify a caution, a restriction (other than a restriction to which paragraph (8) in Part II of Schedule 4 applies), notice (including a priority notice), an inhibition, or a note for which no other provision is made by this Order and for which the Registrar considers a fee should be paid-

for the first title affected £30

—for each subsequent title affected.................... £20

Provided that no such fee shall be payable if, in relation to each registered title affected, the application is accompanied by an application affecting that title upon which a scale fee (but not a fee under article 6) is payable;

APPENDIX VII

(2) To close or partly close a registered leasehold or rentcharge title other than on surrender (whether or not the surrender is for monetary consideration and whether effected by deed or otherwise—for each title closed or partly closed. £35

Provided that no such fee shall be payable if the application is accompanied by an application upon which a scale fee is payable.

(3) To convert from one class of title to another £35

Provided that no fee shall be payable if the application for conversion is accompanied by an application upon which a scale fee is payable.

(4) Application under rule 271 in relation to a lost or destroyed land certificate or charge certificate (in addition to the cost of any advertisement):

(a) where a replacement certificate is issued £35

(b) where a replacement certificate is not issued £20

(5) First registration of a title to a rentcharge........... £35

(6) To cancel an entry in the register of notice of an unregistered rentcharge which has determined on merger, redemption or otherwise—for each title affected £35

Provided that no such fee shall be payable if the application is accompanied by an application upon which a scale fee is payable.

Part II

Services

(1) Official search of the index of proprietors' names—per name... £14

(2) Application by a person other than the registered proprietor for personal inspection:

(a) of the register or any part thereof—per title £7

(b) of the title plan—per title £7

(c) of any or all of the documents referred to in the register (other than documents referred to in paragraph (4) of this Part)—per title £7

(3) Office copy in respect of a registered title:

(a) of the register or any part thereof—per copy £7

(b) of the title plan—per copy £7

(c) of any or all of the documents referred to in the register (other than documents referred to in paragraph (4) of this Part)—per copy or set £7

(4) Inspection or office copy (or both) in relation to

(a) a lease or mortgage referred to in the register, or a copy thereof; or

(b) any document not referred to in a register;
—per document £14

(5) Inspection by the Registrar of the Index Map for the purpose of ascertaining the title number or numbers (if any) under which land is registered where an application is made to which paragraph (3) in this Part applies or (except in the case of an application by a registered proprietor in person) to which paragraph (2) in this Part applies and the applicant has not supplied a title number, or the title number supplied does not relate to any part of the land described by the applicant £7

(6) A search of the register or of a pending first registration application by telephone or telex....................... £7

(7) A search without priority of the register (other than a search by telephone or telex—per title £7

(8) The issue of an official certificate of inspection of the title plan... £7

(9) Subject to article 7(4), an official search of the Index Map:

(a) where any part of the land to which the search relates is registered—per registered title in respect of which a result is given............................... £7

(b) where no part of the land to which the search relates is registered—per application £7

(10) Personal inspection of the Index Map—per application.. £7

(11) The supply by the Registrar of a copy of an Index Map section—per copy £70

(12) The supply of information under section 129 of the Act—per registered title in respect of which information is supplied £14

(13) To take an affidavit or declaration £3.50

(14) To take exhibits to an affidavit or declaration—per exhibit £1

APPENDIX VII 239

SCHEDULE 4

Article 8

PART I

ABATEMENTS

Charge accompanying application for first registration and registered transactions for monetary consideration

Abatement 1 Where, on an application ('the primary application') for;
    (*a*) first registration of land or a lease;
    (*b*) registration of a transfer of registered land, or a transfer of a registered charge, for monetary consideration;
    (*c*) registration of a transfer for the purpose of giving effect to the disposition for monetary consideration of a share in registered land or of a share in a registered charge; or
    (*d*) registration of an exchange;

a charge by the applicant or by a predecessor in title of such applicant (in the case of first registration) or by the transferee (in the case of a transfer or exchange) is delivered either with the primary application or before the primary application is completed, no fee shall be payable for the registration of the charge:

Provided that where the charge also comprises registered land ('the additional land') which is not the subject of the primary application the abatement shall not extend to the additional land so that, in addition to the fee payable in respect of the primary application, there shall be paid a fee in accordance with Scale A in Schedule 1 on an amount calculated in accordance with the following formula:

$$\frac{\text{Value of the additional land}}{\text{Value of whole security}} \times \text{Amount of charge}$$

Reduced fee for certain transactions with registered land

Abatement 2 Subject to paragraph (7) of Part 11 of Schedule 4, in the case of an application for:
    (*a*) a transfer of registered land or a transfer of a registered charge otherwise than for monetary consideration;
    (*b*) a transfer for the purpose of giving effect to the disposition otherwise than for monetary

consideration of a share in registered land or of a share in a registered charge;

(c) a surrender of a registered lease (whether effected by deed or otherwise) where the surrender is consideration or part consideration for the grant of a new lease to the registered proprietor;

(d) a surrender of a registered lease otherwise than for monetary consideration (whether effected by deed or otherwise);

(e) a transmission of registered land on death or bankruptcy;

(f) an assent of registered land (including a vesting assent);

(g) an appropriation of registered land;

(h) a rectification of the register;

(i) a transfer of a matrimonial home (being registered land) made pursuant to an order of the Court;

the fee payable in accordance with Scale A in Schedule 1 shall be reduced to one fifth:

Provided that the minimum fee on any one application shall be £35.

Leases made under the provisions of Part V Housing Act 1985

Abatement 3 Where on an application for first registration of a lease made pursuant to the provisions of Part V Housing Act 1985 (Right to Buy) or to any statutory instrument applying the same for which a fee is payable in accordance with Scale B in Schedule 2 on the largest ascertainable amount of annual rent reserved, the fee in accordance with Scale B shall be reduced to one fifth.

PART II

Exemptions

No fee shall be payable in respect of:

(1) making a land certificate or charge certificate correspond with the register;

(2) changing the name, address or description of a registered proprietor or other person referred to on the register, or changing the description of a property;

(3) registering a discharge of a registered charge;

(4) registering a notice or renewal of a caution or notice pursuant to the Matrimonial Homes Act 1983;

(5) registering a notice, or a withdrawal of a notice of deposit or intended deposit of a land certificate or charge certificate;

(6) entering on the register the death of a joint proprietor;

(7) registering a disposition to which section 145(2) of the Act (dispositions otherwise than for valuable consideration by personal representatives of a deceased proprietor registered as such) applies;

(8) registering a restriction which is obligatory under section 58(3) of the Act;

(9) cancelling the registration of a notice (other than a notice in respect of an unregistered lease or unregistered rentcharge), caution, inhibition, restriction or note;

(10) approving an estate layout plan or any draft document with or without a plan;

(11) a personal inspection of the register or any part thereof, the title plan and any document referred to in the register, made by the registered proprietor;

(12) an official search with priority of the register or of a pending first registration application (other than a search by telephone or telex);

(13) issuing of a summons under the seal of the Land Registry;

(14) an order by the Registrar.

Index

Administration order—
  acquisition of land, 188
  disposal by administrator, 188
  notice, 187
Alteration—
  details on register, 80–1
  instruments, 80
  see also Rectification
Applications—
  cancellation, 14–15
  dealings—
    acknowledgement, 75
    forms, 72–5
    part of land, 74–5
    whole of land, 72–4
  delivery, 5–6
  first registration, *see* First
    registration, application priority, 6
  rejection, 14
Attorney—
  company as donor, 78
  execution by, 78–9
  irrevocable, 79
  joint proprietors, 80
  order, enduring power, 78
  registration of instrument executed by, 78
    delay in completing transaction, 78–9

Bankruptcy—
  creditors, notice, 182–3
  cancellation, 184–5
  dealings by registered proprietor, 183
  deeds of arrangement, protection, 173, 174

Bankruptcy—*contd*
  inhibition, 182–3
    cancellation, 184–5
  inspection of register, 56
  joint proprietor, 183, 185
  Land Charges Department search, 69
  matrimonial home—
    bankrupt's rights, 180–1
    charging order, 185
    wife's rights, 180
  official receiver—
    registration, 183–4
    transfer by, 184
    vesting in, 183
  registration at Land Charges Department, 182
  trustee—
    registration, 184
    transfer by, 184
    vesting in, 183
Boundaries—
  agricultural land, 21–2
  discrepancies in plans, 22
  disputes, 23
  fixed, 21
  general, 21
  generally, 21
  hedge and ditch presumption, 21–2
  ownership of fences and walls, 20
  position, 21
  transfer of part, 75
Building estates—
  absolute leasehold title, 94, 199
  deposited certificate, 196
  discharge of charge, 199
  draft transfers, 199
  easements, 198, 199

243

Building estates—*contd*
  guide for solicitors, 194
  leasehold estates, 194
  metrication, 196
  office copies, 196–7
  plans—
    approval, 194–5
    changes, 195
    filed—
      certificate of official inspection, 58–9, 197–8
      office copy, 196
    information for surveyors, 20
    instrument, 198–9
    layout, 194–5
    reduced copies, 19–20
    searches, accompanying, 60
  plots, sales in, 196
  search against plot, 198
  surveys, 195–6
  title shown procedure, 38
  verifications, 197–8
Building society, 91

Capital transfer tax—
  generally, 159, 161–2
  see also Inheritance tax
Caution—
  application, 169
  assignment of protected interest, 166
  charge's proprietor, effect on, 169
  conversion of title, 167
  damages for injury, 167, 169
  dealings, 167–70
  death of cautioner, 166
  effect, 169
  first registration, 166–7
    leasehold land, 167
  generally, 166
  hearing of dispute, 170
  trust for sale, 168–9
  warning-off, 169–70
  withdrawal, 170
Charge—
  alteration, 119
  caution, effect on charge's proprietor, 169
  certificate, *see* Charge certificate
  company—
    by, 74, 115
    to, 74, 115–116
  covenants, implied, 113
  debenture, 124–6

Charge—*contd*
  debenture—*contd*
    trust deed, 115, 124–5
  description of land, 111
  discharge—
    cancellation of notice, 120
    equitable charge, 120, 124
    floating charge, 124
    form, 119, 120
    generally, 119–20
    in transfer of land, 120
    non-availability of form, 85–6
    only remaining charge, 74
    part of land, 119
    unregistered interest affected, 120
  discount, Housing Act cases, 121–3
  entry into possession by chargee, 118
  equitable, 123–4
  exchange of registered charge,
  execution, 120
  fee, disposition of registered charge, 89
  floating, 125–6
  foreclosure order, 118
  form, 110, 111–112, 223
  further advances, 114, 116–117
  generally, 2–3
  incorporated documents, 111, 112–113
  matrimonial home, occupation rights, 181
  notice, deposit [intended], 126–8
  part of land, 111
  power—
    of charge's proprietor, 110, 117–18
    of land's proprietor, 110, 117
    to create, 110–11
  priorities, 116, 121
  registration—
    application, 114
    completion by, 113–14
    fees, 114–15
    first, 111, 114
      subsisting charges, 120–1
  rule 72, 30, 111
  schedule of stipulations, 111–12
  sub-charge, 118–19
  transfer—
    of charge, 118
    subject to charge, 85, 117
    under power of sale, 72, 117–18
  variation, 119

INDEX

Charge certificate—
  computerised, 12, 219–21
  generally, 10–11
  second charge, 10
  see also Land certificate
Charging order—
  protection by—
    caution, 168
    notice, 164–5
Charity—
  certificate of non-occupation of land, 148–9
  declaration of trust, 154
  exemption from Charity Commissioner's control, 149
  first registration, 153–4
  landlord, Leasehold Reform Act cases, 108, 152
  Official Custodian for Charities—
    execution of deeds, 108, 152–3
    first registration, 153–4
    registration, 151–2
  orders of Charity Commissioners, kinds, 149–50
  powers of, 148
  religious bodies, 150
  restrictions, 148–51
  transfer for charitable uses, 154
  trustees—
    collective registration, 151, 152
    disposition by, 151
    execution of deeds, 152–3
    restriction relating to, 151
Chief Land Registrar—
  judicial powers, 12
Company—
  charge—
    by, 74, 115
    to, 74, 115–16
  execution of deed, 77
    as attorney, 78
  first registration, 32, 34–5
  floating charge, 125–6
    discharge, 124
  liquidation, 186
    inspection of register, 193
  overseas, 90–1
  receiver, *see* Receiver
  registered number, entry in register, 90
  registration at Companies Registry, 115

Company—*contd*
  transfer—
    by, 125
    to, 74, 90
Compulsory registration—
  extension of time, 27–8
  generally, 27
  inapplicable, 28–9
  period for application, 27
  transactions involving, 27, 28–9
  see also First registration
Computerisation—
  generally, 11, 12
  plans, 11, 12
  register, form, 219–21
Contract, 82, 164
Conversion of title—
  adverse claim, 139
  application, 140
  caution against, 167
  easements, showing title, 138–9
  good leasehold, 138–9
  inquiries, 140
  notice, 140
  possessory, 8–9, 139
  qualified, 139
Corporation—
  transfer, party to, 89–90
  see also Company
Covenants—
  implied, 87, 113
  indemnity, 45–6, 88
  leases, 95, 113
  positive, 45–6
  restrictive—
    benefit, 44–5
    burden—
      first registration, 42–4
      registered land, 44
      transfer of part, 44
    Lands Tribunal order, 45
    leases, 95
    modification, 45
    release, 45
    text, 42–3
    waiver, 45

Day list, 68
Dealings—
  application forms, 72–5
  associated, 75
  authorised, 70–1
  caution against, 167–70

INDEX

Dealings—*contd*
  certificates, production, 71–2
  company to be proprietor, 74
  completion, 71
  depositing documents, 72
  devolution of right to be registered, 71
  draft instruments, approval, 76
  expedition, 73
  joint tenants, 74
  part of registered land, 74–5
  refusal to register instrument, 76

Death—
  assent, 158–9
  inheritance tax, *see* Inheritance tax
  joint proprietor, 160–1
    sole survivor entitled, 160–1
  power of personal representative, 158
  registration—
    dealings by personal representative, 158
    personal representative as proprietor, 157–8
    responsibility of personal representatives, 159–60
    restrictions, 160, 161
      cancellation, 158, 160–1
  sole—
    proprietor, 157–60
    survivor, 157–60
  vesting assent, 158–9

Deed—
  delivery, 77
  execution by—
    attorney, 78–80
    company, 77
    foreign company, 77
    individual, 77
  form, 76–7

Defective dwellings—
  repurchase, 41

Destroyed documents, *see* Lost documents

District land registries—
  appropriate, 5
  areas served by, 214–16
  list, 210–13

Draft instruments—
  Land Registry approval, 76

Easements—
  building estates, 198, 199

Easements—*contd*
  first registration, 51
  flats, freehold, 53–4
  generally, 51
  grant, 51–3
  ineffective grant, 53
  leases, 95
  registrable, 3
  reservation, 51–3
  title, conversion, 138–9

Exchange—
  fee, 86
  see also Sale of registered land

Fees—
  cancelled applications, 14–15
  credit accounts, 15
  generally, 15
  Order, 227–41

First registration—
  applicant, 32
  application—
    certificate as to title, 32–3
    completion of form, 31–3
    deeds—
      accompanying, 33–4
      list, 35
      return, 32
    expedition, 32
    fees, 31–2
    forms, 31, 222
    generally, 5, 31
    time of delivery, 6
  completion of, 36–7
  compulsory, 27–9
  examination of title, official, 36
  extent of land, 29–30
  incorporeal hereditaments, 36
  inspection of land before completion, 30
  interests—
    incapable of registration, 3–5
    registrable, 3, 4
  lease—
    absolute title, 7–8
    application for registration, 31, 35
    good leasehold title, 8
    incapable of registration, 4
    registrable, 3, 4
  plan, 17, 30
  priority notice, 172–3
  procedure before completion, 29–30
  rule 72 transfer, 30

First registration—*contd*
  voluntary, 29
  see also Registration of title to land
Flats—
  freehold, 53-4
Forms, 2, 15, 222-5
Friendly society, 91

Housing Act cases—
  defective dwellings, repurchase, 41
  see also Right to buy cases

Indemnity—
  application, 208
  costs, payment, 208
  covenants, 45-6, 88
  generally, 12, 207
  maximum amount, 207-8
  non-eligiblity, 207
  settlement, 208
  time limit, 208
Industrial and provident society, 91
Information—
  inquiries, 15-16
  practice—
    leaflets, 16, 226
    notes, 16
Inheritance tax—
  background, 161-2
  certificate of non-liability, 159, 163
  Inland Revenue charge, 162-3
    cancellation, 162, 163
  notice, 162, 163
    cancellation, 162, 163
Inhibition—
  bankruptcy, 182-3
  cancellation, 184-5
  generally, 172
Insolvency, *see* Bankruptcy
Inspection of register—
  certificate of official inspection, filed plan, 58-9, 197-8
  crime, investigation, 56
  generally, 55
  index of proprietor's names, 55-6
  insolvency, 56
  personal, 56
  receiver, by, 56, 193

Joint tenants—
  powers of attorney by, 80
  transfer, 88
  see also Trust for sale

Land certificate—
  computerised, 12, 219-21
  corresponding with register, 59, 82
  depositing, 72
  generally, 10-11
  loss or destruction, 202-4
  mistakes, 37
  new certificate, application for, 203-4
  production, 71-2, 94-5
  registration of lease or rentcharge, 35
Land charges—
  local, 174-5
  protection, 164, 173-4
  searches, *see* Searches
Land Registry—
  aims, 1
Lease—
  agreement, 94, 102
  assignment, 101
  business tenancy, 101-2
  caution, 167
  company grantor, 125, 126
  completion, 93
  covenants—
    implied, charge, 113
    restrictive, 95
  easements, 95
  first registration, *see* First registration, lease
  form, 92-3
  Leasehold Reform Act, *see* Leasehold Reform Act
  merger, 98-101
  non-registrable, 94
  notice in lessor's title register, 93, 94
  office copies, 57, 96
  options in, 95
  part of land in title, 92
  particulars delivered stamp, 14
  plan, 92, 93
  power to, 92
  production of lessor's certificate, 94-5
  registration—
    generally, 93-4
    incapacity to register, 94
    with lessor, 96
  rent, apportionment, 97
  searches, 93
  shared ownership, 39-40
  surrender, 98-101

Lease—*contd*
  time-expired, Landlord and Tenant
    Act 1954, 101-2
  title—
    absolute, 7, 8
    conversion, 138-9
    good leasehold, 8, 92
    lessor's, 7-8, 92
  transfer, implied covenants, 87
  variation, 96-7
Leasehold Reform Act—
  caution protection claim, 103
  charity landlord, 108, 152
  discharge of charges, 104-5
  disclosure to Registry, 108-9
  enfranchisement, application for
    registration, 104
  extended lease—
    application, 105-6
    registered title, 107
  first registration, disclosure to
    Registry, 108, 109
  floating charge, 105
  investigations, 102
  notice of claim, 103
  rentcharge on landlord's title, 105
  rights and burdens under, 104
  scheme under, 108
  surrender of existing lease, 106-7
  tenant's—
    assignment of rights, 103-4
    claim, protection, 103
Lien, 126-8
Local authorities—
  certificates of title, 39
  defective dwellings, repurchase, 41
  see also Right to buy cases
Lost documents—
  application to register land, 202
  charges, 201
  covenants, inadequate information,
    202
  leasehold, 201
  loss, 200
  possession of land, 201-2
  title—
    given, 202
    reconstruction, 200-1

Map—
  general system, 18-19
  public index, 23-4

Matrimonial home—
  bankruptcy, 180-1
  caution against dealings, 176, 178
    cancellation, 179-80
  change of home, 178
  charge securing further advances,
    178-9
  notice—
    application, 177
    cancellation, 179
    protecting rights, 176
    renewal of registration, 178
  order continuing rights, 177-8
  public index map search, 176-7
  rights of occupation,. 176, 180-1
  search by chargee, 181
Mental disorder, 155-6
Mines—
  indemnity, 207
  registration, 27, 36
Minor interests—
  definition, 54
  protection, 54
Minors, 154-5
Mortgage, *see* Charge

Notice—
  application, 165
  cancellation, 165-6
  deposit [intended], 126-8
  devolution of title, evidence, 166
  entry, 164-5
  generally, 164
  lease, in lessor's title register, 93, 94
  priority, first registration, 172-3

Office copies—
  application, 57-8
  building estates, 196-7
  deduction of title by, 83
  fees, 58
  items supplied, 57
  leases, 57, 96
  mortgages, 57
Overriding interests—
  first registration, 48
  generally, 46
  list, 46-8
  person 'in actual occupation', 48-50

Plan—
  building estates, *see* Building estates,
    plans

INDEX 249

Plan—*contd*
  colouring, 17–18
  computerisation, 11, 12
  deed, 19–20
  defective, 22
  field numbers, 19
  filed, 17–18
    certificate of official inspection, 58–9, 197–8
  first registration, 17, 30
  generally, 17
  'identification purpose', 19, 81
  metrication, 23
  part of title—
    charge, 111
    transfer, 87–8
  preparation, 17
  public index map search, 23–6
  reduced copies, 19–20
  scales, 18
  search, accompanying, 60
  'T' marks, 20
  see also Map
Possessory title—
  acquisition, 37–8
  conversion, 8–9, 139
  generally, 8–9
Proprietors—
  index of names, 11
  inspection, 55–6
Public authorities, *see* Local authorities
Public index map search—
  applications, 24
  certificate of result, 25–6
  description of property, 24–5
  fees, 25
  generally, 23–4
  leases, 25
  matrimonial home, 176–7
  plans, provision by Registry, 25–6
  rentcharge, title investigation, 131

Receiver—
  administrative, 188–9, 193
  agent, as, 189–90
  appointment, 188, 189
  attorney, as, 191–3
  debenture appointing, 188, 189
  effect of liquidation, 190–1
  execution of deeds, 191–3
  inspection of register, 56, 193
  powers, 189–90

Rectification—
  application, 206
  generally, 12, 205–6
  minor errors, correction, 80, 205
  mistakes, 80
Register of title—
  charges register, 10
  classes of title—
    absolute, 7–8
    conversion, *see* Conversion of title
    generally, 1
    good leasehold, 8
    possessory, 8–9
    qualified, 9
  clearing register, 10
  correction, *see* Rectification
  division, 1–2, 9
  form—
    computerised, 219–21
    non-computerised, 217–18
  inspection, *see* Inspection of register
  office copies, *see* Office copies
  property register, 9
  proprietorship register, 10
  separation of titles, 10
  superior titles, 7–8
Registration of title to land—
  applications, *see* Applications
  compulsory, *see* Compulsory registration
  first, *see* First registration
  generally, 1
Rentcharge—
  application for registration, 35
  apportionment, 135
  certificate, *see* Rentcharge certificate
  dealings, 134–5
  definition, 129
  equitable, 131, 133–4
  estate rentcharge, 129, 130
  extinguishment, 136–7
  generally, 129
  incapable of registration, 133–4
  investigation of title, 131
  leasehold land, 132
  notice, 131–2, 134
  prohibition of creation, 129
  public index map search, 131
  redemption, 135
  registered land, 131–3
  registrable, 130–1
  transfer, 134–5
  unregistered land, 131

Rentcharge—*contd*
  variable, 136
Rentcharge certificate—
  deposit, 134
  generally, 133
  see also Land certificate
Requisitions from Registry, 14–15, 81
Restriction—
  application—
    applicant, 171
    entry, 170
    form, 171
    refusal, 171
    voluntary, 170
  cancellation, 172
  compulsory, 170, 172
  generally, 170–1
  liquidation, 187
  modification, 171–2
  withdrawal, 171, 172
Right to buy cases—
  certificate of title, 39
  discount charge—
    generally, 121
    notice—
      cancellation, 123
      form, 121–2
    overreaching, 122
    postponement, 122
    priority, 122
    statutory period, 121
  forms, 39
  lease, 39–40
  registration, 39–41
  shared ownership lease, 39–40
  restriction, 40

Sale of registered land—
  completion, 85–6
  contract, 82
  fee on transfer, 86
  part of land, 85
  registration of transfer, 86
  searches, *see* Searches
  title—
    deduction, 82–3
    investigation, 83–4
    requisitions, 83
  see also Dealings
Searches—
  Companies Register, 84, 125
  index of proprietors' names, 55–6
  Land Charges Department, 68–9

Searches—*contd*
  leases, 93
  local land charges registers, 69
  mortgagee, 67
  official—
    applicant, 60, 64
    application, 60–1, 64–5
    certificate of search, 61–2, 65
    delivery of application, 61, 64–5
    generally, 59, 84–5
    importance, 59
    priority—
      conferred, 62, 65–6
      operation of priorities, 61, 63
      pending first registration
        application, 64–6
      without, 66
    purpose, 59–60, 64
    sub-sales, 63–4
    telephone, 67–8
    telex, 67–8
  part of land, 60
  plan, 60, 64
  public index map, *see* Public index map search
Settled land—
  changes under settlement, 143
  ending of settlement, 144
  forms, 142–3
  minority, 143
  registration, 141–3
  restrictions, 141–2
    cancellations, 144
  trustees—
    death, 144
    new, 143–4
  vesting assent, 158–9
Solicitor to HM Land Registry, 12
Souvenir land—
  dealings, 71
  non-registrable, 5
Stamp duty—
  adjudication, 13
  appointment of receiver, 189
  generally, 86
  non registrable instrument,
    transaction by, 13
  particulars delivered stamp, 13–14, 86
  production of documents, 13–14
  sufficiency, 13
  trust for sale, 145, 147

Sub sales—
    fees, 15
    searches, 63-4

Tenants in common, 88, 145
Transfer—
    covenants, implied, 87
    execution, 77-8
    forms, 87, 225
    generally, 2
    part, plan, 87-8
    sale of registered land, 82-6
    several transferees, 88-9; *see also* Trust for sale
    survivorship, 88-9
    see also Dealings
Trust for sale—
    capital money, payment, 144

Trust for sale—*contd*
    caution, 168-9
    creation, 145
    disposal of land, power, 144-5
    exclusion from register, 144
    notice, 144
    registration, 145-6
    restriction on register, 144-5, 146
    trustees—
        additional, 146-7
        appointment, 146-7
        bare, 147-8
        number, 144
        sole, 147
        survivorship, 145-6
    undivided shares, dealings, 145
    fees, 89
    vesting declaration, 147